D1546084

TINLING

Sixty Years in Tennis

TINLING

Sixty Years in Tennis
by Ted Tinling

Foreword by Richard Evans

SIDGWICK & JACKSON
LONDON

For Gladys Heldman, Joseph F. Cullman III,
and Philippe Chatrier, who, in changing the
face of tennis, also changed my life.

First published in Great Britain in 1983 by Sidgwick & Jackson Ltd

Copyright © 1983 Ted Tinling

Some portions of this book have been adapted from *Love and Faults* © 1979
(U.S.A. and Canada) by Ted Tinling and Rod Humphries, published in
the United States by Crown Publishers, Inc., and in Canada by General
Publishing Company Ltd.

All rights reserved including the right of reproduction in whole or in part
in any form

Frontispiece: Wimbledon, 1925. Suzanne puts silk and sex into tennis —
no one had ever done either before.

ISBN 0-283-98963-7

Printed in Great Britain by Biddles Ltd, Guildford, Surrey
Typeset in Garamond by C. Leggett & Son, Mitcham, Surrey
for Sidgwick & Jackson Ltd
1 Tavistock Chambers, Bloomsbury Way
London WC1A 2SG

Contents

Author's Acknowledgements

I would like to thank the following for their help with this book: the United States Tennis Association, for access to the USTA Library; William J. Clothier Jr for access to his extensive tennis library; Evelyn Dewhurst, Suzanne Lenglen's companion and opponent during their exhibition tour of Great Britain in 1927 for many interesting recollections of Lenglen; and Margaret Willes for her editorial guidance. I should also like to thank W. Norton & Sons of Savile Row for their splendid gold lurex tuxedo that shimmers on the book jacket.

Space has not allowed me to mention all the wide variety of people who have helped me at various stages of my life, but I should like to thank David Gray, the former tennis correspondent of the *Guardian*, who is now General Secretary of the ITF, and Prudence Glynn, former woman's editor of *The Times*, for their wise counsel and trusted friendship over the years.

For the Australian chapter, *The Sunburned Country*, I would like to acknowledge the help of Mike Hurst. My innumerable visits to Australia would never have been so successful or enjoyable had it not been for the many kindnesses paid me by Brian Tobin, Ray Sneddon, Bill and Jenny Owbridge and Karen Scott.

Last, but not least, I am particularly grateful for Richard Evans' patient collaboration in compiling this story.

Foreword by Richard Evans

The man is copyright; stamped, sealed and delivered from above as one of a kind. There has never been a head that shape, encompassing a mind that sharp, a wit that witty, or an eye so perceptive that it can analyse and strip bare the human condition at a glance. Anyone who leaves a conversation with Ted Tinling not knowing more than when he entered into it has to be deaf, because he could not possibly be that dumb.

It is difficult to know whether Tinling was made for tennis or tennis for Tinling. But, as the man and his sport have been intertwined in rapturous harmony since World War I, the question is moot. What we do know is that each has been wondrously enriched by the other and I, for one, am delighted that readers of this book will be able to feast off the fruits of that life-long love affair.

Sixty years is a long time to have worked at anything but few have done so with greater enthusiasm than Tinling. His roles may have rotated over the years – umpire, referee, player, couturier to the game's greatest stars, *chef de protocole*, television commentator, press liaison officer – but his enthusiasm has never waned and it is this quality that I would single out as his greatest gift to the game.

Even now, working as he does with great dedication and eye for detail at the age of seventy-two during the arduous weeks of the French Open and Wimbledon, he will still find time to take his seat on the Centre Court and watch matches of importance that take his fancy. Of course, he could argue that it is part of his job to be *au courant* with what is happening on court. But that is not why he is out there. He is watching because he simply adores tennis. He adores its style and athleticism and grace. He is fascinated by the psychological and technical nuances that are evident only to the connoisseur.

Unlike some of the officials who have been in positions of power in the world of professional tennis in recent years, Ted not only knows the players but can tell you how they won their last match and why. Many times, especially with the girls, he can tell you how they are going to play their next match as well. As a creator of fashion, Ted has never felt it particularly extraordinary to be one step ahead of the future.

For the past quarter of a century, I have been lucky enough to be able to use Ted as my lens to bring things into sharper focus. So many times at Wimbledon or elsewhere I would watch a match, amass all the information I had gleaned about the state of play and the players and come to what I hoped would be a fairly accurate and coherent conclusion. Then, if my deadline would allow it, I would race up those steps to the old players' tea-room to find Ted, cup in hand, about to plant the other large and jewelled one on some sticky bun. Before he could get it into his mouth I would blurt out, 'What did you think?' The answer invariably cut to the heart of anything we had just witnessed on the Centre Court.

'Well, what did you expect with that woman on the line? Billie Jean didn't hit a forehand down the line from the Royal Box end all afternoon because she was scared stiff that anything close would be called out. That was the same stupid woman who gave her all those horrendous calls last year, if you remember. That's why Billie Jean was so upset. She had to alter her whole strategy to prevent herself from being robbed blind.'

It is always like that with Ted: like switching on a light; like focussing that lens. Suddenly everything is so clear, so obvious.

No wonder he rose to the rank of Lt-Colonel in the Intelligence Corps during World War II. He was with Eisenhower in Algiers before joining Montgomery's staff in Germany. When all the revelations about how we had cracked the German code early in the war hit the newspapers a few years ago, I was stupid enough to mention it to Ted as if it was some new conversational tit-bit. He gave me the old soldier's look. It wasn't exactly new to him. He'd known about it from Day 1.

But then he usually knows about most things before anyone else. It is essential to his role as communicator par excellence. If you want to communicate properly it is necessary to know what you are talking about. Even though the very nature of his speech lends itself to occasional flights of fancy, with the odd fact or two finding itself blown happily along on a gust of exaggeration, such a harmless predilection is never allowed to obscure a basic truth. Blessed with something of Noel Coward's talent to amuse, Tinling's deep knowledge of the subjects closest to his heart − tennis, fashion, Wagner − enables him to communicate in such a way that people find themselves compelled to listen ... and therefore to learn.

His knowledge of tennis is truly extraordinary. It tends to be forgotten that he played the game himself at a very respectable level and, indeed, must be the only person ever to have played competitively against both Bill Tilden and Lew Hoad, Wimbledon Champions separated by a full thirty years.

The breadth and depth of that knowledge, stretching back to a now forgotten age, is evident on each and every page that follows. As I have only been professionally involved in helping Ted with the last few chapters, I can wholeheartedly recommend this book as a totally engrossing history of the game; a history that, quite literally, no one else could have written.

London, March 1983

PART ONE

1 Kingdoms in the Sun

For the high-life seekers of the 1920s, whether they were kings or commoners, the French Riviera provided a wonderful and apparently unending honeymoon. The sheer physical beauty of that magic coastline, beginning at Cannes and ending forty miles to the east at the Italian frontier, has never failed to cast an extraordinary, magnetic spell.

Two thousand years ago the Romans aptly named this strip the Azure Coast, and they called the bay that frames the proud city of Nice the Bay of Angels. Today's playground resorts of Cannes, Nice, Monaco, Monte Carlo, and Menton still shimmer at the base of the Maritime Alps like glittering jewels in the hot haze of the day or the particularly intense blue of Mediterranean nights.

Along the countless promontories and inlets of this coastline, dark cypresses and parasol pines blend almost imperceptibly into the edges of the royal blue water. In places, towering cliffs rise directly out of the sea to a height of over three thousand feet, giving the whole seaboard a natural shield against the rain clouds that come traditionally from the north.

The parched lower levels of these cliffs are covered with an effusion of drab olive and locust trees. The English, more accustomed to fresh northern greenery, are often disappointed at their first sight of the Riviera, but it does not take long before this muted tapestry captures everyone with its own particular beauty.

Behind Nice is a stark hillside. Scorched by centuries of burning sun to a bare and arid dome, it gave Mussorgsky the inspiration for his famous orchestral piece, *St John's Night on the Bare Mountain*. Further along the coast the olives and cypresses shade into a more lush and exotic mixture. Tall date-palms tangle with acres of wild figs. Aloes and prickly pear make protective hedges around profusions of tuberoses, freesias, and mimosa. From early spring until late summer the scents of blossom and over-ripe fruit mingle to give off a heady fragrance that is the essence of Provence.

Queen Victoria, seeking refuge from the London fogs, was the first of the European monarchs to journey to this 'fragrant haven', as she described it in her private letters. Although invariably surrounded by

11

her German relatives and her court ladies, a host of foreign ambassadors, anxious to report her every innovative movement to their own masters, closely followed her royal progress to the sunshine.

With Queen Victoria's presence acting like a magnet to the other royal courts of Europe, elaborate palaces and villas were built in exotically laid-out gardens. Eventually there was hardly a crowned head nor a royal courtier who did not spend his winter and spring days established in this sybaritic paradise.

Queen Victoria's middle and old age was the heyday of such French masters as Mistral, Cézanne, and van Gogh. Mistral gives a wonderfully impressionist word picture of Provence. The shimmering light of southern France inspired Cézanne and van Gogh to change the whole course of modern painting.

Lawn tennis took its grasp of England in that same era, but the rich English found their garden lawns survived only a few summer months: they were deprived of their novel pastime by the cold and wet of the English winters. Although there were probably more indoor facilities in London then than there are today, the wealthy and privileged succumbed readily to the pleasanter prospect of chasing tennis balls under Mediterranean skies.

The first tennis courts in France were accordingly laid out by the English in the 1880s, amid the eucalyptus trees, the palms, and the flower beds of the Beau Site Hotel in Cannes. The name was appropriate because the beautiful gardens and the tennis courts remained there unchanged for sixty years, from the days of the Renshaws, tennis's earliest idols, until World War II.

From the 1880s there was an annual migration to the South of France of tennis players from America and almost every country in Europe. Every famous name in the game's history is inscribed somewhere on the rolls of honour of the clubs that still survive there. The records show that on the old Monaco courts the Doherty brothers won many early championships, and in Nice there are still records, salvaged from the old club, which mention the first Central European masters of the game.

The settings were all extraordinarily beautiful because the courts everywhere were sited in a natural milieu of palms, oleanders, frangipanis, and mimosa, with the ubiquitous bougainvillea often climbing up the backstops. The surroundings were as typical of Provence as the gum-tree creeks are of Australia and the bayous of old colonial American plantations.

In the early part of this century palatial hotels, the first in Europe to include three or four hundred rooms, were built in strategic viewpoints in all the main Riviera centres. These were invariably crammed from Christmas until Easter with the complete *Almanach de Gotha*.

Also in those early days, Monaco, the tiny independent enclave in southern France now hereditarily ruled by Prince Rainier, saw the commercial possibilities of organized gambling. The gilded enthusiasts were already there and searching for additional excitements.

Eventually, with the aid of Edmond Blanc, who had already made Hamburg the gambling centre of northern Europe, an ornate casino was built on the rocky plateau neighbouring Monaco. This plateau was dedicated with great ceremony on 1 June 1866, by the reigning prince Charles III, and given the name Monte Carlo.

In turn, Cannes and Nice decided that if they did not follow suit they would be losing out. So, piece by piece, this whole coastline was linked into the most luxurious and cosmopolitan playground ever recorded in history.

And it was there, on this coastline, surrounded by beauty and immersed in the crazy luxury-age of jazz and the Charleston, that I spent my formative years.

2 Thursday's Child

On the 'British Riviera', as the advertisements call it, lies the respected, and respectable, township of Eastbourne. I remember Eastbourne as a windy place with the salt tang of fish in the cold air. I should remember it well because I was born there on Thursday, 23 June 1910.

My father was a well-to-do chartered accountant. By Victorian standards, my mother had travelled extensively and we had an impressive and comfortable home. My mother was enthusiastic about the steam-heat systems she had seen in Sweden and had central heating installed, making ours the first house in all southern England to enjoy this novelty. From romantic journeys to Italy, she brought back seedlings and planted a driveway of the flowering chestnut trees that give parts of Tuscany much of their romantic ambiance.

My parents had good, solid Victorian first names: my father, James Alexander; my mother, Florence Elizabeth. Our establishment was uncompromisingly middle class. In addition to my governess, there was a parlourmaid, housemaid, 'Cook', with her own kitchen maid, one manservant, and a chauffeur. Being independent and humanitarian, my mother never encumbered herself with a personal lady's maid.

In the proper traditions of pre-World War I England, my child life, except for a brief time on Sundays, was controlled exclusively by my governess, Miss Pearce. All my meals were served in the nursery, presided over by Miss Pearce. But on Sundays, when my parents took tea in the drawing room, Miss Pearce would take me to join them. The Sunday tea ritual was a feast of delicate sandwiches and iced cakes. But in Edwardian upbringing there was the stern discipline of eating four pieces of buttered bread before being allowed any cake. I remember quite a few occasions when I failed to reach the target of the eclairs or cream slices.

I was the spoiled child of the family because my eldest brother, Collingwood, ten years older than I, was always away at Radley or Cambridge. My second brother, Banastre, seven years my senior, was usually arriving at the same institutions just as my first brother was moving on.

I was born with a chronic chest problem, which the doctors of the day described as bronchial asthma. As an annual routine I would be put to bed with the first wheezy nose cold of October and most times remained there until the following April. Throughout, I was ceremoniously swathed in layers of lamb's-wool. Frequently I had farthing-sized hives because it was not known in those days that one could be allergic to wool. The chest-rubbing routine with pungent camphorated oil still haunts my nightmares.

World War I was declared a few months after my fourth birthday. By then, my mother had taken it into her head to move us all to Pevensey Bay, and in the summers of the war I spent many long hours with Miss Pearce on the beach where William of Normandy began his approach to the Battle of Hastings. Battle was a favourite picnicking spot for my governess. When it did not rain on Wednesdays, we invariably made the short journey by train and lunched on the grass among the ruins of Battle Abbey.

From 1915 to 1918 bombardments on the Western Front boomed and rumbled night and day across the sea, according to the direction of the wind. On the beach with my governess, I was already familiar in early childhood with bright explosions on the horizon, signifying the sinking of a ship in the Channel. Afterwards the high waterline would be cluttered for days with an endless assortment of goods, from cases of canned fruit to crates of ammunition that floated in on the tide.

The pride of Eastbourne is the picturesque, typically English, green woodland area known as Devonshire Park. Devonshire Park accommodates twenty plus tennis courts and has long been a major stronghold of the British tennis calendar, having staged Britain's largest tournament annually since 1894. Gentleman stars of the Edwardian era played the Eastbourne tournament as a matter of course. My mother was a regular spectator for a decade before I was born.

Probably the first tennis story I ever heard derived from my mother, reading in the newspaper that Papa Lenglen had refused to bring Suzanne to Eastbourne because he was not satisfied with the terms offered. In tennis, the word 'terms' held a horrendous significance in those amateur days.

After the Armistice of World War I my parents took my two brothers and me on a tour of the Flanders battlefields. 'Glory' had been the sentiment of millions of young bloods who went, cheering, to their death for King and Country before 1918. My parents were intent on impressing us that there was no glory in war.

Later we settled for a while in Switzerland in an effort to resolve my chest problem. But my breathing never came to terms with cold air and it was then decided we should experiment with the winter sunshine of the South of France.

First we migrated *en famille* to one of the palatial hotels in Cimiez, behind Nice. Then, when my father's post-war finances showed signs of failing, we were forced to separate, my mother renting an apartment where I lived with her until a few months before her death.

In those teenage years I found it difficult to know what to believe: difficult to know right from wrong. My father was a God-fearing Victorian, the son of a clergyman and a staunch believer in the 'Vengeance-of-Heaven' gospel. My mother was a progressive freethinker, always exploring the most newly-conceived cults. In her youth she had been an ardent follower of Madame Blavatsky and Annie Besant, and later, of Rudolf Steiner.

Meanwhile our friends, the English and American leisured classes, took off on the wild joy-ride of the 1920s. The world turned upside down, and many of the sacred beliefs we were taught at my Catholic day school were tossed recklessly to the wind by the grown-ups. Adolescence hit me just when Hollywood scenes were spilling into everyday life. The rich and famous were finding, on the sun-drenched Mediterranean, whatever stimulus they needed to recover from the hangovers of war. Suddenly saxophones, cocktails, and shiny silk-stockinged legs became the new religion. Cole Porter and the Model T Ford were the new high-priests. Josephine Baker and Mistinguett became Queens of Paris overnight.

Then, of course, there was Tennis.

By the 1920s the earlier aristocratic game had already taken its first downward steps toward being the plaything of the well-to-do middle classes. But from Christmas to Easter, the Riviera remained the in-place for the stars and all the rich who surrounded them. Tennis, dancing, and gambling were the catalysts of the high-fashion winter calendar, and Suzanne Lenglen, the unquestioned Queen of Art Deco, was the Pied Piper who had only to appear on a peal of laughter to have crowds flocking to see her play tennis between the cocktail hour and the *thé-dansants*.

'Prime time' for Suzanne's matches was always arranged to coincide with these rituals. Her matches were invariably concluded in forty-five minutes and everyone would then head for the hotel bars only to reappear at 4.00 p.m., rebeautified and regarbed for tea and dancing at the casinos. After that, the women would ride back to their hotels for a Mah Jong session while the men gambled until it was time to change into their dinner jackets and white waistcoats for the gala evenings.

Every nationality and every type of person met up at the casinos. There were kings, famous financiers, *demi-mondaines* with their lovers, crooks, Hollywood silent stars, and the aristocracy of half-a-dozen countries, all mixed in with the old crones who needed twelve hours of daily good luck at the tables for the price of their hotel bills.

Many of the elegant women preferred to show off their Paris creations and their jewels while dancing, rather than standing behind their husbands or lovers in the gaming rooms. At the back tables round the dance floors, the sleekly handsome professional gigolos sat alone, perusing the scene with unfailing instinct. For them, protocol involved the ultimate in formality, bowing low to the husband of any obviously married couple and saying, 'May I have permission to invite Madame to dance?'

Following the nightly gala dinners, there would often be firework displays to amuse the bejewelled women, while some of the richest men in the world puffed at their cigars. A second migration to the gaming tables would take place about 11.30 p.m., when millions of francs would change hands until sunrise. Then the whole round would begin again with mid-morning champagne and Suzanne's daily tennis match.

I became a part of this now-extinct life-style through my infatuation with tennis. As a child, I had played the usual condescending games with my elder brothers. Then my mother gave me a gift subscription enabling me to become a schoolboy member of the Nice Tennis Club. Years later, I was delighted to learn that Suzanne Lenglen had begun her tennis in the same way, with a school membership at the same club.

At thirteen I lived, and would gladly have died, for tennis. Schoolboy members were allowed to play only in out-of-school hours, which meant on Thursday and Sunday afternoons. To this day, I still recall the agonizing difference between enduring the three blank days from Sunday to Thursday, and the two more blank days between Thursday and Sunday. Every Thursday and Sunday, on the stroke of midday, I was at the Nice Club, either waiting for one of my schoolfriends to arrive, or just standing around staring.

The Nice Club was Suzanne's personal empire and many times I waited for her appearance just to gape at the sight of her. I think now that I already had an affinity with fabrics, colour, and design; certainly the glamour consciousness and the panache she projected already had an inborn fascination for me.

My mother had read me accounts of the great tennis personalities like Tilden and Patterson, and, of course, Lenglen. As some boys collect photographs of film stars, or nowadays rock idols, I adorned my bedroom wall with pictures of tennis greats. Playing in the same tennis club as the Empress herself was very heady stuff in my teens.

Even now I can sense the excitement and electricity Suzanne generated in me the first time I saw her play. She seemed to experience a special joy and abandon just from hitting the ball, with her perfect coordination providing the opportunity for her ballet leaps, and a projection that suggested complete sexual fulfilment from her own flowing movements.

Destiny finally put it all together in 1924. Lenglen was ready and waiting to make her entrance onto the centre court. But no one had thought to arrange an umpire ahead of time.

January 4 was the moment of confrontation when I was unsuspectingly recruited as a tennis umpire, five months before my fourteenth birthday. I was well and truly baptized by fire, for my first-ever experience of officiating in tennis was to umpire a match for the Incomparable Lenglen herself. I was to earn my living in tennis administration on the Riviera for the following eight years.

On that fateful day I was just standing around hoping for a single glance from Suzanne as she passed through the exotic, flower-lined setting of the Nice Club, when a voice said, 'Have you ever umpired a match?'

I felt an immediate electric tremor as I spun round to find myself face-to-face with the Empress herself. I had hardly noticed that the speaker had been Mrs Wollaston Richards, the well-meaning but ineffectual British organizer of the tournament.

'I have never umpired,' I told Mrs Richards, my gaze still riveted on Suzanne. Before I could say another word, Mrs Richards asked Suzanne, 'Would you mind this young man umpiring your match?'

Awaiting her reply, I was already convinced that if Suzanne rejected me, the whole course of my future would be different. Instead, Suzanne flashed a radiant smile and said, '*Mais avec plaisir*, I would be delighted!' This had to be on a Thursday because funny things, like being born, always happen to me on Thursdays.

Thereafter I was incorporated straightaway into Suzanne's close entourage, which consisted of Papa and Mama Lenglen backed by the handsome escorts with whom Suzanne invariably made her entrances. The escorts were dismissed to front-row seats in the stands for the duration of the match, while Papa and Mama Lenglen sat on a court-side bench beneath the umpire's chair. On Mama's lap, perched rather belligerently on a rug, was her pet Belgian griffon, Gyp.

As Suzanne removed her luxurious winter coat, revealing a brilliantly coloured cardigan over a white silk pleated dress, I stood hypnotized until I realized I should already be climbing the steps of the umpire's chair. Suzanne's opponent of the day was quite capable of rallying with her, but, like me, was overawed by the occasion.

Naturally I had never before experienced any situation like this. Papa and Mama Lenglen chattered incessantly on the bench below me. At that age I spoke better French than English and my thoughts wandered repeatedly as I overheard, fascinated, their running commentary on Suzanne's every movement.

'She's not arching her back on her serve today,' from Papa Lenglen.

'I liked last year's cardigans without sleeves much better,' from Mama.

With Gyp yapping with every rising intonation of the Lenglens' voices, it was probably excusable that I became distracted.

The match was already under way when I realized I had not marked the umpire's sheet and did not remember the score. Now, nearly sixty years later, I still recall the stage fright and apprehension I felt, with beads of perspiration falling inside my shirt.

Fortunately, the club's head ball-boy, Victor, who was also the friendly assistant pro', had been keeping an eye on the whole proceedings. Realizing my problem, he manoeuvred himself beside my chair. This gave me the chance to ask his help. He prompted me, and I was saved.

Suzanne was very friendly after the match and introduced me to her parents with the customary French formality of the era.

The next day Mrs Richards told me Papa Lenglen had suggested that I should umpire all Suzanne's matches. The organizers, more accustomed to being scared to death by Suzanne's tantrums, were greatly relieved at this prospect.

There is always one lad in every stable who, by some unaccountable bond of telepathic sympathy, can hold the bridle of the star runner in peace and calm. For two teenage years I was that 'stable-boy' to the greatest tennis star ever known.

Suddenly the old nursery rhyme became appropriate:

> Monday's child is fair of face,
> Tuesday's child is full of grace,
> Wednesday's child is full of woe,
> Thursday's child has far to go ...

3 La Petite Suzanne

From 1919 to 1926 all Europe, as well as the lotusland of the Riviera, belonged to Lenglen. She was the Southern Empress, as unique as the capital cities of Europe and the sun-drenched coastline over which she reigned supreme.

Suzanne spent her youthful years in Nice and she remained faithful to Nice throughout her life as a star. The city recognized her loyalty by giving the Lenglen family use of the Villa Ariem, a comfortable residence in the heart of the exiled Russian community, and directly facing the gates of the Nice Tennis Club.

The original Nice Club consisted of two courts in the Place Mozart, a tree-lined square in the town centre. Suzanne's extraordinary attractions outdated this overnight when she first won at Wimbledon. For once, those in authority had the good sense to recognize this by planning twenty new courts on a beautiful hillside site. From the present clubhouse, built in 1921, the view of the city below the grand sweep of the blue Mediterranean is reminiscent of the set that good opera-houses use for the first act of *Madame Butterfly*!

The Parc Imperial, the name given to the club area by its expatriate Russian neighbours in remembrance of their past glories, contains one of the few Riviera clubs that is not located in the grounds of some luxury hotel. Until the present Monte Carlo Club materialized in 1928, I do not believe there was a tennis club anywhere in the world where the natural beauty of the surroundings was as effectively blended with functional efficiency as in Nice.

The Nice clubhouse is a traditional Provençal *maas*, all flat-roofed pink stucco and white marble. During Suzanne's reign there was usually a long row of terracotta Roman vases, separating the clubhouse from the main courts, overflowing in early spring with torrents of bright pink geraniums. In late March these would be replaced with banks of sweet peas. Later there would be tall hedges of pink roses. The courts themselves were the same shade of terracotta as the rocks of the coastline. Bill Caudery, the first of the present club's secretaries, had the artistic taste to have all the court backstops painted the darkest of dark green, matching the surrounding cypresses.

Into this setting, almost daily from October until March, Suzanne would appear like some exotic bird of paradise. During the pre-Christmas months Papa Lenglen would arrange practice, sometimes inviting the three Burke brothers from Cannes to play doubles with her. After Christmas the round of tournaments, which continued till Easter, would claim all her energy.

Suzanne was born at Compiègne, in northern France, on 24 May 1899, the only child of solid, bourgeois Catholic parents, Charles and Anäis. Papa Lenglen, originally trained as a chemist, had become a pioneer racing cyclist during the sudden Victorian fascination for speed, when ice-skating and bicycling first made possible for everybody the excitement of fast independent movement without the aid and expense of a horse.

Six-day bicycle races became a major attraction of the 1880s and 1890s, and the competitors, coming for the most part from a proletariat background, were professionals. They were not hypocritically shy like the gentlemen sportsmen, but proud of their moneymaking aptitude. So Papa Lenglen generated early on a fixed and unbreakable habit of going after the main prize. On the other hand, if he could not win, he thought it more practical to conserve his energies by giving up the fight.

In the French language, to give up is to 'abandon'. The few times in Suzanne's life when her eventual victory may have been in question from whatever circumstance, Papa Lenglen, from years of practical French logic, uninhibited by any upper-class sporting code, would command his daughter from the court side or from the stands, 'Abandonne'. The introduction of this attitude to the Edwardian code of ethics, which was still law to many of Suzanne's opponents, gave her critics a head start for the repeated accusations of 'quitter' that she endured to the bitter end of her amateur career.

From Suzanne's earliest childhood Papa Lenglen was determined to find, in his only offspring, the world supremacy that eluded his own performances. In Suzanne, destiny gave him the material to fulfil this ambition to the ultimate degree. From Suzanne's childhood days, the only question in Papa Lenglen's mind was at which sport she could excel the most easily. *

Historically, most of the steps taken toward women's tennis evolution – which were to be taken by Suzanne a decade later with such dazzling brilliance – were first traced by the pre-World War I French champion, Marguerite Broquedis. The first public disdaining of corsets and bras by a woman, the first published tennis-fashion

---

*Charles Lenglen's philosophy of his daughter's game is reprinted in the Appendix, page 220.

columns in magazines, the first thoughts of special hairstyles for tennis, the first Olympic Gold Medal won for France by a woman, even the first suggestion that women's tennis should be beautiful, all derived from Madame Broquedis, and were given the added authority of her outstanding personal beauty.

Charles Lenglen inherited from his father a Paris horse-bus network with the convenient inclusion of eight hundred horses. In fact, I well recall some elderly English critics of his tennis concepts referring bitterly to him as 'nothing, really, but a horse-dealer'.

Once tennis was decided on for Suzanne's future, she was given an extra-light racquet when she was ten years old. After the family's move to the Riviera, a strict schedule of training was set up in the Place Mozart with a swarthy young local professional called Negro. Sessions against a practice wall were also arranged under the guidance of Negro, and the ever-watchful eye of Papa. In addition, Suzanne was enrolled in a ballet class, and she spent fifteen minutes every night and morning skipping before an open window. In all these activities, her laughing eyes and natural ebullience seemed to find some sort of joyous satisfaction.

Meanwhile Papa Lenglen was augmenting his income by helping out with the club's secretarial needs and, on Suzanne's twelfth birthday, he gave her an adult-sized racquet, asking her to promise that with it she would one day become champion of the world. He had only three years to wait. By then the migration of tennis enthusiasts to the Riviera had been in full swing for two decades, and Papa Lenglen was never backward in asking the best players to play with his daughter. The evening hours of pitting her ever-increasing skill against much older male opponents became the daily reward for the tedious sessions of metronome rallying with Negro. *'Voulez vous jouer avec ma fille?'* became a familiar parrot cry from Papa Lenglen, but it was never resented because everyone loved Suzanne's spontaneous gaiety and marvelled at the little girl's ability.

Events arranged for the top players of the pre-World War I era were always played on a handicap basis. The current code of sportsmanship demanded that everyone should start with an equal chance, so if one player was better than another, he was automatically 'weighted' in order to give his weaker opponent a good game.

One of my early privileges from being a member of the Nice Club was to have access to the secretary's desk, this by virtue of being Suzanne's stable-boy. The records of all the earliest tournaments were kept there, and from these handwritten pages I could trace Suzanne's extraordinary progress, the amazing speed with which her handicap went down and down in the years leading to 1914.

The previous year, two visiting personalities, both destined to play a leading part in Suzanne's life, arrived on the Riviera: Elizabeth Ryan and Count 'Ludi' Salm. The familiar invitation: *'Voulez vous jouer avec ma fille?'* was readily accepted by both, and in 1914 Suzanne not only won the World Singles title in Paris, but also the World Doubles with Elizabeth Ryan and was the mixed finalist with Count Salm. From that moment on, the doubles team of Elizabeth and Suzanne lost only one set in seven years, while winning Wimbledon six times together, the World championships in 1914 and 1923, and uncountable lesser doubles titles all over Europe.

Suzanne experienced her last-ever singles defeat to Marguerite Broquedis in April 1914, after which she calmly told an astonished pressman: 'I need more strength, more breath and more length on my shots, after which they will become winners.' Two weeks later she became the World Singles and Doubles champion within days of her fifteenth birthday.

Following these Paris triumphs there was great disappointment in England that Papa refused all invitations to the unfamiliar grass courts of Wimbledon. He was much too shrewd a planner to fall for that temptation, whatever the prestige attached, and Suzanne was quickly sent back to practise each day in the Place Mozart.

'You have won two World titles,' Papa told her rather harshly. 'That is nothing, you must win them all.'

So certain areas of the practice court were designated, and Negro was instructed to see that she placed the ball in those areas two or three hundred times in succession. Her ballet training and skipping sessions were also intensified.

In the last years of World War I the French Riviera was offered by the French as a convalescent area for the American forces who had fought on the Western Front. I recall that among these were at least two top-ranking American tennis players. This was fortunate again for Suzanne, as Elizabeth Ryan, although a Californian, was absent, generously working with the British, and Count Salm was away on a crusade very different from that followed by his illustrious ancestors.

'Will you play with my daughter?' must have been specially translated for the convalescent Americans, as Papa Lenglen usually resolutely refused to speak any English, although he understood it perfectly.

In my time on the Riviera, Papa Lenglen had already retired from business and would spend hours, when Suzanne was not playing, watching us juniors and reproving us severely for any casual stroke or signs of frivolity. He was a tall, gaunt man with shoulders that were already bent and a penetrating gaze through very thick glasses. He always wore a hat and was usually muffled to the ears in a heavy coat, which gave him a slightly sinister appearance.

Mama Lenglen was the mother hen, fat, cheerful, and dumpy, and always fussing about something related to Suzanne. Suzanne often referred to her as '*ma poule*'. Nature had played a remarkably apt trick on Mama Lenglen, for she had such an acute astigmatism that both eyes looked outward in opposite directions, saving her the need to turn her head when following Suzanne's shots during the million hours she spent clucking over her daughter from the sidelines.

Papa Lenglen always encouraged us to use table-tennis scoring for tennis, because this gives added importance to every stroke. He never believed in the traditional tennis scoring because, as it still stands, it is possible to win fewer points than one's opponent, yet still win the match. On principle, he found this quite intolerable.

Immediately after the 1918 Armistice, the American forces on the Riviera decided on one last monster tennis spree. Listening to some of the ranking Americans involved, Papa Lenglen heard irresistible whispers about the reopening of Wimbledon and Papa decided this was at last the time for Suzanne to take the plunge. The boldness of taking an already highly strung, twenty-year-old with an almost legendary, but unproven reputation, to Wimbledon with all its starch and inhibitions, should never be underestimated.

Elizabeth Ryan recalls that at that time the women's dressing rooms in England habitually provided a rail near the fire-place on which players could dry their steel-boned corsets. 'It was never a pretty sight,' says Miss Ryan, 'for most of them were blood-stained.'

Unfortunately I never questioned Suzanne about her memories of her initial trip to England, but no one could have failed to be impressed by the purposeful severity of Mrs Dorothea Lambert Chambers, six times Wimbledon champion. Her stance, her predatory shoulders, and the determination illustrated in her every action and incisive comment.

On her arrival in London, Suzanne lost no time at all in making her mark, for after her very first practice-session, most of London's society was agog with controversy about her calf-length cotton 'frocks', and the audacity of her girlish silhouette so 'brazenly' revealed. Quite a large section of the British public initially condemned her as 'indecent', and only a small minority doubted that Mrs Chambers would deal summarily with this French hussy.

Suzanne's capacity to adapt to grass within a few hours of her first sight of it amazed everyone, particularly her first four opponents whom she swept unceremoniously aside, apparently oblivious to the fact that they were themselves world-class players. Yet, in spite of these encouraging beginnings, there still remained the forbidding obstacle of Mrs Chambers, solidly entrenched in the psychological fortress of a twelve-year supremacy. London's Society chatter became crystallized into a single question: Could Suzanne *possibly* beat Mrs Chambers?

By some demanding fate, Suzanne was called upon to play the two greatest matches of her life at the extremities of her career: the first at the very beginning of her stardom; the second at the very end.

In 1919, she responded marvellously to London's question and to Papa's critics by defeating Mrs Chambers after having been twice at match-point down. When at times Suzanne seemed near to collapse, Papa threw her a tiny silver flask of cognac from his seat in the stands. When Mrs Chambers led Suzanne in the deciding set, his imperious gestures ordered his daughter to move forward and attack from the net.

On an unusually perfect day, with King George V and Queen Mary leading the cheering thousands, Suzanne survived and overcame Mrs Chambers's merciless driving to finish victorious in what was regarded as one of the greatest upsets in the record books.

After her victory Suzanne began her champion's life as she ultimately pursued it — by making her own rules and receiving her ecstatic admirers in her bath!

In life, Mrs Chambers adamantly refused to disclose her age. Her death revealed that on the day of this great match she was only two months short of being forty-one years old. Suzanne had celebrated her twentieth birthday a few weeks previously, so it is doubtful which of the two opponents was the most gallant.

After the match Mrs Chambers, with the greatest of generosity, said she had never played better, but years later she told me she considered the outcome of this match to have been a tragedy for them both. Her own case was obvious. She was twice deprived, by a single stroke, of an eighth Wimbledon Singles title, the all-time record achieved only by Helen Wills twenty years later. As for Suzanne, Mrs Chambers considered this particular victory to have given her the taste of invincibility and a subsequent compulsion for it, which brought endless sacrifices and unnatural unhappiness, out of all proportion to the rewards of her fame.

Suzanne's 1919 triumph caused shock waves and a tide of adulation around the world. In the immediate post-war era women everywhere were longing for some release from the restrictions of the Edwardian decade. They worshipped Suzanne for daring to enact their secret dreams, men loved her for bringing them the ballet leaps, the intermittent glimpses of bare thigh, and the sexual connotations of her very visible silhouette, all of which they determinedly denied themselves in their own homes.

This was the beginning of a seven-year period in Suzanne's life in which she blazed trails that were previously unthinkable.

After sixty years of reflection all the experts unanimously agree that she gave to tennis an importance never previously attached to any sport. My own interpretation is that she created a blueprint of tennis patterns that will still be valid in the year 2000.

But there were to be temporary eclipses, of course. The storm clouds gathered when her father's health began to fail; in less than twenty years a terminal illness would afflict Suzanne herself.

In 1920 she returned to England with the new 'bobbed' hairstyle; to keep her hair attractively in place, she conceived what was soon to become the famous 'Lenglen bandeau', two yards of brightly coloured silk chiffon, tightly swathed around her head. Within weeks the Lenglen bandeau was copied by a million women, and for the next six years there was not a tennis girl who did not attempt some imitation of the Lenglen look.

That same year Big Bill Tilden came to Europe from Philadelphia. Both he and Suzanne won the Wimbledon Singles titles in 1920, but from then on he decided to consider himself her rival, if not her superior, as a world star personality.

Mrs Molla Mallory was also present and was fated to play an historic role in Suzanne's destiny. Mrs Mallory was not then making her Wimbledon debut, because she had already played there, inauspiciously, in 1909, when working in London as a masseuse. Originally a Norwegian, she had emigrated to America in December 1914, and in the interim had won the US national championships five times and had become the tennis heroine of her adopted country.

One can be sure that Papa Lenglen, knowing of Molla's reputation in America, made his customary reconnaissance of her game, but in 1920 at Wimbledon she was summarily dismissed by Mrs Chambers, whom Suzanne had already beaten, so he had no cause for concern.

In the spring of 1921 Tilden and Mrs Mallory went to Paris and this time Molla put Suzanne to the test. Suzanne had a difficult match with her, and at one point it even seemed she might give up the fight. But Papa rose dramatically in the stands and commanded Suzanne to go on and win, which she did. 'Just wait till I get her on grass,' was Molla's immediate comment to Bill Tilden at court-side, and well within Suzanne's hearing.

There are pictures for public consumption, in which Suzanne and Tilden appear to be on amicable terms, but this sharp challenge of Molla's was the spoken declaration of a feud that was inevitable between them, with Tilden firmly declared as Molla's ally.

In stage terms, Molla's position was that of an ambitious second lead, needling the established top name in the business. Appropriately, it was petty, one-sided, and often bitchy, and Suzanne was then still able to disdain the whole situation. Logically, in their relative positions, Suzanne and Mrs Mallory were destined to clash, but the intrusion of Tilden's partisan emotions made the rivalry much more explosive.

Tilden appears to have developed a compulsive hatred of Suzanne from the moment of his first Wimbledon success. Whether his championing of Mrs Mallory was due to plain, primitive jealousy of the adulation Suzanne commanded, or to some odd sense of patriotism in favour of the Americanized Molla, may never be understood. At all events, the seeds were well sown for the dramatic circumstances that led, a few months later, to the one really bitter setback Suzanne ever experienced on the courts.

4 La Grande Suzanne

Soon after Suzanne's first Wimbledon win in 1919, she received a letter from America's leading tennis editor, Wallis Merrihew, asking when she was going to the United States. 'I have no plans for doing so,' she replied, *'because my tennis is only a pastime.'*

Suzanne's close friend, Pierre Albarran, has written in his memoirs of the marked change in Suzanne's character that occurred after her second Wimbledon win in 1920, when she was worshipped by British men and hailed by British women as their liberating heroine. Her attitude certainly appears to have somersaulted dramatically as, from then on, her 'pastime' became a compulsion. Suddenly she was determined on an American visit to conquer the New World as she had now conquered the Old.

The opportunity came in the late summer of 1921, when Anne Morgan, whose father had been one of the pioneers of American tennis, invited Suzanne to play a series of exhibition games in the States for the benefit of French areas that had been devastated by World War I.

The proposed trip, and Suzanne's determination to accept the Morgan invitation, led to the fiercest of disagreements within the Lenglen household. Papa Lenglen had always refused to go on any long boat journey, so the major objection was that Suzanne would be separated from him on an important occasion for the first time in her life.

Tennis politics then played, for once, into Suzanne's hands. For the previous seven years the all-European International Federation had been frantically wooing the American tennis administrators to join with them. They wanted to consolidate a truly world-powerful organization, but for reasons of their own, the Americans were still refusing to play ball.

In 1921 the French felt that the participation of their very own Suzanne in the forthcoming American national championships could greatly improve their chances of success. But Papa Lenglen adamantly refused to agree to Suzanne's participation on the grounds that she was not properly prepared. He had acted on this belief when he refused to let her participate at Wimbledon before World War I.

Being twenty-two years old at the time, Suzanne may well have thought the moment had come when her Trilby-Svengali relationship with Papa should end. Decades later Maureen Connolly had a similar experience when she decided, overnight, to split with 'Teach' Tennant; later still, history was repeated when Evonne Goolagong split with Vic Edwards.

There was also a reason for the American authorities to want Suzanne in their championships. The women's US national title had been fought out for thirty-three successive years in Philadelphia. That year the event was captured for the first time by Forest Hills. The New York authorities decided to celebrate the occasion by assembling the most impressive possible parade of champions, past and present.

Anne Morgan accepted that Suzanne would play only in exhibitions, but Suzanne clearly saw wider horizons ahead of her, in defiance of Papa. She had beaten Molla Mallory in Europe. She had also seen Molla decisively beaten by players whom she herself could beat with the utmost ease.

Papa Lenglen's agreement to the journey was extracted only on the absolute condition that Suzanne would not compete in the national championships at Forest Hills. The French Federation was informed, but it seems the message was never transmitted to the right people. Possibly, this was an intentional omission. In the final arrangement, Suzanne was to be accompanied by the vice-president of the French Federation, Monsieur A. R. de Johannis, Mme de Johannis, and Mama Lenglen. For the first time in such circumstances, Papa Lenglen would not be along.

Billie Jean King would say nowadays there were 'bad vibes' around the whole project. To begin with, soon after Suzanne won her third Wimbledon in July, she contracted a summer cold that developed into bronchitis. Her departure for America was postponed twice. Each time Anne Morgan patiently rearranged the exhibition schedule. Then the ship, *Paris*, which was due to sail from Le Havre with the Lenglen party on board, was delayed for two days by bad weather. As the gangways were eventually pulled up, Papa Lenglen yelled to Suzanne from the dockside, 'Whatever else, do *not* play the championships.'

The Forest Hills championships were scheduled to begin on Monday, 12 August. Suzanne docked in New York on the previous Friday, 9 August. Mama Lenglen claimed later she did not think this 'mattered' as, in her understanding, Suzanne had no official commitments until the championships finished.

It seems likely that for their own different reasons, Suzanne and de Johannis plotted privately that she would play the championships, because, on arrival, Suzanne 'discovered' she had been officially entered. In addition, the draw had already been made, making it diplomatically impossible for her to withdraw. From three thousand miles away, Papa never had a chance to enforce his advice.

The draw itself had a fatalistic quality. Seeding, or the separation of the top players from one another in the preliminary stages, was not in force in those days, and by another stroke of perverse chance, no fewer than eight of the top-ranking players came out of the hat in the same half as Suzanne.

Then came the rain that prevented Suzanne from even going to practice on either the Saturday or Sunday. Finally, her first-round match, against Eleanor Goss, the fifth-ranking American, had to be postponed from Monday until Tuesday to allow Suzanne a few hours for her first warm-up since landing.

Tuesday, 13 August 1921, must have combined some of the worst vibes of Suzanne's life. First, Miss Goss called to say she was ill and could not appear. Then the committee, seeing the chance of making up the day lost by rain, scheduled Suzanne's second-round match against Molla Mallory. Eventually, late in the afternoon, and before eight thousand expectant spectators, Molla played the game of her life and humiliated Suzanne.

After a shaky start Suzanne began coughing conspicuously. She was mentally unprepared and physically unfit for Molla's unexpected onslaught. This time Papa's command, '*Abandonne*', was not forthcoming. In the circumstances it would have seemed totally appropriate to Suzanne, so she made the decision herself and retired ignominiously in the middle of the match.

As Suzanne left the court sobbing, supported by de Johannis, the match umpire, Edward C. Conlin, and the referee, J. M. Jennings, hissing was heard from several sections of the crowd. The national press was to coin the bitterly appropriate barb, Cough and Quit. Suzanne never again wore the peacock-blue bandeau she had chosen for that match.

Tilden proudly proclaimed the hatred he had for Suzanne, boasting how he had kept Molla in an armchair for sixty minutes before the match, and during this time had brainwashed her with comments about Suzanne calculated to inflame Mrs Mallory.

Suzanne's own intimate thoughts are described in one of her close friend Coco Gentien's most treasured possessions: a pencilled note from her bed on the day after the match. 'I am dreadfully unhappy,' she confided. 'America thinks of me as a monster and I am afraid of Papa. If only I had accepted his advice! As always, he was quite right.' Suzanne probably felt the urge to stick pins in Molla Mallory's effigy every night during the first six months of 1922.

When their rematch became inevitable, in the 1922 Wimbledon final, such was the surrounding climate that Molla's husband bet $10,000 on his wife's renewed victory, and Mike Myrick, head of the American authorities, felt himself obliged to issue a formal statement denying the derogatory remarks about Suzanne that were being attributed daily to his close friend, Mrs Mallory.

In the eventual match, Suzanne took exactly twenty-seven minutes to avenge herself with a 6-2, 6-0 victory. Suzanne met Molla again six months later in Nice. There she took only twenty-six minutes to repeat the execution by 6-0, 6-0. The umpire's sheet for the match is still framed on the wall of the Nice Club, whose members justifiably wanted a permanent reminder of their Empress's achievement.

One of the most beautiful girls in the world watched Molla's humiliation of Suzanne at Forest Hills in 1921. Some days earlier she had won the Junior national title. This was Helen Wills. Helen climbed the ladder of tennis fame very quickly, and by late 1923 she was already considered good enough to lead the American women's team – ahead of Mrs Mallory – in the first-ever international match between English and American women. Wimbledon in 1924 was the occasion of Helen Wills's first trip to Europe, and the fact that she had been so recently rated above Mrs Mallory gave rise to the usual sensational speculations about her meeting with Lenglen.

In April 1924 Suzanne contracted jaundice during a visit to Spain with Alain Gerbault. Wimbledon was to begin on 23 June, yet her doctors refused her permission to pick up a racquet before 5 June. All went well in the first week of Wimbledon when she scored three successive 6-0, 6-0 victories in the opening rounds. This in itself was a record, but her very short convalescence medically validated her subsequent claim that she was still unfit and should never have entered an event as demanding as Wimbledon.

At the start of the second week, Elizabeth Ryan, playing the game of her life, came within six points of beating Suzanne. A questionable line call, given the other way, would have put her even closer. The set conceded to Miss Ryan in this match was one of only three sets Suzanne lost in singles in the seven years of her star reign.

The shock, and the effort of survival, proved too much for her nerves, and once again she decided to abandon the whole tournament. Her emotional resources may have been exhausted, but her physical reserves were still sufficiently intact for her to ask Miss Ryan to go shopping with her the next day, adding insult to injury and certainly giving renewed fuel to her critics.

Needless to say, the critics lost no time in accusing Suzanne of running scared from her first risk of a meeting with Helen Wills. It was a complete replay of the 'Cough and Quit' episode three years earlier, they said. The 'aftermath of jaundice' was the reason quoted in the formal club bulletins. Then Papa Lenglen himself went on record saying, 'Next year my daughter will play better than ever.' This unusual intervention proved, I think, his remarkable understanding of Suzanne's nature, his mastery of what is now known as public relations, and the confidence he had in his own extraordinary influence over his daughter's game.

The year 1925 was to become the very zenith of Suzanne's life. She won the French championships with the loss of only seven games, and won six rounds of Wimbledon with the total loss of five games. Her opposition included at least three players – Diddie Vlasto, Kitty McKane, and Elizabeth Ryan – who would certainly win some of today's $200,000 tournaments, yet Suzanne's financial rewards from these triumphs totalled just two weeks' hospitality, a medal, and less than £25 in non-negotiable prize vouchers.

My association with Suzanne started at the beginning of 1924. After umpiring the first few of her matches and overcoming my stage fright, I became accustomed to Papa and Mama Lenglen's constant arguments on the court-side bench by my chair. These concerned Suzanne's every action, and at first were disconcerting as the yapping of Mama's lapdog, Gyp, always grew in intensity when they themselves raised their voices. But the Lenglen parents were unfailingly fair to me, Papa always asking immediately if I was sure of my call when either of them thought I had made a mistake.

Never, in all the 104 matches I called for her, did Suzanne say a cross word to me. When she changed ends, she frequently took a nip of cognac from the silver flask that by then was kept either in the pocket of her usually lavish fur coat, or on Mama's lap on the rug beside Gyp. Once, when I made an obviously bad call, she waved the flask at me and said laughingly, 'When you're older, we can share this and you will see better.'

In 1925 she taught me the lesson of my life in the essential need for common sense and tact in handling the great stars. As usual, she had just won the singles final in Nice and had gone off to the Villa Ariem to change her ensemble. I never recall meeting anyone who saw her play two successive matches in the same coloured bandeau and cardigan. To her, this would have been a let-down to her public.

Her next opponents on that particular day were probably the world's best mixed-doubles pair at that time: Randolph Lycett and Elizabeth Ryan. We all waited patiently for Suzanne's return – 're-entry on stage' would be a better description in her case. However, Lycett had reservations for an overnight berth on the Blue Train to Paris within a few hours, and he told me to go to fetch her. Somehow I fell for that one, and it is no excuse to remember now that

I was only fourteen. Knowing Suzanne, I should have known better, even then.

I reached the tall iron gates of the Villa Ariem at the exact moment that Suzanne opened them from the inside. She was radiant in a flaming orange bandeau and cardigan. 'I came to fetch you, Mademoiselle,' I said, very foolishly. Her expression turned instantly from sunshine to thunder. 'Fetch *me?*' she said. 'Let them wait.'

I knew that even in that lightning flash of temperament she would not slam the iron gates in my face, but she turned and disappeared inside the Villa. Ten minutes later she emerged laughing apologetically, but Lycett was so incensed at the delay that he hardly hit one good shot, giving poor Miss Ryan no chance to exercise her wonderful expertise in mixed doubles.

After four years at the top, Suzanne's flare-ups became more frequent and more distressing to her friends. There were also times when she was found retching over the dressing-room basin before playing and having hysterical outbursts after losing two games in a match. One should remember, of course, that when Suzanne lost two games in singles it made world-headline news.

The press started to ask questions about what made Suzanne's character so compellingly magnetic and what were the secrets of her life off the courts.

It is now generally accepted that other than a few normal infatuations with her mixed-doubles partners in 1919 and 1920 her personal circle was purposely restricted to a few intimate and presumably 'safe' young male admirers. These included, primarily, two contrasting young men. The first, Pierre Albarran, a brilliant brain, one of the world's leading card-players, and an accomplished tennis player, was at one time on the verge of marriage to her. It seems that only her first Wimbledon success and the new horizons it offered caused her a change of heart. The second, Alain Gerbault, also an accomplished tennis player, was later to become the lone Atlantic sailor of 'Firecrest' fame. Gerbault subsequently developed such a compulsion for heroic withdrawal from life that he could appropriately have been called the 'Lawrence of Arabia' of tennis. Later these two young men were joined in Suzanne's affections by a delightful socialite playboy, Coco Gentien.

Meanwhile Albarran, who won no fewer than seventeen successive mixed-doubles events with Suzanne, was shocked into detailing how much celebrity and fame had changed not only Suzanne's character but her physical appearance. In one sense at least, this was obviously true, because year by year she developed her star status to the point of transforming herself physically and dresswise from the ugly duckling of her beginnings to the bird of paradise she became.

Her close friendships with Gerbault and Gentien appear, in retrospect, to have been the memorable, *joie-de-vivre* experiences of three delightful and sophisticated young people linked by a common love of tennis. Her teenage romance with Albarran was probably as close as she ever came to a true love affair until she left the competitive tennis scene in 1926.

On another plane, Suzanne's entourage included a selection of highly influential people, notably Lady Wavertree and Lady Crosfield from London's Society set, and Lady Wavertree's paramour, the Honourable F. M. B. Fisher.

'There's a Len-Glen Trail a'Winding,' the waiting lines outside Wimbledon sang to pass the time, parodying the 'Long Long Trail', a war-time hit the British soldiers sang on their marches to and from the Flanders' trenches. But under the amateur tennis rules of the 1920s, not even Suzanne's immense box-office attractions were allowed to bring her a legitimate income. Even the most modest endorsements had to be secret in those days, and for the most part, were not worth having anyway. Her parents were what the French call *petits rentiers*, which means those who derive an unearned income from a pension or from modest capital investments.

Yet for ambitious hostesses, Suzanne was the ultimate catch in any European capital. There is no doubt that she and Sophie Wavertree had a far deeper mutual affection than this implies, but it was also true that Sophie's constant companion, 'F. M. B.', as he was always called, was the managing director of one of Europe's most progressive sporting-goods manufacturers. With the best goodwill in the world, Lady Wavertree's close friendship with Suzanne, as with many other top tennis stars, could never therefore be entirely divorced from the commercial interests of 'F.M.B.'

Both Lady Wavertree and Lady Crosfield had sumptuous London properties where tennis stars could enjoy the capital's hospitality at its most glamorous. Lady Wavertree also had a beautiful home by the lake in Aix-les-Bains, a favourite French summer resort at that time. In earlier days King Edward VII had been a regular visitor to Lady Wavertree's London mansion. The annual socialite mixed doubles in Lady Crosfield's garden always attracted a gathering of cosmopolitan royalty: the event was won in 1922, for example, by the Duke of York, later to become George VI. Kings, princes, and aristocrats, butlers and footmen, painted ceilings, champagne and roses every day ... such was the scene London presented to Suzanne in the years of her triumphs. Yet she invariably returned with relief to her beloved Nice and to the companionship of her tennis buddies.

Some say the tremendous exertions and the constant invincibility demanded of her by Papa Lenglen eventually reduced her to a frail, nervous wreck. Others think that early repressions by both her parents, who felt any normal life might impair her performance, were the real cause of her decline. At the time of my Riviera association with her, she certainly seemed to spend her whole life on her toes, unable ever to relax.

After a close friendship during the fifteen years that preceded her death, my feeling is that from childhood on, she became slowly but inextricably caught in a spotlit destiny that she could never have anticipated, nor have been mentally prepared for in the short years available. Papa Lenglen drove her relentlessly toward the goal of absolute supremacy, which was compulsive to both their egos. To maintain this, Suzanne began very early to deprive herself of all the joys of a normal existence.

Eventually, some compulsion seemed to develop in her that might be compared to the renunciations of a person taking the veil. By the fourth year of her stardom, probably exacerbated by the Mallory debacle in America, she was confronted by the realization that to stay in the life she had come to adore, and retain the public's adulation she now depended upon, would involve the total sacrifice of all natural life.

She was not yet twenty-five when I first saw her almost daily from close quarters, but the transformation, which had shocked Pierre Albarran, was fast taking place. Her face and expression already bore the traces of sleepless nights and deep emotional soul-searching. After her jaundice in Spain and the abandoning of the 1924 Wimbledon, it even seemed as if the sleek escorts were becoming mere stage props, and the habitual peals of laughter just a façade for the fans.

In 1925, she reached a stage where to lose two successive points in any game automatically implied to her that she was ill. If she missed one shot, Mama, of course, would immediately say, 'But what is the matter with you?'

Nevertheless, all this resulted in the tennis miracles she performed in the summer of 1925, the true summer of this marvellously glittering but artificial period in her life. Papa predicted it, and between them, they made his prediction a reality. After Wimbledon of that year she made a Grand Tour of Europe. She was welcomed and fêted in half-a-dozen palaces with an uninhibited enthusiasm which monarchs themselves seldom experience.

Yet the following year was still to provide the most triumphant – and tragic – climax to everything that had gone before.

5 The Bandeau and the Eyeshade

For a hundred years the names Ritz and Carlton have been synonymous with everything that is luxurious and grand in hotel life. The Carlton Hotel in Cannes is no exception, but by some quirk of fate, it reached an unlikely summit of its fame on 16 February 1926. On this Tuesday, the small, rather inconspicuous tennis club, which faced a side-street entrance of the Carlton and shared its famous name, staged one of the most dramatic encounters ever seen in the history of tennis.

The simple programme was content to announce in French:

`à 11 heures:`

Mlle Suzanne LENGLEN   c   Miss Helen WILLS
France   Etats-Unis

For three years Papa Lenglen's immediate response to any tournament invitation involving Suzanne was already 'What is the proposition?' The implications of this question were endless, and his inquiry became increasingly logical as more and more spectators wanted to pay more and more money to see his daughter perform. Suzanne's Grand Tour of the royal palaces of Europe a few months previously led to the initial questions as to how she maintained her exotic plumage and her luxurious modes of travel.

Since '23 Helen Wills, now twenty years old, had climbed the top rungs of the tennis ladder by several victories over Molla Mallory, by coming to within a few points of winning the 1924 Wimbledon after Suzanne's withdrawal, and by winning the American championships three years in succession, in 1923, 1924 and 1925.

In announcing that she would play the Riviera spring circuit in 1926, Helen's instinct must have told her the time had come to challenge Suzanne's reign and that she was ready to do so on Suzanne's own territory. Henceforth, a showdown somewhere along the Lenglen coast was inevitable.

Probably, from San Francisco six thousand miles away, Helen Wills and her mother, being quiet dignified people, had no opportunity to appreciate the absolute pride of place Suzanne occupied in French national prestige. Had they done so, they might have foreseen the world-wide interest Helen's invasion of the Riviera would arouse. In the minds of sports editors, memories of Lenglen's 'Cough and Quit' incident in 1921 made this new encounter, between the French Empress of tennis and the American successor to Molla Mallory, potentially big news, and they sent countless hard-nosed journalists, who had never previously seen a tennis match, hot-foot to the South of France.

On 15 January 1926, Helen Wills, accompanied by her mother and fifteen unstrung tennis racquets, arrived at Le Havre on the liner *De Grasse*. Somewhat to their astonishment, the two ladies were met on their arrival in Paris by the President of the French Tennis Federation, Pierre Gillou, accompanied by Jean Borotra, France's male star performer, and an unusually large muster of sensation-seeking journalists.

Later they boarded the Blue Train for Cannes, and on arrival, were again surprised by another welcoming crowd. Among these was Charles Aeschliman, probably the best player Switzerland ever produced. He had been married to a delightful American girl, Lesley Bancroft, at one time ranked No. 2 in her country ahead of Helen Wills herself. This apparently gave him the feeling he should have a part in the arrangements for the Wills' visit. No one could have foreseen that he would soon play the most controversial of all roles at the climax of the forthcoming drama.

Helen told the welcoming party she planned a nine-week schedule of singles and doubles on the Riviera, beginning with the Metropole tournament in Cannes. She said she intended to play every week; so the burning question was which week would the Empress Lenglen submit herself in singles to the Wills challenge. They had never played against each other, so their first meeting would be interesting, even in doubles. But what all the newsmen in the world were waiting for was their first face-to-face confrontation in singles.

In the first week of Helen's schedule, she won the singles of the Hotel Metropole event, but was disappointed to find Suzanne had entered only in doubles.

The Lenglen parents, however, wasted no time in making a microscopic inspection of the newcomer's form. They sat wrapped in rugs in the V.I.P. seats. These overlooked the Metropole courts from a high escarpment, and Helen recalls that while playing below she felt very self-conscious under the combined scrutiny of the Lenglen trio.

Helen scheduled her first tournament immediately on arrival to accustom herself to the slow French clay surface, and was far from showing the peak form she reached three weeks later.

Conversely, Suzanne, determined to impress Helen to the utmost, put on one of her most dazzling displays and lost only seven games in winning the eight matches of the two doubles events partnered by Diddie Vlasto and Toto Brugnon.

Meanwhile, all types of writers, from tough newsmen to best-selling authors, were swarming to the Riviera to a point where regular sports-aces could not find a room in an appropriate hotel. Blasco Ibáñez, famous Spanish author of *The Four Horsemen of the Apocalypse*, was commissioned by a South American newspaper to report the anticipated Lenglen-Wills singles match for today's equivalent of £50,000, allowing for inflation, although he had never seen a tennis game in his life.

The second week of Helen's visit coincided with the Gallia tournament. That week Papa Lenglen became ill and was unable to attend. The significance of this fact did not emerge until later because, as it turned out, he never again saw Helen Wills play singles. I always thought his appraisal of her at the Metropole, before she had found her land legs after six days on the Atlantic, gave him an inaccurate picture of her true potential. Moreover, Suzanne announced that because of Papa's illness she would not play any events at the Gallia, which meant that her own appraisal of Helen Wills in singles was also confined to Helen's first performances at the Metropole.

The announcement of Suzanne's non-participation at the Gallia tournament became a signal for the impatient newsmen to start suggesting that she was deliberately avoiding a possible final against Helen Wills. Suzanne's 'aftermath of jaundice' had caused her to withdraw from Helen Wills's first Wimbledon, and also the 1924 Olympics. These were their only previous opportunities of meeting. The old accusation of 'quitter' was quickly revived and the spectre of Molla Mallory loomed in almost every tennis report from the Riviera.

The tournament in Helen's third week was in Nice. Suzanne responded sharply to the bad press image she was getting by entering the singles before Helen even had time to do so. Now it was Helen's turn to play catch-as-catch-can.

On arrival Helen had said she would play every week. Her entry form for Nice was received, but at the last moment she said she intended to play doubles only. The tournament referee, George Simond, inquisitioned by all the reporters, said that Charles Aeschliman, in entering the mixed doubles with Helen Wills, had also entered her in the singles. But George conceded that this may have been without Helen's authority.

The reason Helen did not play the Nice singles when it was known that Suzanne would play, is still only partly answered in her own statement that said, 'I may *or may not* have entered.' In her memoirs she adds, significantly, that she may *also* have thought, 'Why play Suzanne on the one court she knows best in the whole world?' The likely answer seems to be in her additional thoughts.

From the journalists' point of view, the Nice week was a near fiasco. By entering the singles before she knew that Helen was not playing the Nice singles event, Suzanne refuted all the 'quitter' accusations and successfully spoiled their stories.

Suzanne, too, went to great lengths to disprove theories that she was antagonistic toward Helen. Helen stayed in her Cannes hotel during the Nice week but drove to Nice for the doubles. On her arrival, Suzanne was seen to wave gaily to Helen from the Villa Ariem, across the street from the club. Later she went to the club to greet Helen personally, playing to perfection the role of gracious Empress receiving an honoured guest in her own palace.

The atmosphere of this waiting game built to fever pitch during the week of the Nice tournament. The whole world was now asking whether the showdown might come the next week at the Carlton in Cannes. Helen Wills signified early on that she would play singles there, but Suzanne gave no hint of her intentions. Researchers discovered that she had not played the Carlton singles for the past three years, though she had won one of the earliest tournaments of her life there at the age of fourteen.

No promotional expert could have planned a better build-up. Meanwhile, more than two hundred frustrated journalists drowned their anger daily in bars the whole length of the Riviera. And the world waited.

Some small consolation was derived in Nice from the possibility that Suzanne and Helen might find themselves on opposites sides of the net for the first time in the mixed-doubles final. Suzanne was again in dazzling form, winning five rounds of singles with identical scores of 6-0, 6-0. Sixty games won to none lost must have impressed Helen Wills.

Helen Wills won the ladies' doubles in which Suzanne did not play. But at last they met in the mixed final, for which I was appointed one of the linesmen. Suzanne and her partner, the Italian, Hubert de Morpurgo, inflicted a crushing defeat on Helen Wills and Charles Aeschliman.

Meanwhile, the crowd of newsmen were frantically phoning their editors for instructions. They had no story and still did not know if and when they would get one. Should they stay or go? It was even thought for a time that Suzanne and Helen would never play each other in singles. But since Suzanne's unparalleled triumphs of 1925 she had been considering several professional offers for exhibition tours of the United States, so it was obvious she must play – and beat – Helen somewhere if she was to push up the pro' offers.

Two dominant personalities in this complex situation were Lady Wavertree and F. M. B. Fisher. The Riviera had been the natural winter habitat of this pair and it was more than coincidental that their presence greatly enhanced the promotion of Dunlop tournaments and the adoption of the Dunlop brand of balls. Moreover, Suzanne was Sophie Wavertree's close personal friend. Another relevant fact was that the Carlton Club was the private enterprise of the three Burke brothers, Suzanne's lifelong sparring partners and friends. Still another consideration was that all three Burkes, Albert, Tommy, and Edmond, were also friends of the Dunlop executive.

Towards the end of the Nice week, George Simond at long last announced that both Lenglen and Wills had entered the Carlton Club singles. From that moment on, the Dunlop people were publicly involved and this placed 'F. M. B.' in the spotlight of full centre-stage.

Many of the newsmen sent to the Riviera were being introduced to the brittle veneer of the tennis scene and thought it clever to demand answers to basic money questions that had been tactfully, and purposely, avoided in the past. John Tunis, a tough, ace reporter for Wallis Merrihew's *American Lawn Tennis*, and also a good player who enjoyed access to the Riviera dressing rooms, was already terrifying many of the stars with his bloodhound professionalism.

'How can you afford to live here?' Tunis asked the perennial English finalist Phyllis Satterthwaite, who was in fact on the payroll of an important chain of Riviera palace hotels. The circumstances surrounding the Lenglen-Wills confrontation seemed likely to present the greatest stimulus for his probing character.

With Tunis leading the pack, the journalists immediately attacked Fisher in strength. Every awkward question conceivable was asked about the finances of the match. Tunis had done his homework with great care. He calculated the gross receipts would approximate half a million francs, the equivalent of almost £300,000 by today's standards. He was prepared to allow 350,000 francs (about £180,000 today) for expenses and taxes, already a generous calculation. But these were 'amateur' days according to the Establishment, and Tunis wanted to know 'what the hell' was going to happen to the balance of the money.

'F. M. B.' was big, fat, and jovial, with a broad face, a strong handshake, and a slap on the back for most people. He originated from a well-known sporting family in New Zealand, but had adopted an authentic English manner and behind the joviality could be detected a feeling that there would be no holds barred in any business arguments. It was typical of his character that he arranged for these awkward press questions to be asked in the same Carlton Hotel suite in which the Prime Ministers of Great Britain and France, Lloyd George and Aristide Briand, had argued for days at the International Cannes Conference in 1921, and that he also conducted the press conference from the same chair that Lloyd George had used.

So the whole question of under-the-table payments to 'amateur' stars, and the then dirty word 'shamateurism', were first publicly aired in the discussions about the Lenglen-Wills match. The arguments were reported in newspapers across the world. Was Suzanne making a personal profit out of the match? And what was to be Helen Wills's benefit? Were the Dunlop Company, by virtue of providing a few dozen balls, and the Burke brothers going to make it rich at the expense of two girls? There was also a long argument about the newsreel rights. Finally, both Suzanne's and Helen's advisers agreed the whole world should have the opportunity of seeing the match and the Burkes were told they could not sell the sole newsreel rights to any one company.

Tilden was shortly to be suspended by the American tennis authorities for having a 'writing arrangement' with the newspapers, but no one seems to have noticed that Helen Wills had a contract to report for the American International News Service and was, consequently, already on their payroll.

Two of the questions F. M. B. carefully sidetracked at the press conference were the means by which Helen and her mother had recently moved into luxury accommodation at the Carlton Hotel and how Helen, meanwhile, had been outfitted by a leading Paris couturier with a wardrobe that today would have cost at least £10,000.

Papa Lenglen, having got up too soon from his illness in order to see Suzanne's matches in Nice, was again ill at home. From the Villa Ariem, however, he told George Simond there must be no Americans officiating when his daughter played Helen Wills. The American press (without involving Helen and her mother, because this was not their way) made a public demand that there should be no Frenchmen either.

At that time I had in two years umpired 104 of Suzanne's matches. The question of my umpiring this match was very tactfully broached by my boss, George Simond, immediately after Helen's arrival in France. I was only fifteen and he foresaw that the eventual clash of these two stars would be of such importance that my age would preclude me from the all-important role of umpire.

Very sensibly, he also said that if any questionable incident should arise, my close association with Suzanne would immediately be raised and could create embarrassments for all concerned. For sixty minutes I was heartbroken. But then a great sense of relief set in. In retrospect, and since the full drama has become history, I have been eternally glad of Simond's decision.

Some years after women were first allowed to take part in the early Wimbledon championships, Commander George Hillyard, then the Wimbledon secretary, decided he would convey to the ladies' singles what he considered the 'honour' of having the male club secretary umpire their final. This set up a long precedent by which for over thirty years he umpired most of the Wimbledon ladies' singles finals and many other important women's finals in Europe.

As a player Hillyard won an Olympic Gold Medal for Britain in 1908 and, by strange coincidence, finished his playing career winning the handicap mixed, at well over sixty years of age, in the Gallia tournament while Helen was playing there in the second week of her Riviera visit.

So it was not only inevitable, but a natural choice for George Simond to ask Hillyard to take charge of the Lenglen-Wills match. Simond was also faced with finding a crew of linesmen who were all British or, at least, of non-French and non-American nationality. I was British, but again Simond took into account my close association with Suzanne and we agreed that I should not be included.

The importance of the event made Simond feel that staunch supporters of tennis, well-known people who had been faithful to the Riviera tournaments, should be rewarded by involvement in this historic event. A rather strange cast of characters therefore became linesmen for this match. Some of these were to play, as is usual in climactic events, unsuspecting but leading parts. The first was Lord Charles Hope, a brother of the Viceroy of India, who made the most controversial call of the match. The second most controversial call was made by Cyril Tolley, one of England's top golfers. Another linesman was Sir Francis Towle, president of the Grosvenor House and Mayfair hotel chain that employed Phyllis Satterthwaite and in whose Riviera hotel gardens many of the top tournaments were staged.

Among the remainder was Victor Cazalet, a famous English racing trainer whose family had been involved in tennis for years. A German, a Russian, and four others whose names I have forgotten, were involved only in routine calls. No foot-fault judge was considered necessary.

Riviera tournaments began every Monday morning and, supposedly, finished with the finals the following Sunday afternoon. But on this occasion, the heavens opened at midday on the first day and the rain did not stop until Thursday night. All the handicap events were cancelled. The tournament proper did not get under way until Friday, when the real countdown began. The four days of waiting to meet Helen Wills's challenge obviously imposed an almost unbearable strain on Suzanne's nerves.

The early rounds were foregone conclusions and, in spite of the delay, Suzanne seemed calm, especially in a photograph I took of her on 12 February, four days before the big match. After that the strain began to show outwardly in her appearance.

The final, instead of taking place on the usual Sunday, could not be played until Tuesday, and by Saturday night Suzanne had only reached the last eight.

Suzanne's favourite Nice club, and almost every other Riviera club or casino, held a *thé-dansant* on Saturday afternoons. I can still see Suzanne returning from Cannes on this particular day looking drawn and deathly pale. I remember her standing by the bar of the club with only a ghost of her customary public smile, even this made with an effort. She also had the dry, tickle cough that normally only came on when she was tensed up on court.

Everyone around me commented on how ill she looked. One of her close friends even whispered to me, 'She looks to me as if she's not going to play that match.' This was just three days before the final.

On 15 February, the day of the semis, the two Greek cousins, Hélène Contostavlos and Diddie Vlasto, played Suzanne and Helen Wills respectively. Even in Suzanne's obvious state of high tension, Contostavlos was unable to take more than two games from her. Helen's comparable domination was demonstrated against Diddie Vlasto. Diddie had been champion of France in 1924, the year of Suzanne's jaundice, and in that year was runner-up for France against Helen Wills in the Paris Olympics. On this day in Cannes Vlasto only managed to take five games from Helen Wills. Suzanne and Helen Wills were head-and-shoulders better than any other girls in the world.

So 16 February, the day of the 'all-time' confrontation, came at last.

One of the distinctive features of the Riviera is that a heavy spell of rain nearly always lasts for four days. It is a sort of purging of the whole coast, and afterwards the scene looks even more beautiful than before. This Tuesday was one of those peerless days that seem, in one's memory, only associated with the French Riviera and Lenglen.

6 Day of Reckoning

The six courts of the Carlton Club were sandwiched into a small square of ground beside the Carlton Hotel. There was a centre court with a permanent stand down one side that could accommodate about fifteen hundred spectators. Behind this was a garage with a sharply pointed tin roof. The Carlton Hotel towered over one end of the centre court, while at the opposite end was a street edged with small villas. These were all roofed with red tiles. Growing astride the street and the backstop of the court by the villas, was a tall eucalyptus tree.

In those days Riviera finals usually drew five or six hundred spectators, maybe a couple of thousand when Suzanne played in singles. The unprecedented interest in the match against Helen Wills meant that the seating accommodation around the Carlton Centre court had to be doubled. A temporary stand for two thousand more people was hurriedly erected on what was normally the second court. How well I remember the carpenters still hammering long after the start of the match. As we sat there, the temporary structure rocked alarmingly.

As I was not to take an official part in the match, Simond said to me, 'Enter the tournament and you will then have a competitor's pass.' My mother rarely went to tournaments outside Nice, but she, too, was caught up in the wild enthusiasm of the occasion and also took Simond's advice.

With my mother I took the train from Nice in time to reach the Carlton by 10.00 a.m., a good hour before the appointed time of the match. We were confronted with total chaos. Both streets beside the club were already jammed with jostling crowds trying to squeeze through a single gate where Albert Burke was attempting, in vain, to check the tickets and prevent a total invasion of the club. Albert told me later that the waiting lines had been five abreast since early dawn, and dozens of the leading journalists, who had been waiting for weeks for this moment, seemed likely not to see it at all.

This was one of the times in my life I was glad of being 6 feet 5 inches tall. With my mother right behind me and with some encouragement from Albert Burke, we managed to reach our seats on the temporary stand amongst the hammering carpenters.

44

By this time, about twenty people were precariously perched on the summit of the pointed roof of the garage opposite, and when they attempted the perilous manoeuvre of moving along to allow even more friends to join them, they received a loud ovation from everyone, glad to have some comic relief from the growing tension.

About 10.30, there was a crash of tiles in the street of the small villas and two heads suddenly appeared through a hole in one of the roofs. Thereafter, this operation was repeated at about two-minute intervals until the pavement below was a sea of red tile dust and the roof of each villa looked like some cocktail-party centrepiece, from which dark olives on toothpicks protrude from cubes of red cheese. As the minutes went by, the holes in the roof were progressively enlarged to allow arms with flags and handkerchiefs to wave to their neighbours and indicate their support for Suzanne.

The next invasion was of the tall eucalyptus tree. Some ten local boys climbed to the highest branches and were about to settle for their front-row view when a squad of police went after them. A pitched battle took place in the branches until the police ejected the original occupants. Then all six policemen decided to remain in the tree themselves to cheer their French heroine.

Another ovation greeted F. M. B. Fisher when he walked on to the court, solemnly carrying three boxes of six Dunlop tennis balls as piously as any acolyte approaching an altar. As I recall, he was then joined on the court-side bench by the faithful Lady Wavertree, Charles Aeschliman and Sir Arthur Crosfield. The most expensive reserved seats, costing £3 compared to half a guinea for the best seats at Wimbledon at the time, were located immediately behind the umpire and the court-side benches.

At about 10.45, the front row began to fill with some of the world's best-known faces: the former King Manoel of Portugal, the two Princes of Orleans, Grand Duke Michael of Russia, Prince George of Greece, the Rajah and Ranee of Pudukota, the Bourbon Parmas from Spain, the Aostas from Italy, and, among many other celebrities, Britain's largest landowner, the Duke of Westminster. The business tycoons included Gordon Selfridge, escorted as usual that season by the Dolly Sisters, laden with diamonds, while everyone asked which was Rosie and which was Jenny. The arrival of each celebrity was greeted with an ovation usually associated with a Hollywood first night. Helen Wills's mother sat alone, calm and dignified on the opposite side.

From beyond the barricades of the club, murmurs and shouts of the seething mass of people still outside the gate suddenly changed to loud cries of '*Suzanne! Suzanne! Voilà Suzanne!*' All the flags and handkerchiefs from the roofs across the street started to wave frantically like mechanical toys in a store display at Christmas. To those who were outside the club, as Suzanne's car inched through the still hopeful fans, she blew kisses right and left, and was obviously deeply moved by the fervour and patriotism of their greeting.

Helen's memoirs recount that the night before the match she dined on *filet mignon*, ice cream and cake, and also recall that although the Carlton Hotel orchestra blared out the song of the hour, 'Valencia', she very soon went to sleep.

Superstition always forms a large part in a game-player's thinking. In Suzanne's earlier years she would not play a match without a particular gold bangle worn on her left arm. Mrs Mallory would never play without the triangle of diamonds that surrounded her monogram. As previously mentioned, Suzanne never again wore, at any time – day or night – the peacock-blue colour of the bandeau in which she retired to Mrs Mallory. In 1926 her 'lucky' ensemble was the delicate shrimp-coloured 'ombré' bandeau and cardigan that she chose for this vital match.

A moment before 11.00 a.m., the two champions appeared. Suzanne's entrance was that of the complete prima donna with full war-paint, a long white coat with white fur collar and fur cuffs. Her confidence seemed to be unimpaired, and she acknowledged graciously the marvellous ovation she received. Helen looked the clean, uninhibited all-American college girl in starched cotton, with the cerise cardigan she invariably wore, and the 'Wills eyeshade'.

Suzanne stood bowing and posing while Helen Wills, possibly out of some sense of respect, kept slightly behind the Empress. There was a battery of photographers already on the court, and the first pictures show Suzanne with her full stage smile and in the ballet pose she always assumed on such occasions.

But the moment the razzmatazz died down, Suzanne's face changed. At last she was confronted with the moment of truth. Being the extraordinary professional she was, her whole image altered. It seemed as if the change transformed the outward façade to the revelation of the inner soul. Suddenly the circles under her eyes were much darker, she looked ill and her expression showed a degree of apprehension that was quite unnatural for her in normal circumstances.

There was still a great deal of noise from the crowd as well as continued hammering in the temporary stand. One official addressed in English and in French the spectators, asking for quiet. He received a public brush-off for his trouble. There were too many Frenchmen new to tennis, and more important, they had come to applaud their heroine, *La Grande Suzanne*.

Eventually, the Empress herself spoke. '*Un peu de silence, s'il vous plaît'*. Later she repeated this on a more pleading note and finally reproved her subjects harshly for not acceding to her requests.

Tommy Burke spent many hours of his later life recalling the famous eighty minutes he spent next to Mama Lenglen during the match. It seems Mama Lenglen also had totally misread Helen's real ability and repeatedly reproved Suzanne for not winning more easily. Tommy recalled that on one change of ends Suzanne told Mama, 'I can't see properly today.' On another, she said, 'I have no strength in my legs.' How different things would have been had Papa Lenglen been able to foresee Helen Wills's improvement in the past weeks and had been present, with his hypnotic influence over his daughter.

Papa's absence must also have told heavily on Mama Lenglen. It is said the frayed nerves of both mother and daughter gave rise to a bitter argument that endured late into the night before the match. Tommy Burke declared that he repeatedly implored Mama Lenglen to calm herself, as her nervous state was communicating to Suzanne at each change of ends.

The first set took about twenty-five minutes, and I think the score of 6-3 to Suzanne was predictable from the girls' form on the day. What came as a shock was the second set, when Helen managed to speed up her shots, and on two or three occasions, Suzanne seemed close to physical collapse.

There were several crisis points in that second set, the first when Suzanne trailed 1-3. All the experts said that Helen then 'let her off the hook' by changing from an attacking strategy to an attempt to slow down the pace.

The many instructional manuals written by Suzanne all put great emphasis on the importance of winning the seventh game of any set. She always referred to this as the 'gateway to victory'. So she must have been deeply discouraged to lose the vital seventh game after a struggle that involved fourteen points.

After this it became increasingly apparent that Suzanne's strength was ebbing fast and that she would face almost certain defeat if forced to a third set. She was having frequent spasms of the famous dry, tickle cough, and was also clutching sporadically at her heart between points. Suzanne's silver flask of cognac was never more in evidence than in this match. During the first set she took liberal sips during each change of ends. In the second set she took swigs between every game. I wondered what Helen Wills thought of this procedure, so far removed from anything she might do herself.

The next crisis occurred when Helen led 4-3 with Suzanne at 30-30 on her own serve. Suzanne hit a shot to Helen's forehand line that Helen clearly thought was out. As the umpire called '40-30', Helen asked the linesman, Cyril Tolley, 'How was that?' When he told her he had called the shot 'in' in Suzanne's favour, Helen exhibited probably the greatest degree of expression her 'poker face' ever allowed in her career, an expression of total disgust.

If Cyril Tolley had given this ball out – as Helen obviously thought – she would have had a point for 5-3. With Suzanne clearly at the end of her resources, this advantage could have changed the whole outcome.

The last, the most contentious, and the most dramatic moment of all came when Suzanne finally reached 6-5, 40-15, match-point on her service.

Helen, who had resumed her hard-hitting tactics, hit a blazing cross-court forehand, which landed either just on the sideline in front of Suzanne, or just outside in the tramlines. The exact answer defied all the experts.

However, there was a cry of 'out'. Suzanne threw the two spare balls from her left hand into the air, then ran to the net to shake hands. Helen accepted Suzanne's hand rather ruefully, and Commander Hillyard announced, 'Game, set, and match.' Although the match took place in France, his calls were in English throughout.

With the invasion of photographers about to take place, and an accompanying army of page boys and deliverymen carrying floral tributes for the heroine, I recall seeing Charles Aeschliman go toward the foot of the umpire's chair as if to take control, once again, of the situation. He would soon have had to move in order to allow Hillyard to leave the chair, but while still standing at the base of the steps, he noticed the side-linesman, Lord Charles Hope, making a semaphore with his arms as he came across the court toward Hillyard. I played Aeschliman many times in my life and always felt that he had an exaggerated sense of the dramatic, which many other players considered an ego trip. He was an extremely imposing figure of a man, outstandingly good-looking with the rugged aura of a Swiss Alpine guide.

Aeschliman, from the foot of the umpire's chair, then made what was probably one of the most incredible utterances ever made on a tennis court: '*Attention, le match n'est pas terminé*'. The nearest equivalent to this in English would be, 'Just a moment, the match is not over.'

Lord Charles Hope had made Hillyard understand that he had not called Helen's shot out. He had seen the ball 'in', and the cry of 'out' had come from the crowd behind where he was sitting.

By this time Suzanne had sunk onto the court-side bench, and was already disappearing behind six-foot floral tributes and the army of photographers and page boys. Hearing Aeschliman's statement, Suzanne tensed and her face framed the largest question mark in the world. '*Alors il faut continuer?*' she asked blankly. Again, the sense of this can be expressed only in English as 'Then, must we go on?'

Hillyard, taking his cue either from Charles Hope's frantic gestures or Aeschliman's incredible statement, or both, resumed his seat. To everyone's amazement he announced that Helen's shot had been in and the match would continue at 40-30.

Aeschliman's intervention must remain one of the most incredible in the game's history, particularly coming from an international player who would be – or should have been – immediately conscious of the implications of his action. Hillyard, being over sixty and a Victorian gentleman, was probably too taken aback to react as he might.

In fact, the match had positively and formally ended. Helen had accepted the umpire's announcement, right or wrong, and the players had shaken hands. There was no reason on earth why Hillyard could not have told this to Charles Hope, and particularly to Charles Aeschliman, and left things as they were.

There cannot be a player today who would not claim that such a point should at least be replayed. Suzanne, instead, after her initial amazement, removed her coat. Looking straight ahead and without a word or a gesture, she went back to serve at 40-30 from the left court.

She lost the point, lost the game, and was in obvious danger of losing the set, which in everybody's observation would have meant losing the match because she was so close to total collapse. But she fought back and, a good ten minutes after having thought she had won the first time, she stood at match-point again, with the score at 7-6, 40-15.

Double fault!

In all Suzanne's years of supremacy, she was known to have served only six double faults. Then the game went to deuce and it was almost unbelievable that after such traumatic setbacks, she was able to win the match for the second time, with two blazing winners. The final score was 6-3, 8-6.

Once again, all was total chaos on the court. This time Suzanne collapsed sobbing on the bench. Blinded with tears, she avoided the hundred hands proffered in congratulation. Even the immense floral tributes seemed unnoticed until, as she recovered, a French army officer offered the miraculous compliment that she had really won 'two matches in one morning'. By then the area was so surrounded with a clogging mass of photographers and admirers, Helen hardly had room to raise her arms to put on the cerise cardigan.

On Helen's first day in Cannes, she had noticed a good-looking young man with his mother, but at the time they had not spoken. Standing alone now and ignored behind the hysterical throng and the banks of flowers that surrounded Suzanne, Helen was surprised to see the young man leap the barrier, force his way to her side, and say, 'You played awfully well.'

This was Freddie Moody, and on 28 January 1929, *Time* magazine announced Helen Wills's engagement to Frederick Shander Moody, Jr, stockbroker of San Francisco.

It had been arranged that the winner's cup be presented by either Mama Lenglen or Mrs Wills, according to who won. This was, of course, impossible in the circumstances. There was no presentation and for many minutes, Suzanne remained prostrate amid the floral tributes and the outpourings of admiration.

Helen left the court alone and unnoticed; nobody even seemed to care that she had gone.

Suzanne was assisted from the court. She was taken to the small wooden clubhouse that revealed, when unlocked, a scene of wild disorder, because the thousands of francs in paper money that had been taken at the gate had yet to be counted and checked.

Once in private, Suzanne's nerves finally gave way, and her friends recount a bout of terrible hysterics in which Suzanne lay on the floor screaming and clutching fists full of the banknotes. It has often occurred to me that the sight of the piles of money, when she was making so much for everybody else and so little for herself, may have unconsciously set off her hysterics.

Eventually Suzanne reached the suite allocated to her in the Carlton. But there was still no peace for her because her private room was invaded by Ferdy Touhy of the *New York Times*. A more outstanding contradiction between forceful reporting and the ultimate in cruel bad taste has yet to be imagined!

Needless to say, Suzanne upbraided him in a torrent of hysterical French, fenced all his questions, and told him with angry bravado that she was still Empress of the Courts and intended to remain so for a long time to come.

Meanwhile, the crowds below her sixth-floor Carlton suite were shouting and calling for her to appear. This she was quite unable to do, and all the victory celebrations that had been planned for that evening were firmly cancelled by Mama Lenglen.

It is perhaps difficult to recall that these were days before news of events was immediately relayed by radio, and that Mama Lenglen had to telephone the result to Papa's bedside. Hopefully she did not tell him, as she had told Suzanne at the moment of her greatest triumph, '*Mon dieu*, how badly you played!'

Recounting her feelings later to her friends at the Nice Club, Suzanne said of the match:

'I never tried to impose my game; I never tried to win points.'

My parents, James Alexander and Florence Elizabeth Tinling, in their 'going-away' outfits after
their wedding, 2 November 1898

Cannes, 1923. The Beau Site Hotel courts in Cannes, showing the surrounding palm and eucalyptus
tree setting. Left to right: King Manoel of Portugal, Suzanne Lenglen (back to camera), Mrs
Geraldine Beamish, and King Gustav V of Sweden (back to camera). This was a game these same
four played annually for five years on this same court

Beautiful Marguerite Broquedis, the first pin-up girl in tennis history, known as the 'Goddess'. She is shown here at the age of sixteen, when she won her first French championship at Villa Primerose, Bordeaux, in 1908

Mrs Dorothea Lambert Chambers in play at Wimbledon, 1919

Left to right: Jacques ('Toto') Brugnon, Mrs Wollaston Richards, the 'instrument of destiny' who changed my life by suggesting that I should umpire for Suzanne Lenglen, and myself. New Courts Club, Cannes, 1925

Left to right: Elizabeth Ryan, Suzanne Lenglen aged thirteen, Miss O. Ranson, and Miss M. Stuart, Monte Carlo, 1913. This was the first time Elizabeth Ryan and Suzanne Lenglen ever played together, in a handicap ladies' doubles event. They gave points to their opponents and lost 7–5 in the third set. They were never again beaten together throughout their playing careers.

Suzanne Lenglen, aged fourteen, with Count Ludwig ('Ludi') Salm, World Hard Court championships, mixed-doubles finalists, St Cloud, Paris, 1914 (Courtesy USTA)

Wimbledon ladies' singles final, 1922. Mrs Molla Mallory with Suzanne Lenglen before the match. Suzanne won 6–2, 6–0 in twenty-seven minutes. This was the great 'revenge' match, on which Mrs Mallory's husband had bet ten thousand dollars that his wife would win

Two of the greatest stars tennis has ever known: Suzanne Lenglen and Bill Tilden in a very rare pose. Wimbledon, 1920 *(Courtesy USTA)*

Suzanne Lenglen with Helen Wills before their historic match. Carlton Club, Cannes, 16 February 1926 *(Courtesy Mirropic)*

Suzanne Lenglen after beating Helen Wills: the floral tributes are just beginning to arrive *(Courtesy USTA)*

Suzanne in Rome in 1926

Elizabeth Ryan preparing her famous 'chop' shot, Wimbledon, 1930

Wimbledon, 1926. Left to right: Suzanne Lenglen, Diddie Vlasto, Mary K. Browne, and Elizabeth Ryan, leaving Centre Court after the historic ladies' doubles. Suzanne and partner had two match points, Elizabeth and partner won. Neither had ever previously lost a doubles match at Wimbledon, as they had always played together and were never beaten *(London News Agency)*

'Big Bill' Tilden's wonderful grace is demonstrated in this backhand drive, with both feet off the ground. Wimbledon, 1928 *(The Times)*

This photograph of Bill Tilden and myself was specially taken to prove which one was the taller. Gallia Club, Cannes, 1930

'Little Bill' Johnston (left) with 'Big Bill' Tilden (right). They opposed each other six times in the finals of the US championships *(Courtesy USTA)*

Wimbledon, 1920. Big Bill's 'woolly bear' sweaters fascinated the English spectators *(Courtesy USTA)*

Brian (Babe) Norton with Bill Tilden after their challenge round 'enigma' match at Wimbledon, 1921 *(London News Agency)*

'I contented myself with returning the ball the best I could.'

'I did not deserve the applause or the flowers that I received because I was ashamed of my performance.'

Helen's comment was, 'There will be other tennis matches, other years.' This was essentially the remark of a young aspirant at the sunrise of her career. She could not know that she would never again meet Suzanne in singles.

That afternoon Helen was to lose once more in doubles to Suzanne. Suzanne had changed to a brand new bandeau-and-cardigan ensemble in rose pink, but she was so exhausted that she was almost carried through the match by her partner, Diddie Vlasto.

After the match, Helen shook hands with Diddie but appeared to ignore Suzanne altogether.

Between 1914 and 1938 Suzanne's and Helen's careers as Queens of Tennis overlapped for three years, from 1924 to 1926. Everyone expected that in these years they would meet many times. Extraordinary sets of circumstances, which could have been decreed only by destiny, allowed them just three meetings in which Suzanne won all three matches – one in singles, one in doubles, and their first-ever clash in mixed doubles in Nice.

Later that evening, with the victory celebrations all cancelled, Suzanne withdrew to the lone company of her most intimate confidant, Coco Gentien. Coco recalls that they dined at a restaurant near the old Nice port. During the evening some guests at a neighbouring table, recognizing Suzanne, commented proudly, 'Our Suzanne is still Queen.' It was tragic that Suzanne should overhear this remark, for the moment seemed to reveal her innermost soul. She whispered almost inaudibly, as she looked into the far recesses of the restaurant, 'Yes, but not for much longer now.'

So ended 16 February 1926. Helen Wills, a more gallant loser than anybody predicted possible: Suzanne, for a short while still the Empress, not only of her Riviera coastline, but now of Europe and the whole world.

John Tunis, a first-class tennis player and reporter, had an acid pen, which was reflected in his almost daily comments about all of us. Tunis and I disagreed on many aspects of tennis, but on one point we agreed completely: his assessment of Suzanne's silent resumption of play after having already been awarded the most important match of her life. 'Never in her long and luminous career,' Tunis reported, 'did Suzanne so justify her claim to greatness as she did at this moment.'

The party was also over for the world corps of journalists. One British newspaper summed up succinctly, in bold headlines, the ending of this four-week episode, unique in sports history: 'The Universe Can Now Go On As Before.'

7 Wimbledon's Classic Tragedy

For Suzanne Lenglen, Wimbledon's fiftieth jubilee in 1926 had every ingredient of a Greek tragedy. Those interested in the dynamics of Greek tragedies may recall that their customary format features a Hero or Heroine of brilliant achievement, a Messenger of Destiny, a Chorus, who describe and elaborate on the action, and finally, an inborn and self-destructive flaw in the Main Character. Heavy significance is also attached to Auguries, Omens, and Fates.

Suzanne's experiences at her last Wimbledon could well have inspired the classic writers of the fifth century BC. Like the Greek theatres of old, the open stage of Wimbledon provided a backdrop of which early Greek audiences would have approved.

Suzanne, at the beginning of the 1926 Wimbledon, was certainly a heroine of unmatched achievement. The previous year she had won Wimbledon with the loss of only five games in the whole singles championship. She had also won the doubles and mixed, Wimbledon's 'triple', for the third time in her life, an achievement unsurpassed to this day. She had beaten Helen Wills, her only possible rival, in Cannes, and two weeks before Wimbledon, won the French championships for the sixth time, literally demolishing the past American champion, Mary K. Browne, in the final.

But the Auguries, essential to Greek plays, had already made their appearance on the stage of Suzanne's life. There were five.

The first recalled the traumas of the Cannes meeting with Helen Wills. This match foreshadowed, for the first time, the possibility that Suzanne's world supremacy in singles might be near its end.

The second revealed a more complex situation, which implied the possibility that her supremacy in doubles might also be over. In all her Wimbledon years, Suzanne's partner had been the Californian, Elizabeth Ryan. At the start of the 1926 Wimbledon they had never been beaten together in an open event, and at Wimbledon alone their record stood at thirty-one wins without the loss of a set.

However, the French Federation had been itching for years to force Suzanne to forsake Elizabeth Ryan for a partner of her own French nationality. There was only one woman player in France even remotely capable of partnering Suzanne at international level. This was Diddie Vlasto, a confirmed base-line driver, and a stark contrast to Miss Ryan, then the world's greatest volleyer.

From Miss Ryan's side the proposed break-up was also extraordinary, although she had expected some sort of situation comparable to Suzanne's. Since 1924 the American authorities had been making similar demands about her partnering an American. Molla Mallory, in particular, had been vociferous in questioning Miss Ryan's qualifications to represent the United States so long as she persistently partnered Suzanne at Wimbledon. Personal and official jealousies played a major part in all aspects of these devious manoeuvres.

The third Augury spoke of money. For nearly a year the American impresario, 'Cash and Carry' Pyle, had been trying in vain to assemble a tennis 'circus' of which Suzanne would be the unquestioned superstar. And there were many other proposals. For Suzanne, the question of which offer to accept, and when to accept it, had become a daily poker game with the whole family's future at stake. The 'amateur' rules of her era precluded her from accruing any appropriate rewards for her incomparable skills. The Lenglens' finances were often thought to be insecure, and now Papa was seriously ill.

The fourth Augury appeared when the French Federation made a very unwelcome proposal. This suggested a completely new event, an international match between French and American women, to be played at the end of May. The heart of the affair was that it would inescapably involve Suzanne in a rematch with Helen Wills.

Suzanne had risked her all the first time, and won. This time she had everything to lose. There would be no title at stake, no money could be mentioned. It would be 'just another match', yet one involving immense effort and intolerable risks to her future.

The proposal clearly found its way into Suzanne's waste-paper basket for, simultaneously, she was accused by her Federation of having 'emotional caprices'. The match never materialized, but she had provided fresh grounds for French Federation anger at her wilful disregard of their wishes.

The fifth Augury caught Suzanne in a trap. During Wimbledon's preparations in 1926 it was announced that, because of this special occasion, all overseas players would be invited to the jubilee championships as Wimbledon's guests. Less publicized was that this gesture would replace the usual arrangement by which Wimbledon allocated official monetary 'grants' to foreign associations, a proportion of which filtered down to the players.

This change in arrangements touched Suzanne very closely. In past years she had assumed a fair share of the French allocation. Under the 'jubilee guest' system, she would become a two-time loser. There would be no Wimbledon money to distribute and, since she had a standing invitation to be Lady Wavertree's house-guest, she would lose again by not availing herself of the alternative hospitality. Any allowable funds for Suzanne would thus have to come from the French Federation itself, and this gave her Paris antagonists their long-awaited leverage. At last they were able to say to Suzanne, 'A French partner. Or else!'

The agonizing decision she had to make was the break-up of her partnership with Miss Ryan. It was unlikely she would win the Wimbledon doubles with anyone else while Elizabeth Ryan was still in the field. And this proved true.

Meanwhile, on the Riviera, Helen Wills was finding plenty of consolation for the loss of her first Lenglen challenge with a full round of socialite activities, now always escorted by young Freddie Moody.

After the nerve-racking exhaustions of the Carlton match, and with five nagging problems unresolved, Suzanne retired to Italy for some rest. A communiqué announced ironically that she had gone there to 'prepare for an ever-more brilliant success in Paris and Wimbledon'.

The brilliance she expected was reflected in the Royal Command to be presented at Court in London in July. Suzanne's formal appearance at the Court of St James's was to be the crowning glory of her personal achievements. She ordered a special Paris creation for the occasion, but it was really her future and the Helen Wills problem that occupied her attention. By May, after a long rest in the Italian sunshine, she seemed confident that she could beat Helen Wills in the French championships and again at Wimbledon, so perhaps things would work out.

She had not taken the Omens into account.

Eventually the French championships began on 2 June. Suzanne was expecting to meet Helen Wills in the final. The Auguries and Omens remained offstage until 4 June, but then Helen Wills was rushed by ambulance to the American Hospital in Paris. A few hours later she was operated on for acute appendicitis.

No doubt with bitter memories of the Mallory incident, Suzanne's first reaction was to give an acid press-release, in which she said, 'I am sure France will be as sympathetic to Miss Wills as America was to me when I was ill in that country.'

Though by now she had decided that she could beat Helen Wills anyway, Suzanne would have been less than the star she was if she had not felt a sense of relief on hearing of Helen's illness. Henceforth, she would be spared the effort and risk of the actual matches, not only in Paris but also at Wimbledon. With the dawning of this realization,

Suzanne quickly made amends for her spontaneous bitter comment by being the first of Helen's visitors and surrounding her hospital bed with bouquets of flowers.

The first act in Greek classics often ends with a Chorus elaborating on the unsurpassed achievements and dazzling feats of the heroine. Such was the case with Suzanne in the days surrounding the 1926 Paris final.

With the announcement of Helen Wills's removal from the immediate scene, Suzanne seemed suddenly in a state of euphoria and inspired to repeat the best tennis of her life. She won the French championships more easily than ever before. Mary K. Browne, congratulating her after being able to gain only a handful of points in the final, told Suzanne in utter frustration, 'You're just too damn good!'

But moving to the next act, which was Wimbledon in June, the tone of the Chorus changed abruptly, and foreshadowed impending storms. The first storm involved Suzanne in a minor arm injury, and on her arrival in London she was already nervy and saying she needed to see a doctor. The next storm broke when the Wimbledon draw was announced. With every player's name tossed in the hat in those days, the Messenger of Destiny made his first speech in announcing that not only had Suzanne drawn the Paris finalist, Mary K. Browne, in her first-round singles, but the artificially formed teams of Lenglen-Diddie Vlasto and Ryan-Mary Browne would meet in their first match in the doubles.

Omens and Auguries were both ominously on stage at this point. The draw Fate decreed was close to being unbelievable. Neither Suzanne nor Elizabeth had ever lost a doubles match at Wimbledon. Now one of them must inescapably lose in the very first round. Suzanne's only public comment was to ask, 'How could they be so tactless?'

On the first Monday of the jubilee championships, King George V and Queen Mary presented commemorative gold medals to every past and current champion of Wimbledon's fifty years. Nine of the twelve lady champions from the whole history of tennis were still alive and made their curtsy to the royal couple, but on the afternoon everyone agreed that Suzanne received the greatest ovation from the crowd.

One wonders how the Greek writers would have made it known to their audience that, after seven years of adulation, this was the last time Suzanne would find favour with the fickle British public, that she had already played her last Wimbledon final the previous year.

Following the ceremony, a one-set exhibition doubles match was arranged in which Suzanne and Elizabeth Ryan opposed Kitty McKane-Godfree and the Dutch champion, Kea Bouman. This was

55

the first and only time in the history of championship tennis that Suzanne and Elizabeth were beaten. It was also the last time they were ever teamed together on court as partners.

In her state of tension this first defeat, although only in a one-set exhibition match, assumed an altogether out-of-proportion effect on Suzanne's morale because of the fateful pairings of the draw, the pain in her tennis arm, and the unaccustomed absence of Papa.

To the connoisseurs it was another Omen. Still another appeared when Suzanne lost five games to Mary K. Browne in her first-round singles the next day, the same total she had lost in the entire Wimbledon singles championship the previous year.

Wednesday, the third day of Wimbledon, was the day of the doubles with her young partner Diddie Vlasto against Elizabeth Ryan and Mary K. Browne.

Realizing she would have to exert every ounce of her strength and skill if she were to pull Diddie through this match, she made a point of asking the referee, F. R. Burrow, about his programme, to be sure she would not be required to play a previous match on the same day.

On leaving the club on Tuesday evening, she also confirmed that the incredible doubles match was scheduled for the Centre Court around 4.30 p.m. on Wednesday. Suzanne was not told, however, that Burrow's Wednesday order of play was not yet final. Certainly nothing was said to her about playing an ealier match.

Eventually, about 7.00 p.m., Burrow's final order of play was distributed to the press and dispatched, as a nightly procedure, to the royal residences of London, which included Buckingham Palace.

But meanwhile, after Suzanne's departure, Burrow performed the act that became the main single factor in the ending of her amateur career and her exit from Wimbledon. He added to his final programme the additional match Suzanne had particularly asked not to play. This was a second-round singles against the champion of Ceylon, Mrs Evelyn Dewhurst. Burrow's excuse for his disregard of Suzanne's expressed wish was, 'This was an unimportant match and should not have bothered Suzanne at all.'

Theories have differed for over fifty years as to whether or when Suzanne became aware of this addition. Burrow's final programme was published in most, but not all, the London newspapers the next morning. But it is still agreed by all the members of the French team that Suzanne never read the newspapers during Wimbledon.

Here again the name of Commander George Hillyard appears in Suzanne's life, and again at a peak moment affecting her whole future. Hillyard had been succeeded as Wimbledon secretary the previous year by Dudley Larcombe. In all the years of Hillyard's secretaryship, he made a point of Victorian courtesy by informing the

Empress of Tennis each evening of her following day's commitments. This Tuesday evening in 1926, there was no communication between Hillyard and Suzanne. For some years this gap in communication was attributed to the change of command in the secretary's office and the possibility that Hillyard no longer felt himself responsible to Suzanne.

Sometime later it appeared that a deep rift had arisen between Suzanne and Hillyard because of Hillyard's conduct in the vital last games of the Lenglen-Wills match in Cannes. Suzanne believed that, in forcing her to resume the match against Helen after he had already declared Suzanne the winner, Hillyard put her entire future recklessly in jeopardy and she never forgave him. In her mind Charles Hope and Charles Aeschliman were bracketed in that same extraordinary incident and it is said she never again spoke to any one of the three.

On the night before the contentious first-round doubles, Suzanne dined quietly with friends in London. Her enemies have suggested she already knew about Burrow's late addition to his order of play at that time. Yet, she made a date with her doctor for noon the following day.

To my personal knowledge Suzanne was always extremely punctilious about her match timings. It was known that she often spent a full hour arranging her bandeau and her make-up. Every match was a stage entrance to her so she certainly would not have made this midday date with the doctor had she really believed she had to be at Wimbledon early the same afternoon.

At 11.30 on Wednesday morning, Diddie Vlasto played the classic role of Messenger when she read an obscure newspaper and was obliged to tell Suzanne she was scheduled to appear in the one singles match she had asked not to play. Moreover, this was listed for two o'clock. There were no immediate hysterics, but the resentment of an Empress, hearing that her express wishes had been disregarded, can easily be imagined.

It has been said that with her doctor's appointment still thirty minutes away, Suzanne had time to contact Burrow personally. Instead, from a mixture of haste, disbelief, and probably some anger, she asked her team-mate Toto Brugnon to reach Burrow and explain she would not be there for the singles, but would arrive, as arranged, in good time for the 4.30 p.m. doubles.

Throughout the rest of his career, Burrow refused to accept that he ever received Suzanne's message, though Toto Brugnon confirmed that he had transmitted this to his office.

Burrow had refereed the Wimbledon championships for seven years. Just as it would not have occurred to Suzanne that her personal request would not be respected, it would not have occurred to Burrow that his decisions would be questioned.

Burrow's late addition to the programme in deliberate disregard for Suzanne's particular request was the key to the whole tragedy to come: a fundamental clash of personalities combined with a total breakdown of vital communications.

On Wednesday at 3.00 p.m., Queen Mary came to see Suzanne, but Suzanne did not arrive until 3.30. All the officials were summoned to a meeting, and the only temporary solution they could reach was that the empty Centre Court should be rolled in an attempt to make it appear that the break in the proceedings was a routine necessity. Eventually, the court was rolled for twenty minutes under Queen Mary's hopefully unsuspecting gaze.

By this time almost the whole Wimbledon Committee was assembled on the doorway looking toward the gates for Suzanne's car. Although Suzanne did not know her message to Burrow had served no purpose, she must have gone to Wimbledon prepared for a showdown with him. To say she stepped from her car into a wasps' nest would be an understatement. Recriminations flew in all directions to such effect that after fifteen minutes of public haranguing, she ran sobbing to the dressing room.

In those days, one of the cubicles in the ladies' dressing room was reserved with the words 'The Lady Champion' on the door. Locked firmly in the star cubicle, Suzanne refused all entreaties by Diddie Vlasto. Meanwhile Queen Mary was still watching a perfectly rolled, but empty court.

Discussing this whole episode with Jean Borotra at the Wimbledon Centenary fifty years later, Jean said it was at that moment he arrived at Wimbledon. He told me that as captain of the French team he was immediately pounced on by numerous angry committee members who implored him to use his influence with Suzanne in the hope she might still appear.

Even in his account of this tragic confusion, Jean's unquenchable Gallic humour somehow managed to inject some comic relief. He said that going upstairs to the ladies' dressing room, he was given a towel to put over his head in deference to the other girls' modesty. A game of Blind Man's Bluff ensued with Diddie Vlasto guiding him by the finger to Suzanne's locked door.

Unfortunately, even Jean's unique powers of persuasion had no effect whatsoever. Suzanne had become hysterical. There was no longer any question of her playing anything at all, singles, doubles, or whatever else.

Borotra then offered to be the spokesman who would make the corporate apologies of the French team to Queen Mary. He did this in the Royal Box, telling Queen Mary that Suzanne had suffered a sudden indisposition.

Burrow, of course, wanted to scratch Suzanne from the doubles and proposed to do so. However, Elizabeth Ryan, supported by Mary K. Browne, adamantly refused to accept a walkover. After a long argument, the committee bowed to the pressure of Suzanne's opponents and agreed to postpone both her matches.

On Thursday it was thundery and wet but, in spite of all that had gone before, Suzanne achieved one last victory over Burrow. Priority was given to her vital doubles match, and the single against Mrs Dewhurst was again postponed.

Suzanne and Diddie Vlasto appeared for their fateful Centre Court doubles in defiant battle regalia, Suzanne complete with yards-long chiffon scarf and flowered corsage pinned to her furs. Even more than the rest of the tennis world, Diddie affected a replica of Suzanne's outfits. This time both French girls carried identical silver flasks of cognac to fortify them in the coming struggle.

For a short time the Auguries seemed propitious to the French pair. They won the first set and, after an intervening thunderstorm, reached 5-2, with double match-point on Miss Ryan's service.

In the early part of the match, Mary K. Browne had been badly beset with nerves and was outstandingly the worst of the four players, but during the thunderstorm break, Miss Ryan was able to restore her partner's confidence to such effect that the American pair won the second set and eventually the whole match.

It was an incredible situation for Suzanne to lose any match, least of all a first round, and from such a commanding lead. The result, which itself had arisen from amazing circumstances, was a last and bitter twist of fate in Suzanne's and Elizabeth's twelve-year relationship.

Meanwhile, on her way from the Centre Court, Suzanne stood back respectfully for Queen Mary's exit from the club. For years, Queen Mary had been very cordial to Suzanne. Indeed, one of Suzanne's greatest prides was the friendliness shown her by both Queen Mary and King George V since the day of her first Wimbledon victory in 1919. On this occasion in 1926, passing within handshake distance of Suzanne, Queen Mary appeared not to notice her. This was quickly interpreted by her detractors as a deliberate royal snub.

The press 'Chorus', fulfilling its classic role of elaboration, publicly disgraced Suzanne in all the newspapers the following day. It was even reported that Suzanne had deliberately kept the Queen waiting to show that she recognized no peers in the world of women.

Against Evelyn Dewhurst on the No. 1 Court Suzanne lost four games – the last Augury – and forthwith complained of being ill.

When Suzanne returned to the Centre Court on Saturday for a mixed doubles with Jean Borotra, she received a hostile reception for the first time in her life. She had 'insulted' the Queen, and her myriad fans turned against her in an hour. The situation was marginally salvaged by Jean Borotra's sensitivity to the unpleasant atmosphere. Once again his inspired Gallic charm provided some measure of clowning relief when he deliberately served half-a-dozen wild services yards outside the court, gesticulating in mock despair, at the start of the proceedings.

But on Monday, the Messenger announced the final lines. Suzanne would withdraw from all events at Wimbledon, she would excuse herself from being formally presented at Buckingham Palace and would return to Paris at once.

Molla Mallory, finding her possible path to the final unexpectedly cleared by Suzanne's withdrawal, must have derived some cynical pleasure from the whole play.

As is often the case, history was corrected many years later in an unusual way. Wimbledon's earlier secretary, Norah Cleather, was asked by one of the palace equerries to send a copy of her book, *Wimbledon Story* to Queen Mary. Later, Norah received a letter from the Queen, thanking her for her gift. However, the Queen also conveyed her sorrow at reading, in the account of the Lenglen incident, that she had allegedly snubbed Suzanne. Queen Mary emphasized that the day following Suzanne's indisposition she had, in fact, commanded the French Ambassadress in London, Madame de Fleuriau, to inquire about Suzanne's health on her behalf.

It became clear, once again, that a complete communications breakdown had occurred, but this time the reason was no mystery. During Suzanne's many visits to Sophie Wavertree's London mansion, Mme de Fleuriau made no attempt to disguise her antagonism toward Suzanne. She considered her socially inferior and deeply resented the enormous popularity that made Suzanne France's 'First Lady' in London, a position Mme de Fleuriau considered should be reserved for her personally.

This was the opportunity for Mme de Fleuriau to give full rein to her personal dislike. Instead of placing emphasis on the press blow-up of the alleged snub to the Queen, the Ambassadress should more correctly have complied with Queen Mary's command to convey her personal sympathy to Suzanne. Had she done so, she might have discovered in the ensuing diplomatic proceedings that Suzanne was still welcome at Buckingham Palace. Instead, she told her abruptly she had become *persona non grata* and advised her to go home.

This was the final blow to Suzanne's reign in Britain.

To Mme de Fleuriau fell the role of the last Fate to appear in this long cast. Suzanne's susceptibility to high-tension hysterics at the great climaxes of her career was the inborn and self-destructive flaw required of all classic Heroines.

In retrospect, Burrow's conduct seemed to have stemmed from his dedication to an outdated concept of sporting ethics. The players of his day often found him something of an autocrat. I had one or two sharp brushes with him myself on the circuit. His thinking certainly derived from the pre-World War I era before there were empresses to make tennis into the big-money spectacle it was destined to become.

Burrow's published account of these two stormy weeks begins with pages of unmitigated praise for Suzanne. He speaks of her uniqueness, of her supremacy, and her contribution to Wimbledon in the most glowing terms – only to contradict this whole picture in one short statement, 'No one should expect me to give priority to the wishes of any one player.'

As early as 1920 London's infallible monitor of Society, *Punch* magazine, was saying, 'Wimbledon is packed for Suzanne alone.' In the intervening years it was unanimously agreed she gave an importance to tennis never previously attached to any sport. In so doing she brought millions in cash and a wonderful flowering to Wimbledon.

In the world that Suzanne had done so much to build, her supremacy had been absolute. Yet Wimbledon, having benefited enormously from Lenglen's stardom, delivered the final blow against her.

Papa Lenglen's comments are best left to the imagination. But Suzanne's life history proved that in the absence of his domination over her, things invariably went wrong. In late July 1926 Suzanne decided to accept 'Cash and Carry' Pyle's offer to embark on an exhibition tour of America. Thus she became the first world star to do so. With this step she was taking a leap into the unknown. At that time, professional sports performers were regarded as tradesmen; many of them came from a background of manual work. Because of this, French reporters made a strong point of saying that Suzanne was not denigrating herself but uplifting the world of sport.

Suzanne, now without the need to win at all costs, and with the family finances more secure, could turn her thoughts to a happier existence. The roses would still be there and the admirers would still ply her with champagne. Moreover, romance and sex could henceforth play a part in her new life.

Asked by reporters about her future plans as a professional, the secret of her years of strain and sacrifice came out at last.

'First let me live a little!' she cried out.

8 The Two Bills

'Big Bill' Tilden was already in his mid-fifties when he served two prison sentences related to homosexuality. 'Contributing to the delinquency of a minor' was the official charge.

Both times he was sentenced to a year in prison; the first after pleading guilty to interfering with a fourteen-year-old boy while allowing him to drive Tilden's car in Los Angeles shortly after World War II. The second, again in his car, for interfering with a sixteen-year-old hitchhiker in the same city three years later.

Before receiving his first prison sentence, Tilden told the judge he had not been involved with boys from the time he left college until recent years, when a car accident 'frayed his nerves'.

To me, Tilden seemed obviously attracted by blond 'young hopefuls' in tennis, right down to ball-boys and the like. In my job as tennis organizer of many tournaments in which Tilden took part, it was impossible, from close quarters, to overlook the situation. When Tilden toured the Riviera in 1930, there were incidents which, in their blatantness surprise me to this day.

The thread of Tilden's associations with young boys was to weave through his entire life and began, in tennis at least, with his 'protégé', the blond, budding star, Vincent Richards. They won the American national doubles title together in the last year of World War I. Tilden was twenty-five at the time and the boy, Richards, only fifteen. Later he was to develop another protégé, Arnold Jones. After that still another 'young hopeful', Wilbur Coen, who was called 'Junior'.

A great deal has been written about Tilden's friendships with young boys but, since in the 1920s the word 'homosexual' was never referred to and the word 'gay' had not yet assumed its present associations, it is not clear what 'friendships' implied in the minds of the writers.

On the tennis courts there was no denying Tilden was a genius. What has been forgotten with the passing years is that Big Bill was *a genius of his own making*.

Big Bill always had a big serve, but he realized in his teens that his service alone would not make him a champion. His ideal was to be a

62

baseliner and a volleyer; in fact, the all-court master he became. 'Everyone, including my friends, told me I was foolish,' Tilden said in an interview. 'They said I couldn't have everything, but I was pig-headed enough not to believe them and kept at it.'

So Bill worked and worked at his game and by 1918 was ranked in America's top ten. By then he was already twenty-five. As late as 1919 he was still not pre-eminent in the States because, although he had twice reached the last round of the national singles championships, he failed to win a set in either final.

As a result, he spent the entire winter of 1919 hitting thousands of backhands in an indoor court belonging to a millionaire friend, Jed Jones, of Providence, Rhode Island. This was one of the few private indoor courts in the US and Tilden was supposed to sell insurance for Mr Jones's company, The Equitable, in return for his keep. Tilden's sparring partner each day was Jed Jones's son Arnold, the US national boy champion of that same year.

The arrangement worked out well, because Big Bill put the finishing touches to his game during that winter. Thereafter he became the ultimate tennis craftsman, the only player I ever saw who could use three complete tennis styles, flat, top spin, and slice, to destroy an opponent.

But while his game was improving, Big Bill's personality was far from popular in America. His natural arrogance and the air of superiority he projected were too different from the Philadelphia gentlemanly image to be understood by his peers. Tilden had undoubted charisma that ordinary mortals had not seen outside the great silent movie stars who seldom emerged from Hollywood. Hollywood and Philadelphia were quite different worlds.

William T. Tilden was born in Germantown, Philadelphia on 10 February 1893. Twenty-one months later, on 2 November 1894, William M. Johnston was born three thousand miles away in San Francisco. For more than a decade they were rivals, partners, friends, and were eventually to be opponents six times in the finals of the American national singles.

With both players inevitably being called 'Bill', some extra distinction had to be found. At 6 feet 1½ inches Tilden was 'Big'; Johnston, at 5 feet 7 inches, was 'Little'. Both came to national prominence almost simultaneously. In 1913 Little Bill won the first of seven Pacific Coast championships. That same year the American singles title holder, Mary K. Browne, was asked to partner a promising young Philadelphian in the national mixed-doubles championships. 'He is not that good, but he has a big serve,' she was told. This was Big Bill and they won. 'The Establishment certainly figured Mary pulled me through that tournament,' Big Bill said later. 'Because, in spite of being national mixed-doubles champion, they still ranked me somewhere between fifty and five hundred the next year.'

From then on Little Bill stole a march on Big Bill, winning the US national singles championships in 1915. Big Bill did not even compete at Forest Hills until the following year, and did not win his first US national singles until 1920.

Their face-to-face confrontations began in 1919. Strangely, Tilden won their first meeting, but for the next eighteen months Johnston won all their clashes when it really mattered.

In 1920 Johnston and Tilden were ranked Nos 1 and 2 respectively in the States and in consequence were sent to regain the Davis Cup from Australasia, a combined team representing Australia and New Zealand. On the way they made their joint debuts at Wimbledon, and London was to see the first real flowering of Big Bill's career.

In the United States everybody loved Little Bill. Tilden was a very late bloomer, whereas Johnston came to prominence much younger and, in so doing, assumed the image of a contemporary gentleman sportsman of pre-World War I vintage. The dissimilarity of their temperaments was unfavourable to Big Bill and contributed conspicuously to the American public's affection for Johnston, in strong contrast to their dislike of Tilden.

At Wimbledon the whole concept was reversed overnight. When Tilden arrived in London, staid old Worple Road Wimbledon was still recovering from the shell-shock of Lenglen the previous year. To the English Bill was a romantic, Hollywood-style figure with the rangy stride of a hero from some early Western. They were fascinated by a man who some genuinely thought was a cowboy. Tilden's coat-hanger shoulders, the arrogant grace of his long legs, even his 'woolly bear' pullovers, were things the English had never seen except in silent movies.

By comparison with Tilden, the English found Johnston uninspiring and dull. Despite beating Tilden in the final at Queen's Club on the eve of Wimbledon in 1920, and actually going on to win Wimbledon in 1923, Little Bill as a personality never really had a chance. England was worshipping Suzanne and Big Bill.

At their first Wimbledon in 1920, both Big and Little Bill found themselves in the same section of the draw and were expected to meet in the third round. However, Johnston's wife became ill and he was so worried that he lost an earlier round, leaving a relatively easy path to the final for Tilden.

For Big Bill this was curtain up on a decade of dazzling world stardom. In his first Wimbledon final, Tilden had to challenge the rugged Australian, Gerald Patterson. Patterson was a man who looked as if he had come straight from a prize ring. On the centre court Patterson was the boxer and Tilden the fencer. Tilden used his racquet as a rapier and in a short time parried his way to the Wimbledon championship.

At twenty-seven, an age when many players are already past their best, Big Bill was only at the start of a period of tennis glory.

Once again Wimbledon fervour exploded overnight. Big Bill was a hero who brought a new connotation of showmanship to men's tennis. The Dohertys had won everyone's hearts at the turn of the century with their sporting chivalry. Tilden commanded people to admire him through the challenge of his personality. He was a frustrated actor who used the tennis court for his stage and the English loved every moment of his act. After Wimbledon, the two Bills travelled to New Zealand to capture the Davis Cup from Down Under, and to retain it in the United States for the next six years.

But on returning home, Tilden discovered that despite his Wimbledon and Davis Cup successes, and despite the adulation the English had given him, the American public still preferred Little Bill. The previous year Tilden had lost to Johnston in the Forest Hills final, winning only eleven games. Little Bill was still not only the American national champion but close to everyone's heart because of his purist, sporting demeanour. His many American fans were still unable to understand Johnston's loss at Wimbledon and were certain the record would be put straight if he and Tilden were to meet again in the forthcoming US championship.

Ten thousand fans packed the old wooden stands at Forest Hills for the showdown. The Irish tenor John McCormack, bet a large sum on Big Bill to win, but nearly everyone else felt Little Bill was a certainty.

The match had every possible element of drama. The two Bills split the first two sets 6-1, 1-6, and split the third and fourth sets 7-5, 5-7 – after four sets a dead tie, although at one stage Tilden had been only two points away from winning.

At that tense moment a plane taking aerial photographs of the match crashed, and both occupants were killed within two hundred feet of the spectators. The impact of the crash was such that Tilden felt the ground tremble under his feet. The umpire feared a panic, but both players agreed to carry on.

In that momentous final, Tilden served twenty outright aces and Johnston could never get control of the match. At last Big Bill beat Little Bill in a major championship. He was now champion of America and Wimbledon and stood unchallenged at the summit of world tennis.

9 Tilden, The American Mountain

For Big Bill the spring of 1921 represented the sunrise of a glorious era. He was champion of Wimbledon and the US, but had not previously competed in the so-called World championships on hard courts, which were still played at Saint-Cloud on the outskirts of Paris.

On 12 May Tilden, with his friends, Jed and Arnold Jones, sailed from New York to Cherbourg on the then fashionable S. S. *Mauretania*. Molla Mallory and her friend, the ninth-ranking American, Edith Sigourney, travelled separately, and they all met for a romantic spring amid the flowering chestnut trees of Paris.

At last Tilden enjoyed the rewards of his long years of hard work. The highest authorities of the French Tennis Federation treated him like some sort of god. Soon after their arrival Tilden introduced the Jones's to Suzanne at the Racing Club, and thereafter there were ceremonial lunches each day at which the crowned heads of tennis, Lenglen and Tilden, placed side by side at the top table on every occasion, were the subject of formal eulogies.

After five days at sea and two weeks in Paris the Americans were still complaining of not having found their land legs. Their practice matches were so much below form that the whole party decided to drown their sorrows in a visit to the Folies Bergères. History records that Tilden was 'reluctant' to go. Nevertheless, everyone was in much better form the next day.

On 27 May, Suzanne was again Tilden's lunchtime neighbour and, with all the speeches and the hilarity, she allowed herself to be drawn into a one-set challenge in singles with Tilden.

The French were so impressed by Tilden's presence they would only let him practise on their centre court, a unique honour at Saint-Cloud. Suzanne and Tilden played their challenge set there, 'amid a great furor'. Not one to be upstaged, even by an Empress in her own country, Tilden inflicted an ignominious 6-0 defeat on Suzanne. On being asked the result afterwards in the dressing room, Suzanne, always the star of stars, replied elusively, 'Someone won 6-0, but I don't recall who it was.'

In revenge, Suzanne immediately challenged Tilden to play the next day with his protégé, Arnold Jones, against her and Max Decugis, eight times French champion. She realized it would be degrading for two men to lose to a mixed-doubles team. The rivalry between Suzanne and Tilden, which was to become so deeply antagonistic very soon afterwards, had already been set in motion, and Suzanne assured her vindication by beating Tilden and Jones with a one-set, 6-4 victory.

Suzanne's vindication turned out to be all the more impressive because Tilden and young Arnold fought their way through several internationally known doubles teams to reach the semi-finals of the World championships, against the top French team of André Gobert and William Laurentz.

Tilden beat the Belgian champion, Jean Washer, in the singles final. But, with the social rounds and the strain of completing his triple victories of Wimbledon, Forest Hills, and Paris, he developed a serious attack of boils and spent two weeks recovering in hospital.

While the English were falling in love with Tilden, and Americans were at last forced to show him the respect he thought he deserved, Tilden was becoming infatuated with yet another protégé. This time it was an amusing twenty-one-year-old from South Africa. Brian Norton, or 'Babe,' as Tilden nicknamed him, with fair hair and an impish face, was originally just a raw South African boy. But he was a fine natural player and a born show-off. In these respects he was a miniature of Tilden himself.

Norton revelled in the fame and attention his tennis brought him, but his apparently romantic association with Tilden was the spark that really lit up his talent. For a few short years Tilden made him an international celebrity. This relationship produced one of the most controversial matches ever seen at Wimbledon, when Tilden defended his title against Norton in the 1921 challenge round.

In accordance with the system operating before 1922, Tilden, as current champion, had to sit around for two weeks waiting for a challenger to emerge from the 'all-comers' event, and this could not have helped his condition. Incidentally, he declared from the outset his challenger would be Norton.

Because of his physical condition, Tilden did not enter the men's doubles with either of his protégés, Norton or Jones, and only survived two rounds of mixed doubles with Molla Mallory. Thus, before the challenge round, Tilden played only three matches in four weeks, and Wallis Merrihew recounts that he had still not 'regained his wind' when the time came for the eventual confrontation with Norton.

The Wimbledon referee, F. R. Burrow, who had attended every Wimbledon championship since 1886, told me the public's behaviour at that match was the most disgraceful he ever saw. Norton won the first two sets and in desperation Tilden started to drop-shot. At one moment he played three untouchable drop shots in four points. A section of the crowd began to voice its disapproval of Tilden's tactics and the situation reached boiling point when a spectator rose in his seat, shouting, 'Play the game, Tilden!' Arguments broke out among spectators until they were strongly admonished by the umpire.

At one stage, parts of the crowd were so anti-Tilden, Big Bill told the umpire that if the spectators could not be controlled, he would leave the court. Norton, jumping to the defence of his mentor, said that if anyone was going to retire from the match, it would be he. Clearly Norton had a deep infatuation for Tilden, and it is widely accepted that 'Babe' deliberately threw the next two sets. The throwing of whole sets amazed and disgusted the Wimbledon spectators, who had never seen anything like this before in their gentlemanly game. Norton obviously felt his idol was being disgraced and their relationship could be destroyed as a result.

It has been suggested that Norton could never bring himself to defeat Tilden. This theory is probably correct, but in the fifth set Norton nevertheless returned to the attack and led 4-2 and 5-4, reaching double match-point.

The first match-point produced one of the strangest incidents of all. Tilden chanced a daring drive to Norton's sideline. The ball looked to be sailing out, but fell dead on the line. Tilden followed his shot to the net, but not, as Norton supposed, to volley. In reality, Tilden had resigned himself to the fact that his shot missed the line and was running forward to congratulate Babe. He had even transferred his racquet to his left hand.

Did Norton realize? At all events, he tried a difficult passing shot and missed. Thus reprieved, Tilden made short work of the second match-point with an ace and went on, in two quick games, to retain his title. The final scores were 4-6, 1-6, 6-1, 6-0, 7-5.

Sixty-two years have now elapsed since this unfathomed mystery but, by many accounts, the match held an unusual and strange quality throughout. I have known several connoisseurs who were present and all accepted the fact that a psychological, probably homosexual, relationship affected the result. Merrihew described this last Wimbledon challenge round, which took place on 2 July 1921, saying, 'It will always remain one of the great enigmas of tennis.'

The year 1921 saw the last of many old traditions on which lawn tennis had been raised: the last Wimbledon championships at Worple Road; the last challenge round; the end of the vicarage-garden-party atmosphere. In 1919 the advent of Suzanne had outdated Worple Road overnight, and the ovations for Tilden the following year confirmed its legitimate demise. Suzanne's startling debut caused five thousand applications for the five hundred bookable seats and the Wimbledon Committee decided forthwith to commission an architect to design a 'grand new stadium' on a larger site. By 1921 the excitement of Lenglen plus Tilden overtaxed to bursting point the Worple Road seating capacity of seven thousand. The committee must have been relieved that the following year the new stadium would provide for seventeen thousand spectators on the Centre Court alone.

Another feature of 1921 was the deep rivalry that developed between Suzanne and Bill. Lenglen and Tilden both had the same strong drive for success, the same extraordinary instinct for showmanship, and the same reading of public taste. Both also had boundless technical knowledge of the game, induced by determination to excel and an unbelievable capacity for practice. Tilden actually invented strokes never previously conceived. To this day, his book *Match Play and the Spin of the Ball* remains the outstanding masterpiece of technical tennis analysis.

Meanwhile Suzanne became such a dominating figure that the world was automatically her stage. Everything she did was scrutinized in detail by the world press. She did not need to seek adulation. Tilden, however, had to draw attention to himself, and did. I remember Tilden once becoming infuriated and stopping an entire match because he noticed a woman spectator in the second row repairing her make-up from her compact. This upset Big Bill mostly because she was not concentrating on him. The excuse for his anger was that the reflection from her mirror was distracting him.

Suzanne's pride of performance also stood in direct contrast to Tilden's in that she regarded it as the ultimate sin to miss a shot. Bill, in his prime, would throw a whole set for the sole purpose of showing spectators how he could then demean his opponent at will.

When I played Tilden on the Riviera in 1930 I took one game in the first set and three in the second. There is not the slightest doubt that if he had wished to beat me 6-0, 6-0, he could have. I remember praying that his flat first serve would come in because there was a chance of blocking this back. His second serve kicked from outside my right foot to well over my left ear, and even on soft clay courts many good players found this impossible to handle.

It was inevitable there should be clashes between Lenglen and Tilden. I do not believe Suzanne ever felt the same degree of antagonism toward Big Bill as he toward her. Possibly Tilden felt the enormous publicity given to Lenglen's bandeau upstaged the almost equal publicity his 'woolly bear' sweaters were attracting. Tennis clothing has always caused out-of-proportion emotions with the British press and the spectators, and Bill seemed to dress for maximum effect.

From 1921 on Tilden never passed up an opportunity to denigrate Suzanne in public or in conversation. At the same time he never missed the chance of backing Molla Mallory in her feud with Suzanne, culminating in his famous brainwashing session before her historic match against Suzanne at Forest Hills in 1921.

One aspect that Suzanne and Tilden had in common was a special magnetism that caused other great personalities to want to watch them. Just as Suzanne's audiences invariably included kings, rajahs, and international tycoons, Tilden always attracted the queens of Broadway and Hollywood. Tallulah Bankhead was a great Tilden devotee. I remember during his Wimbledon semi-final against Réné Lacoste in 1928, Tallulah chewed a pink rose down to the thorns in sheer nervous excitement as Tilden lost in five sets.

In 1921, after winning Wimbledon for the second time, Tilden returned to the States and conducted his activities out of Philadelphia, confining all his tennis to America. At last he had established unanswerable proof that he had brought the US to the summit of men's tennis, and made himself champion of the world. From Philadelphia he looked down and declared that if there were any aspiring Mohammeds around they would have to come to the American Mountain.

The American Mountain remained impregnable for six years, during which Tilden led the US Davis Cup team to victory every year, and won no fewer than forty-two consecutive matches in the US national singles.

He was the absolute monarch in what is now called the Golden Age of Sports. On the courts he was the complete autocrat, and away from them he indulged a luxurious life-style that he considered appropriate to his status. From tournament organizers he demanded only the best in travel, hotel accommodation, and food, but they knew Tilden's name kept the turnstiles clicking merrily and most often obliged. Tilden did what pleased him and did it when he wanted to, trampling on tournament committees and officials in general. Above all, he incurred the wrath of the Establishment, which continually tried to make him toe its line.

But in America of the 1920s 'Tilden and Tennis', in that order, was the catchphrase always associated with the game. Whether or not he was homosexual, whether or not he antagonized people with his abrasive manner, I have still to meet anyone of Tilden's era who would not rather watch him on court than any other player of his time.

The dawning of professionalism in tennis after World War I brought an unprecedented set of problems because the majority of the leading administrators of the game were volunteers. The very essence of the words volunteer and professional implies contradictions in schools of thought. Long before the revolutionary period in tennis in the late 1960s, Tilden on the one hand and Lenglen on the other indulged in almost day-to-day confrontations with the USTA and the French Federation. The professional postures already adopted by Tilden and Lenglen in the 1920s, when both were theoretically amateurs, put the American and French Establishments in a state of shock.

Money, of course, was considered the villain of the piece by the administrators, but considered the just reward for their efforts by the stars. Tilden is said to have spurned outwardly the 'taint' of monetary reward for playing tennis. However, he thoroughly enjoyed writing for the press as an ego trip and it seems that he did not refuse the considerable sums the newspapers offered to stars in those days. Lenglen naturally had her share, though she never considered it a fair share. The administrators, as volunteer protectors of the amateur code, considered both Tilden and Lenglen as something close to criminals for earning anything whatever from their tennis.

In *My Story*, written by Tilden five years before his death, he says, 'I must own to a special dislike of amateur sports officials.' One way and another the mutual recriminations between all concerned never let up until Suzanne and Big Bill decided to become 'legitimate' professionals; Suzanne in 1926; and Tilden in 1930.

So Bill, arrogant and single-minded, fought the Establishment continually through his amateur days in the 1920s. Throughout this period he had a running feud with the 'strong man' of the USTA, Julian (Mike) Myrick, who had been trying unsuccessfully to gag him for years. Myrick and Tilden were so polarized in their thinking that they were constantly at each other's throats. The US authorities were also scared that the original effete image of American men's tennis that they had been at such pains to obliterate since its pioneer days, could be revived by the world's No. 1 player projecting a homosexual aura.

The bitter feud came to boiling point in 1928. While I was watching Tallulah Bankhead nibble her pink rose down to the stem at Wimbledon, Tilden was reporting regularly for the American press on the championships. On learning of Tilden's defiance of the rule that precluded players from writing about events in which they were still competing, the US authorities finally suspended him on the eve of the 1928 Davis Cup semi-final against Italy, scheduled to take place in Paris. Beating Italy was considered a formality for the

71

Americans, so that the controversy really centred about the final round against France. France, with its Four Musketeers – Brugnon, Borotra, Cochet, and Lacoste – ready to defend the Cup for the first time since toppling Tilden in Philadelphia the previous year, were shocked and amazed when Tilden's suspension was announced.

First, the French had just completed their new Roland Garros Stadium in Paris and were relying on Tilden's box-office power to help pay for it. Second, they could not believe anyone in his right senses could be so uncommercial as to suspend his top star performer. The French, on receiving absolute refusal to cooperate from the USTA, appealed in the first place to their own Department of Foreign Affairs, the Quai d'Orsay. This meant, in effect, the controversy would soon reach the Secretary of State in Washington.

In the days following, the cables between Washington and the Quai d'Orsay resembled a ping-pong game. Eventually, the US Ambassador in Paris, Myron T. Herrick, fortunately a sportsman himself, realized that though time was short, no real progress was being made. Through his personal efforts the case finally came to the President of the United States. This was no storm in a teacup.

Herrick clearly advised that in the circumstances, Tilden's absence from the American team would seriously damage American/French diplomatic relations. This was not the first time a President of the United States felt obliged to intervene in Tilden's squabbles with the USTA, who were incapable of considering the country's international relations. Tilden was unpopular at home and the American tennis Establishment was never willing to admit that abroad Tilden was a fine ambassador of goodwill for his country. In 1921 USTA president and tough guy, Mike Myrick, had refused Tilden's conditions for going to Europe, but President Harding intervened personally and over-ruled Myrick.

In 1928, again on behalf of international relations, President Coolidge put pressure on the USTA, at the same time giving Ambassador Herrick an unofficial nod from the White House. Eventually it was the Ambassador himself who renominated Tilden to the team. Herrick did an on-the-spot deal with Tilden to go ahead if he would take the consequences later.

Big Bill won the only match of the challenge round for the United States. Roland Garros was packed to overflowing and the USTA derived considerably more money from the box office than if Tilden had not appeared.

Meanwhile, within the minds of the tennis Establishment, rules were rules, discipline was discipline, and Tilden was suspended for the rest of the year.

By a curious twist of fate Lenglen and Tilden simultaneously created a new concept of tennis, their stardom attracting thousands of young players from areas never previously exposed to the game. Just as curiously, the lights of both were dimmed within months of each other in 1926; Lenglen's by her tragic exit from Wimbledon; and Tilden's in New York, where he experienced his first-ever loss to Jean Borotra. On that day Borotra became the first European to dent the glory that was American tennis and Tilden.

Tilden was then thirty-four, and before the year's end two of the other Musketeers, René Lacoste and Henri Cochet, were to beat him in major American events. Lacoste beat him in a Davis Cup match for the first time and Cochet dethroned him in his own kingdom of the American singles championship.

In 1926 three of the four Musketeers dominated the semi-finals at Forest Hills and the final was all-French. The coming of the Frenchmen was an ominous danger sign for Big Bill.

But it was to spark a new challenge.

10 *The Return of the Master*

After six years' absence, Bill Tilden returned to Wimbledon in 1927. This was also a red-letter year for me on three counts: it was my first sight of Tilden; my first sight of Paris; and later my first sight of Wimbledon. I was invited to umpire at the French championships in May. This led, unexpectedly, to my first Wimbledon job in June, which lasted until the controversy over Gussy Moran's panties in 1949.

In 1926, after six years of absolute supremacy, the French challenge spurred Big Bill to re-emerge from the United States to campaign again in Europe for his lost prestige.

For nearly a year his knee had been bothering him. This was diagnosed as a torn cartilage and on several occasions he was advised to have it removed. However, in those days the success of a cartilage operation was notoriously questionable and Tilden was very hesitant to accept a risky interruption to his career.

Tilden was thirty-four when he decided to make his comeback. It is fascinating to compare Tilden's determination to reassert himself at this age with Billie Jean King's similar determination (which she called her recycling) at the same age in 1978. Both had experienced a comparably unexpected series of defeats and in both cases their losses related to knee trouble.

Tilden's on-court character was a strange paradox. He would allow himself to become uncontrollably upset over some trivial irritation like a dog barking two courts away or, as we have seen, a woman powdering her nose in the court-side seats. But I do not recall his ever mentioning that a physical injury or even quite severe pain bothered him.

In 1926 he played many of his matches with a damaged knee, but he never once used this as an alibi. Instead, he decided to set out on a tour of Europe with Frank Hunter. Hunter first gained notice as a young naval officer in exhibition matches for the Red Cross in London a few months before the Armistice of World War I. Hunter had sporadic major victories in the early 1920s, reaching the singles final at Wimbledon in 1923 and winning a gold medal in doubles with Vincent Richards at the 1924 Paris Olympics. He understood

Tilden's eccentricities, and at his suggestion they paired together as a regular team in 1927. On their Grand Tour of Europe early that year, Tilden and Hunter had a long run of success, winning almost everything on their way to the French championships at Saint-Cloud.

I was determined to make my first trip from Nice to Paris on the Blue Train. This luxury took a large bite of my youthful savings, and it was a year before I could convince my father, although his fortunes were well on the mend, that it was not an inexcusable extravagance. My father had rented a small house in Passy so that my mother could be close to her doctor. The house was on the right side of Paris for the long journey to Saint-Cloud, and this made it easier for me to accept the invitation to umpire at the championships.

Saint-Cloud, on the fringes of a medieval hunting forest, provided the greatest possible contrast with the exotic aura of the South of France. The Club, known as the Stade Français, had been laid out at the turn of the century and was styled after the original Worple Road Wimbledon. There were the same creaky wooden stands and the same tall, ageing trees, which, for all their beauty, cast disturbing shadows on many of the courts.

But a new and faster pulse was already beating in French tennis. The young 'Musketeers', Borotra, Lacoste and Cochet, had already beaten the great Tilden and successfully stormed the hitherto impregnable mountain of American Tennis.

Awaiting the doctors' daily verdicts on my mother, I was not able to go to Saint-Cloud every day. So my first sight of Tilden was in a very erratic mixed doubles. In this, partnered by the Spanish star, Lili de Alvarez, he escaped defeat only when the South Africans, Pat Spence and Billie Tapscott, missed a sitter on one of their two match-points. This was a disappointing anti-climax to the excitement I had anticipated. It never occurred to me that my first sight of my boyhood idol, Tilden, would be in barely surviving defeat.

Because most of the occupants of the Saint-Cloud court-side seats of those days were English or American, umpires who were bilingual were very much sought after and I was asked several times to umpire on the centre court.

I had no means of knowing that on the Thursday of the second week, I was being observed by a special visitor in the committee box. Coming off court, the assistant referee, Fifi Lefebure, told me that Dudley Larcombe from Wimbledon wished to see me. I had never before met Larcombe because I had not then been to Wimbledon. But on the way to the committee room where he was waiting, I felt an exhilarating sense of anticipation.

When I arrived, Larcombe was pacing the room and with the

directness I came to know so well, he came straight to the point. 'I hear you know all the players,' he said. 'Would you like to come and help us at Wimbledon?' I do not recall any preliminary greeting or introduction. That was his way.

He was a small man with a bullet head. I was only sixteen, but something about the gimlet quality of his blue eyes gave me immediate confidence and I accepted without a moment of hesitation. At that time in my life the long string of what would be fateful Thursdays had not accumulated enough for me to sense their significance for the future.

Major Larcombe told me the Wimbledon championships started on 22 June and that he would expect to see me that morning. He made no reference at all at that time to the disastrous Lenglen incident of the previous year. But he did mention that Wallis Myers had recommended me for a new Wimbledon post he was thinking of creating. I was so thrilled at the prospect of going to Wimbledon in any capacity that the matter of what I was supposed to do when I got there never occurred to me.

My early disappointment over Tilden at Saint-Cloud was only emphasized in the final, when he failed by a hair's-breadth to achieve the first goal of his comeback, losing to Réné Lacoste after squandering two match-points.

Tilden's loss cast a pall of gloom over the whole American colony in Paris. Harry's Bar was twice as packed as usual with American sportswriters drowning their sorrows, while chagrined American hostesses were actually cancelling their parties at Maxim's.

However, Wimbledon was still to come. The Wimbledon title seemed up for grabs, but in London many of the English, as well as the American colony, remembered Tilden's glories of 1920 and 1921 and were keyed up for the return of the Master.

22 June 1927, began my long infatuation with Wimbledon. I was going to be seventeen the next morning and I thought I cut a dashing figure in my best navy blazer, white flannel pants, and the straw boater that was worn by all the aspiring beaux of that era. I had to be there by ten o'clock and went straight to Dudley Larcombe's office where I found him sitting behind his desk. Once again there were no formalities, not even 'Please sit down'. After all, I was there, I was not applying for a job, I already had one.

So I hung my straw boater on the office clothes-peg and his opening words were, 'Don't think you are going to hang your hat there'. I was taken aback, and rather embarrassed, but I suppose, in retrospect, 'he regarded it as an impertinence that I appeared to be setting up shop in his inner sanctum.

In that first year I was assigned to the referee's staff, doing odd jobs and filling gaps when linesmen were in short supply. Evidently I did not blot my copybook for, when I was invited to return to Wimbledon the following year, I found that I was to fill the post that Larcombe already had in mind before he spoke to me in Paris.

The tally of countries represented at Wimbledon had doubled in a very few years. Larcombe felt that with so many new faces coming from countries that were new to tennis, his committee was losing the close touch with the players they had in earlier years.

It was not until I had worked for Larcombe for ten years that he took me completely into his confidence and revealed how deeply he had shared in the tragic Lenglen exit of 1926. He said he felt it was a lack of communications organization resulting from his own shortcomings and those of his committee. Apparently he had sworn to himself then that the situation would never again arise. He felt the need for a personal go-between on whom he could depend to report to him every complaint or grievance overseas players might have about the complexities of the Wimbledon championships. This was my primary task from 1927 to 1949. How strange it would have seemed, could I have foreseen that I would be invited to resume the same job in 1982!

Although Suzanne's absence gave it sad overtones, my first Wimbledon will always remain vivid in my memory because of the unbelievable feat of my original friend in tennis, Henri Cochet. Cochet did what no other player has done at Wimbledon this century: he came back from two sets behind in all three of the last rounds to win the title. In his quarter final, Cochet first beat Frank Hunter, Tilden's partner, who seemed to have everything in hand when he led by two sets to love. In the next match, the semi-finals against Bill Tilden, Cochet was again two sets down and 1-5 as well. What followed remains the greatest Wimbledon enigma since the Norton affair. Cochet won seventeen consecutive points, and went on not only to win the set but the match. Then, in the final his opponent Borotra had six match-points, and the question of whether or not he actually won one of these is yet another enigma. On this particular match-point, the players had a quick volleying exchange close to the net and half the people there, including Borotra, thought Cochet had spooned back one of his volleys with an illegal double-hit. However, Cochet's controversial volley was allowed by the umpire, E. W. Timmis, whom I came to know very well. Unlike some, Timmis was a very fair and able umpire. But no one on earth could have envied him his decision. Not only that Wimbledon title but the whole sequence of tennis history would have been changed had he decided differently.

During the subsequent Wimbledon Ball speeches, Borotra made

one of the most generous possible tributes, 'The Roll of Wimbledon winners would not be complete without the name of Henri Cochet.'

Borotra and Lacoste had already won the singles title, Brugnon the doubles title, and it was this extraordinarily high degree of national pride in each other that enabled the French Musketeers, two months later, to mount an unforgettable assault on Tilden and the citadel of American tennis.

11 One for All: The French Musketeers

'All for One and One for All.' A philosophy born from a motto or, was it more likely, a motto born from a philosophy? Either way, this was the heart, soul, and dedication of the four adventurous Gallic tennis characters, the French Musketeers.

Jacques (Toto) Brugnon, Jean Borotra, Henri Cochet, and René Lacoste climbed individually, but side by side, to a summit of achievement unequalled by any one band of men before or after them in the world of tennis. In their day, the most highly regarded tennis titles were the championships of France, England, America, and Australia. Above all, the team event of the Davis Cup stood highest in prestige. In 1922-23 they won their own championships in Paris for the first time. In 1924-25 they won the French championships and Wimbledon. In 1926 they captured the French, Wimbledon, and American titles. In their peak year of 1928 France took every major tennis honour. Borotra and Brugnon won the Australian singles and doubles, so the vertical red, white, and blue stripes of the tricolour fluttered triumphantly over every championship court in the world, plus the Davis Cup.

Concurrently, their individual efforts were no less memorable than their team victories. In the period from 1924 to 1932 the Musketeers collected no fewer than nineteen major titles. In the Davis Cup after chipping away at the might of Australia, then America, their additional team triumph was to hold the Davis Cup from 1927 to 1933.

Together, they gave a golden era to France. With Lenglen, they created joint legends never to be forgotten in world sport, and their struggles with Bill Tilden and Helen Wills will forever remain classics of the game.

There is only one possible comparison to the legend of the Musketeers, the Australian teams of the fifties and sixties, so carefully selected and nurtured by their captain and coach Harry Hopman. But even the Australian teams, spread over a much larger stable and also a longer time period, fell at times to the challenge of the Americans.

The phenomenon of the French quartet was the span of a decade in their ages and the fact that all four emerged from quite different social backgrounds. Brugnon and Lacoste were Parisian, Cochet was from the provinces, while Borotra was from the Basque country. As a team, each one of the Four Musketeers made so essential, yet individual, a contribution that it is difficult to give pride of place to any particular one.

On reflection, it is probably logical to think first of the oldest. This was Brugnon, though, of the four, he made the least impact in singles. Brugnon's amenable personality made him the cornerstone of the Musketeers' success. He was 'Mr Dependable' in this mix-and-match, a model team member, always ready and willing to help iron out any problems with his friends on the practice court, as well as to advise or comfort them. Cochet, the most successful major tournament winner of them all, said, 'In the victories of the French team, Toto had a role that surpassed all he had already done with his racquet.'

Brugnon was a master of doubles play, brilliant on the volley and remarkable on the return of serve. His only weakness was overhead, but he was able to cover this against most opponents with a high, round-arm 'slap'. Brugnon was the perfect foil for all his team-mates in doubles, always encouraging whichever partner he might have, and apparently incapable of a moment of bad humour.

I remember taking a line for Toto when he played Gerald Patterson on Wimbledon's Centre Court in 1928. I infuriated Patterson by mistakenly calling one of his cannonball services a fault when it was in. At the change of ends, he picked up a roll of adhesive tape from the umpire's chair and threw it at me. Brugnon was actually embarrassed for me. 'I'm not going to dispute a present,' he said with a smile. 'But that is not the way to behave and I apologize for him.'

It was the combination of Toto's many charming characteristics that made Papa Lenglen decide he would be the ideal mixed-doubles partner for Suzanne, and together they were never beaten. And it was through this partnership that I had the pleasure of becoming a close friend of Toto's.

Jean Borotra, a master showman, and a magnet of appeal in every country, could not have been more of a contrast to Brugnon. Charm was the mutual trait of all Four Musketeers, but Borotra had his own unique expression that set him apart from his colleagues. He was an extrovert in both personality and tennis style.

Borotra did it his way. His effervescence on and off court was both astounding and exciting. The English loved all the things he represented in French chivalry, from his invariable hand-kissing to the unending flattery he bestowed on all.

Jean would always announce his arrival at Wimbledon by sending Norah Cleather, Dudley Larcombe's assistant, a gigantic basket of crystallized fruit. A pioneer of air travel, he would fly into London accompanied by his secretary, Suzanne Duboy, and his faithful chauffeur/valet, Albert, setting up residence at the old Carlton Hotel. Wimbledon was a continual whirl of engagements for Jean, and Mlle Duboy always had to be on hand to grapple with his personal business, shielding her boss from the adoring hostesses who deluged him with invitations for their parties and official functions.

Typical of Borotra was his showering of gifts on those around him. Even after he lost to Cochet in the great 1927 Wimbledon final, he sent Norah a gold trinket with the very sporting inscription, 'From Your Most Troublesome Runner-Up.'

The corporate chivalry of the Musketeers made the perfect

complement to Norah's own charm. She happened to be a very beautiful woman, and the setting in her office, much of which was provided by the Musketeers, made a perfect backdrop to her beauty. Borotra's six-foot-high centre-piece of crystallized fruit was usually surrounded by yard-square boxes of chocolates put on the floor because they were too big for the tables. And I remember on one occasion counting no fewer than eighteen floral offerings that almost muffled the incessantly ringing telephones.

It was also a typical Borotra gesture that, as early as my second year at Wimbledon, he should present me with an autographed gold fountain pen.

Albert, after parking a much-travelled Hispano-Suiza car, was always in attendance, carrying an armful of racquets and the huge tennis kit complete with a hat-box full of Jean's traditional berets. Habitually, Jean took six berets with him when he had a long match in view. Changing berets as he changed ends (and sometimes when he was not changing ends) was a danger signal for his opponents because it meant he was really getting down to business.

Borotra had a natural flair for tennis, with a flair for showmanship as well. He delighted the crowds, more often than not infuriating his opponents. One such display of showmanship occurred in a Wimbledon doubles with Toto Brugnon in the early 1930s. In this game Borotra chased a wide ball that most players would have ignored, and finished the stroke in the laps of two startled female spectators in the second row of the East Open Stand. He managed to get the ball back into play. Then, helped to his feet, found time to kiss the ladies' hands while Brugnon kept the rally going, miraculously, for three shots. Seemingly from nowhere, Borotra then swooped from the stand to put away a winning volley. One can imagine the reaction of the pro-Borotra crowd! I saw the incident over fifty years ago, and still find it difficult to understand how he managed it. It was vintage Borotra at its best!

This kind of dramatic escapade always annoyed Tilden intensely and produced another of the bitter feuds of tennis. Tilden thought that he alone should be master of every stage, and once declared that he never lost to anyone he hated, and he certainly hated Borotra's 'antics', as he called them. He once described Borotra as 'the greatest faker in tennis history'.

One might suppose that Borotra and Suzanne would have been involved in a comparable clash of personalities. They did not share any great affection for each other, but because they were both French and Tilden despised them equally, they fought for France as a common cause. It was the tricolour versus the Stars and Stripes. Fortunately for the tricolour, Molla Mallory was never quite good enough to make her partnership with Tilden comparable to either Lenglen and Borotra or Lenglen and Brugnon.

The effervescent smiles, the gallantry, and the hand-kissing routine made Borotra a hero in England. To the English he represented the actions, grace, and charm that English women rarely received from their own men. However, underneath the extrovert behaviour, beat the heart of a real competitor, a man who never recognized Papa Lenglen's philosophy of giving up in the face of defeat. It was his enormously competitive spirit that made it possible for Borotra to become the first-ever Frenchman, not only to reach the final at Wimbledon, but to win it.

Borotra's rather ungainly tennis style derived from the game of pelota (*pelote basque*), the native game of his own Basque Country. In pelota, players use a 'chistera', a sort of banana-shaped glove made from wicker, to project the ball against a wall. This results in an awkward gesture from the backhand side and needs a sharp twist of the wrist, which looks very unnatural when performed with a tennis racquet. There certainly seemed to be a carry-over of pelota into Borotra's tennis.

However, Jean's athleticism, his unique capacity to move laterally across the net (only comparable in my experience with McEnroe at his best) made Borotra almost impossible to pass. His knack of exploding from the starting blocks, enhanced by his already telescopic reach, fully justified the nickname the 'Bounding Basque' that the English press was quick to give him. In French newspapers *'Basque Bondissant'* sounded equally appropriate and impressive.

Henri Cochet, from Lyon, was essentially the product of that industrial, hard-working city. He was the tough little 'bantam-cock' of the four, a fighting mixture of aggressiveness and determination when the chips were down but with a dry wit that spilled over irresistibly whenever something unusual or incongruous caught his eye. Henri's wit was based on keen observation and a sharply sarcastic mind, but his wisecracks were never delivered in a sarcastic way.

When I finished my first stint as assistant referee of the French championships in 1928, I marked the occasion with a gold identity bracelet. Bracelets for men were a novelty in those days, and on mine I had engraved what I thought was a natural souvenir of some outstandingly happy days. The inscription read: 'Championships of France, 1928,' and I often looked at my wrist with pride.

As soon as I began wearing it, Henri observed the inscription without any appearance of noticing it at all. Then, quite innocently, he asked with his usual dry grin, 'Which event did you win in the French championships, Ted?' No sarcasm, no snide comment, such things were unknown to him. He was a true 'copain'.

As a copain, he was always prepared to help out if possible. I was running one of the late 1920s Riviera tournaments in George Simond's absence and I hoped desperately for the status of Cochet's entry. However, with his forthcoming international schedule it seemed an impossibility. But when he understood how much his participation meant to me, he immediately agreed to rearrange his plans.

I remember one evening in that happy week when he even suggested we have a knock together, and he concentrated on showing me the great tactical value of a cross-court forehand dink. I went around like a dog with six tails for the next two weeks thinking about my Cochet dink. I lost it all again because it had been learned too quickly. But in later years I did adapt it to my own game, and it served me a thousand times in doubles when I became a circuit player. For years I always remembered Henri whenever I heard my opponent swearing as the ball drifted sweetly across him into the right-court tramlines!

Cochet had that rare quality of being able to lift his game whenever a situation arose that triggered the necessary reflexes. At Wimbledon in 1928 I was filling in for an absent linesman on Centre Court when Cochet was playing his semi-final singles against Christian Boussus. Boussus was heir apparent to the French Musketeers and was edging into world class. In this particular match Cochet had won a long first set, lost the second set and looked as if he could well lose the third.

I had the outside line, the farthest removed from the umpire. This is a long way away at Wimbledon because of the unusual length of the runback. Cochet appeared totally bored with the whole proceeding, and at one point, ignoring the ball-boys, he wandered aimlessly toward my corner to pick up some stray ball himself.

As he came toward me, I spoke to him in French. 'Henri, you are a bore to take so long. I have seats for the theatre tonight and really wanted to get there.' His eyes lit up immediately. Some new and totally extraneous interest had appeared that was the signal to rub the Aladdin's lamp of his genius. 'Ah,' he said. *'Tu veux aller au théâtre?'* He lost only three more games and turned to me from the umpire's chair with the wry grin I knew so well. 'Will you make it now?' he asked, as I ran off the court like a scalded cat.

Even against top-class players, Henri's miracles derived from his amazing capacity to half volley, which was a natural reflex to Cochet on both wings. The foot-fault rules of the 1920s precluded any net-rushing, but with this technique he could reach his favourite net position without any visible attempt to get there. He probably had the world's finest overhead, and once installed at the net, it was pretty much 'curtains' for any opponent other than a Tilden, Borotra, or Lacoste. Even Tilden went on record as saying, 'Cochet plays a brand of tennis I shall never understand.'

Henri had a very sharp eye for everything, including pretty girls. In mixed doubles he invariably partnered the prettiest of the good players in the tournament. Pretty girls were the only influence likely to subdue his determination to win. This is probably why Henri never won a mixed-doubles title at Wimbledon and only two in Paris, in sharp contrast to Brugnon's seven.

The greatest contrast among the Four Musketeers was René Lacoste, a pale, studious, young man with soulful dark eyes, and a Semitic profile. He was the archetypal student of everything. Everything he did was pre-thought out and pre-planned to the utmost detail.

He was a frail teenager, and at fifteen his father told him to give up sport altogether. It is a testimony to Lacoste's extraordinary dedication that, by the age of twenty, he was the Wimbledon champion and at twenty-one was also champion of the United States. From the outset, René knew in his heart that he had the makings of world supremacy, provided he was allowed enough time to study the mechanics and technique of tennis. Even the dimensions of different areas of the court always figured in his calculations and he would sit for hours taking copious notes on every player he was likely to meet in a match.

There was definitely something machine-like in his approach to the game. He was a dyed-in-the-wool baseliner, but with the same inexorable determination as Suzanne's to work and win at tennis.

In fact, he gives credit to Suzanne for showing him the importance of 'target grouping' his shots. One of my clearest memories of umpiring Suzanne's matches is of her ability to place three consecutive shots within an inch of each other, the marks being clearly visible on the deep red French clay courts.

Never satisfied he was getting enough practice, René was one of the first to conceive a ball machine against which he spent countless hours a day, working at whatever shot he thought needed strengthening or tuning, even after the longest matches. Tilden said he sometimes thought he was playing the ball machine and not Lacoste at all.

Then, after hours on the court, he would return home to practise his strokes in front of a full-length mirror. During a spell when he thought he had lost his service swing, he saw a photograph of himself serving with a bent elbow. With his usual studiousness he traced the bent elbow. In practice in his bedroom he had been avoiding the chandelier. From then on the French team captain, Pierre Gillou, always insisted on a room for Lacoste with no hanging lights.

In René's youth, and with this studious approach to the game, Tilden's unsurpassed knowledge made him Lacoste's idol, eventually the man to beat at all costs. From the day at Saint-Cloud in 1921 when Lacoste first set eyes on Tilden, to beat Big Bill became the all-consuming passion of Lacoste's youthful life. It took him five years to achieve this. The year 1926 saw the first fatal piercing of Tilden's armour. Borotra had already thrown down the French glove by beating Tilden indoors, but Tilden had never previously lost to a Frenchman on an outdoor court.

Lacoste, who had been in poor health in the spring, took three months away from tennis, even foregoing Wimbledon, to tune up for the assault on America, although he was the defending Wimbledon champion at the time.

Tennis always came first and last with Lacoste. During most Wimbledons the French team would be houseguests at Lady Wavertree's Regent's Park mansion. However, Lacoste would separate himself as much as possible from the social round of her life. Wimbledon is a peak of the London Season and the price he paid for being Sophie Wavertree's guest was having to endure, on the way to Wimbledon in her car, an endless flow of socialite chatter, whereas his normal inclination before any match was for two hours' meditation, or at least silence.

Lacoste's single-mindedness and his style of play made him the least flexible doubles player of the Four Musketeers. He won one Wimbledon and two French doubles titles, with the mercurial Borotra compensating for his inflexibility, but while Lacoste's team-mates revered him as a singles player, Cochet and Brugnon considered themselves the crack team and never thought they should lose to him in doubles.

I have an amusing memory of the relationship amongst these outstanding characters. I was walking back to the dressing room with Henri some hours after the second French doubles title won by Lacoste and Borotra against Brugnon and Cochet. As Brugnon came toward us from the opposite direction and passed us, without a turn of the head or a change in expression, their eyes met and they simultaneously said 'Merde'. This single utterance from them both illustrated their feelings about their loss more vividly than any argument or subsequent inquest could have done in hours.

It was in 1923, in a Davis Cup match in Dublin, that the famous Musketeers conducted the first of their memorable campaigns. Brugnon*, the eldest, was a month past his twenty-eighth birthday and Lacoste, the youngest, was still a month short of his nineteenth.

*Jacques Brugnon died in Monte Carlo, 22 March 1978, aged eighty-two.

During the Wimbledon Centenary, knowing full well the complexities of Jean Borotra's character, while at the same time remembering our half century of friendship, I asked him, 'Jean, from your long years in tennis, what do you now regard as the ultimate highlight which gave you the most pleasure?'

With his normally instant reflexes, I was surprised when he took quite a few moments before replying, 'Of course, winning Wimbledon and being the first Frenchman to do so.'

Then he dipped deeper into his memory. Fifty-five years had passed since his Davis Cup debut and an expression of great nostalgia crossed his face. 'I think the most treasured memory of all,' he said, 'is the wonderful unity of spirit we evolved in the French team. In today's circumstances nothing comparable is even conceivable. Our winning the Davis Cup in Philadelphia was a crowning moment of national pride and emotion that has to be incomprehensible to those who never experienced it.'

The team spirit and the crowning victory referred to by Jean derived from long-thought-out and preconcerted battle plans. The French boys had decided the beating of Tilden was the heart and soul of the affair. The Musketeers knew from previous experience that in the 1927 Philadelphia challenge round they would need more than one hero to achieve their dream.

They knew Tilden would be called upon to play all three matches: two singles and the double. Tilden was then thirty-four, and the French plot was that by wearing him down in the first two days, they could conceivably deliver the fatal sling-shot on the last day.

Little Bill Johnston had been called out of semi-retirement because of Frank Hunter's previous failures against the Frenchmen, and did not appear to pose any great threat. One falter by Tilden was all they needed for victory.

The French team was calm and deliberate in its preparations. Only the ultra-perfectionist Lacoste complained first of losing his backhand, then his forehand, then both together. His team-mates knew him well. He would be ready when the moment of truth came.

In Philadelphia, chance gave them the draw they most hoped for: Tilden against Cochet on the first day, a fresh team of Borotra and Brugnon to play Tilden and partner on the second day, and the one Tilden then feared most, the imperturbable Lacoste, for the showdown on the last day.

In the opening match, Cochet played his pre-planned part by running Tilden into the ground for four tough sets while Lacoste quickly disposed of Johnston in three.

Meanwhile Tilden was also being emotionally drained by his own selection committee, who were unable to make up their minds until one hour before the doubles whether to pair Johnston or Hunter with Tilden. Eventually Hunter was chosen and Borotra-Brugnon further blunted Tilden's armour by keeping him on court for the full five sets. Rather tactlessly I mentioned this situation to one of the US selection committee a few years later and his reply was, 'You can't win a match when one of the team thinks he's God.'

Big Bill, at loggerheads again with his own administrators, knew that he had to blast Lacoste off the court in quick sets if he were to survive the last singles. He played like a tornado in the opening set, but Lacoste, more than twelve years his junior, bided his time until Tilden had spent his all before moving in for the *coup de grâce*.

Lacoste won in four sets. Cochet also beat Johnston in four sets. Thus the French Musketeers became the first and only team reared on slow hard courts ever to capture the Davis Cup from a home nation reared on turf. Brugnon dropped his pipe, Cochet grinned quizzically as usual, Borotra became his 'Bounding Basque' self again, while Lacoste, allowing himself one brief moment of celebration, left immediately for some more practice.

The record says there were only thirteen French patriots in the Philadelphia crowd of thirteen thousand. But these thirteen included Suzanne Lenglen. She had been an integral part of the technical scheming and thus felt that she had finally repaid Tilden for Molla Mallory's victory over her in which he played such a psychological part in 1921.

On 20 May 1927, Paris danced in the streets when Lindbergh landed after his historic first lone flight across the Atlantic. On 10 September 1927, Paris again danced in the streets, this time jubilant with its own national pride. There was dancing in the streets a third time the following year. The USTA did its best to hand the French the Davis Cup on its medallioned plinth by suspending its top player, Tilden, on the eve of the confrontation. This was not the first time Tilden controversies with the USTA had reached the White House and, once again, Tilden was restored to the team at the last moment and at the personal instigation of the President of the United States.

However, the rest of the team consisted of Frank Hunter and a newcomer, John Hennessy. Tilden's achievement in taking revenge on Lacoste was not enough and he succumbed to his old jinx, Cochet, who led the French to their second victory.

That was the last challenge round for Lacoste. In his memoirs, Lacoste's close friend, Coco Gentien, recalls that almost immediately before the 1929 match in Paris, Lacoste was admitted to hospital with pneumonia. The French team captain, Pierre Gillou, visiting his sickbed and offering some would-be consolation, said, 'Don't worry, your place in the team will always be waiting for you when you recover.' In reply, Lacoste, who had just turned twenty-five, delivered one of the greatest-ever shocks to the French Federation, probably to the tennis world at large, when he replied, 'I shall not be back. I am giving up tennis!' Maybe Björn Borg reads tennis history!

Lacoste was the ultimate in single-mindedness. He achieved the goal set for himself as a boy, after five years of preparation beating Tilden and winning the Davis Cup for France. Now his thoughts could stray to other things, his health, his business future, both of new concern as he had recently fallen in love. The beautiful golf champion Simone Thion de la Chaume became his wife. It then took a great deal of persuasion for him to accept the captaincy of later Davis Cup teams.

With Lacoste in retirement, the royal flush of French Tennis was broken. Without Lacoste they needed the advantage of their home courts to retain the Cup until 1933, when the British team of Fred Perry and 'Bunny' Austin ended France's period of glory, initiated fourteen years earlier by Suzanne Lenglen.

12 *Twilight of an Idol*

Bill Tilden went through 1927 without a victory in any of the world's major tournaments. Except for winning his seventh US national singles in 1929, those last years of the twenties must have been a heavy disappointment for him in terms of the top-level comeback he had planned.

In 1930, within days of his thirty-seventh birthday, any lesser mortal could have been excused for giving up hope. But this was not Big Bill's way. There was to be one more try, and even this started inauspiciously with two covered-court defeats by Borotra in Paris at Christmas, 1929.

Billie Jean King's famous theory of 'vibes' may have played a part in what then occurred. If so, they changed very much for the better for Tilden with the coming of the New Year, for in the next six months Tilden was to lose only two singles matches. Once he had recovered from his rage over his double loss to Borotra in Paris, Tilden seemed to blossom under the blue skies of the French Riviera, just as Suzanne had done.

His protégé on this occasion was 'Junior' Coen, whom Tilden had selected at the age of fifteen for a Davis Cup tie against China, making him the youngest American ever to play in this international team event.

It was an echo of the past for me to see Tilden showing off in the sun, just like Suzanne, when I had served my apprenticeship umpiring for her on the same centre courts. Now I had three years' experience as assistant referee to George Simond on the Riviera circuit. So for the best part of three months I saw Tilden every day as we shuttled from one famous resort to another along the coastline.

The South of France opened up a whole new life for Tilden. He found a new doting audience ready and waiting to listen whenever he wanted to hold court, which was from early morning until well into the night. The Mediterranean could not have been farther removed from the effects of the Great Depression in the United States and Bill obviously felt revitalized by the attention he received that winter on the Riviera.

We lived in the same hotels week after week and Tilden loved nothing more than to sit around the club or the lounge all day holding the stage or playing his beloved bridge. As soon as tennis began at 9.00 a.m. he would be at the club, laughing and joking with all of us. So I got to know him very well on a casual basis.

Bill recognized instinctively that I was not critical of him, that I always enjoyed a good laugh at his pranks. At nineteen, I was preconditioned to hero worship and not an unattractive admirer myself. This gave us an automatic bond of sympathy that was reflected in our many subsequent meetings. Obviously we both evolved with the passing years, but until the last time I saw him, on his pro' 'circus', we were always the best of friends.

Tilden went to the Riviera recognized not only as a giant of the courts but a giant in stature. Apparently he was asked in two or three press interviews whether he was as tall as Ted Tinling. This may have irritated him because he said, 'Let's stop all this. Let's have a picture taken together so we don't have to answer these damn fool questions.'

It was at the Gallia courts in Cannes that the photograph was finally taken. This revealed that Tilden was 1.84m while I was 1.92m. I have always found being so tall both inconvenient and expensive, and would gladly have exchanged heights with Bill.

It was also at the Gallia that George Simond first noticed Tilden taking an unusual interest in the thirteen-year-old blond son of the teaching pro'. George was even more astonished when Tilden asked him to enter them together in the handicap men's doubles event.

On the Riviera the handicap events were important to the finances of the tournament. Simond was delighted with these extra appearances of his top box-office attraction, but for a star of Tilden's stature it had become almost unheard of to play the handicaps. Even the boy himself was surprised.

With my French/English background and the liberal attitude towards sex my progressive-thinking mother had allowed me, I was personally quite open-minded about Tilden's predilections. So the young Riviera tennis reporters usually came to me to ask if I knew who Tilden's 'protégé' would be the next week. My invariable answer would be, 'Who can know the true secrets of the bedroom?'

Before long the new young blond boy became Tilden's constant companion, surprisingly transformed from a working-man's child to an immaculately turned-out young man who was extolled daily by Tilden as an overnight tennis prodigy.

In addition to this, Tilden seemed concerned on many occasions to have the boy sit on his knee. He undoubtedly had very roving hands, to such an extent that the boy once asked me in French, from Tilden's knee, '*Qu'est ce qu'il me fait?*' (What is he doing to me?) Needless to say, my answer had to be distinctly evasive.

At the Carlton tournament, Bill was complaining of 'fish poisoning' and, though never using this as an excuse, he lost to Eric Peters on the same court as Helen Wills lost to Suzanne four years earlier. Peters thus became the only Englishman ever to beat Tilden while Bill was still an amateur. Leaving the court, Tilden said to me, 'Thank goodness that's over for six months.' I looked at him, not understanding. 'I only have one bad loss every six months,' was his explanation.

Bill had a facial expression that suggested he was always ready for a prank. He had very clear, appraising eyes with a searching look, a feature he shared with Suzanne. His mouth seemed to tilt up at the corners at the slightest pleasure. Both Bill and Suzanne had a unique luminosity in the eyes, which, I believe, came from within, as if always hoping for something to admire or interest them in the person they were talking to.

I remember vividly one conversation with Bill in which he dwelt particularly on the necessity of *enjoying* one's life. I believe he thought of his tennis more as a catalyst yielding pleasure than an end in itself. It was then the height of the Gatsby era, when the main philosophy of life was to laugh and have fun. If one could afford them, fun and laughter were the things that counted.

During the week of the Monte Carlo tournament, when we were both in the Hermitage Hotel, Tilden was in very good spirits. One night Tilden was in particularly good form, and he described, with all the animation of the theatrical performer he craved to be, his greatest ambition at Wimbledon. This was to make his entrance to Wimbledon's Centre Court, not only carrying his normal load of racquets but also a rifle! Spurred by his own momentum, Bill laughed heartily at the imaginary picture in which he propped the rifle against the net post and checked it at every change of ends, at the same time giving a long look toward any linesman who had given him a doubtful call.

I remember Tilden telling me how he and the world famous tenor, Enrico Caruso, were delighted and surprised to meet at a European train terminal. They embraced, of course, and Caruso said, 'Why walk when we can ride?' Caruso then jumped aboard a pile of luggage on a porter's cart, dragging Tilden after him. The whole station came to a halt as they careered the length of the platform, on their backs, their legs flailing the air and the voice of Caruso echoing through the dome of the huge building as he let forth his golden tones in some tremendous operatic aria.

On another evening Tilden used one of our neighbours, an elderly English dowager who resided regularly at the Hermitage for the whole winter season, as the butt of a prank. This 'Lady X' invariably wore long, sweeping evening gowns for dinner. She had a bird's nest of hennaed hair swathed in a cloud of pink tulle and clasped with a vast diamond cluster. Each night she would go through the grotesque ritual of one solemn dance with the hotel gigolo.

At that time all French money was paper. A great deal of this was torn and dirty and there was a large variety of designs for every denomination. Legend had it that Lady X would deliberately tear a sizeable note in half, give one half to the gigolo and invite him to pick up the twin half from her suite later.

Lady X was at the table next to us on this particular evening and Bill was so disbelieving when I told him this story, I challenged him to put it to the test by inviting Lady X to dance. 'Why don't you ask her yourself?' I said. 'But I don't dance her way,' said Bill.

However, I saw the light of a coming prank in his eye, and as we got up to leave Bill approached Lady X saying, 'Excuse me, ma'am, I understand you have a very interesting collection of French notes. I make a hobby of these and would be very interested to see yours.'

Looking up, Lady X examined him through her lorgnette for at least a full minute. 'Are you a cowboy, young man?' she asked. 'No ma'am,' said Bill, 'but I would be very interested to see your collection.'

This time two minutes' examination through the lorgnette took place while she pondered her decision. 'All right,' she said finally, 'you have permission to ask the concierge for my suite number.' Bill, of course, never took up the invitation, but was fully satisfied with his prank.

On another night Bill came to my rescue. Warned by now of the perils of Riviera fish, he had ordered his more customary steak. I had asked for breast of chicken, but when the waiter arrived with a leg of chicken I remonstrated that this was not what I wanted. All the waiters at the luxury hotels spoke reasonably good English. Mine replied, very derisively: 'I regret, monsieur, breasts of chicken are reserved for the ladies.'

Bill, with immediate indignation on my behalf, said to the waiter, 'We are both ladies. Bring two breasts immediately!' The command was surprisingly obeyed.

During those memorable days on the Riviera, it was obvious from my many discussions with Tilden that he had a passionate desire to climb once more to the top of the Mountain. Obviously, his main target was Wimbledon.

It had been the French Musketeers who finally broke the six years of supremacy of Tilden and the US. Now, at thirty-seven, Tilden was to throw himself into one last challenge to the six years of French supremacy at Wimbledon.

After leaving the Riviera, Big Bill eventually reached Paris. The record books show that of all the Musketeers, it was Cochet who could usually beat Tilden. In the Paris final Bill went down once more to Cochet. Nevertheless, it was only the second single he had lost in six months.

The seedings at the 1930 Wimbledon were Cochet 1, Tilden 2, Borotra 3. Tilden carved his way through the early rounds and secured a semi-final position against his longtime antagonist, the man to whom he sarcastically referred as the 'greatest faker', Jean Borotra.

Sometime before, Big Bill made a brash forecast that he would never lose to Borotra on an outdoor surface. This was his chance for national and personal revenge.

After seeing fifty Wimbledons, I am convinced that the spectators of the thirties were more understanding of the real essence of tennis than at any other time in its history. So, for the Borotra-Tilden semi-final of 1930, the spectators came fully understanding the background of bitterness and years of personality clashes between these two master showmen. They knew in advance that high drama would be as inevitable as the sunrise — and their forecast proved correct.

The extraordinary showmanship of the two antagonists showed itself from the outset, when, instead of appearing on court together, Borotra made a lone entrance, weighed down with innumerable racquets and bath towels and a clutch of his famous berets.

Tilden was then seen at the entrance making an imperious appraisal of the Centre Court, alone and without racquets. At least three minutes elapsed before he made a deliberately planned entrance, and this time with Ellis, the dressing-room attendant, dutifully carrying his racquets. The ritual of the dressing-room attendant carrying the players' racquets has now become accepted as part of the ceremony of the men's singles final. But at that time it was unprecedented, certainly in any of the pre-final rounds.

Tilden's arrogant disdain of accepted custom caused a buzz in the crowd and fully confirmed the anticipated dramatic atmosphere. But Tilden's initial arrogance rebounded against him. Borotra, sensing the sympathy of the crowd in his favour, began in a blaze of unbeatable tennis, allowing Tilden only a handful of points in the first set.

Two hours later the scoreboard showed Borotra leading two sets to one, but it was clear that Borotra had given nearly his all to obtain this advantage. In the long struggle Tilden had always been the first out and ready to serve, while Borotra squeezed every precious second of rest, towelling himself that one extra time at the umpire's chair.

Eventually these tactics infuriated Tilden, and his rage together with Borotra's exhaustion made the fourth set a formality, which Tilden won 6-0 in little more than fifteen minutes.

By this time the spectators were almost as spent as the players, but the stage was set for a fifth-set victory that nobody could forecast. At that time even the bookies refused any bets.

Borotra fought his way to 4-2, but Tilden performed a near-miracle, alternating deadly drop shots and perfect lobs to reach 5-4. The crowd was reduced to silence as Borotra made one last superhuman effort to level at 5-5, finishing with an incredible smash that left Tilden stupefied. But this was the end. Borotra had no more to give.

Tilden, who had proclaimed that he would never lose to Borotra outdoors, kept faith with his brash promise. In the last two games Borotra was punch-drunk with the punishment the old master had inflicted on his junior. Tilden won 0-6, 6-4, 4-6, 6-0, 7-5.

The public was also punch-drunk, and there was prolonged silence before they realized the match was really over. When realization came, the applause was deafening as the vast crowd rose to its feet and gave Tilden and Borotra a standing ovation. Dan Maskell and I, who invariably sat together on the court itself, were so limp we could hardly get to our feet.

I remember that even in these circumstances Borotra was as gallant as ever. He had played the finest match of his life, yet he had lost. But a genuine smile of admiration for Bill never left his face. When the applause finally died down, it was I who carried Borotra's racquets, while Tilden, imperious in victory, strode off the court with his winning weapons.

Again, in the final, the master's momentum was not to be stemmed. With Cochet, Tilden's jinx, conveniently removed in the quarter-finals by the popular Texan, Wilmer Allison, the final was little more than a formality, the execution taking just over an hour to perform.

It does not require much perception to imagine Tilden's feelings at this crowning moment of his comeback, probably the greatest triumph of his career.

On the last day of 1930 Bill turned professional. The early pro' tours, particularly in England, took some of the world's greatest tennis to cities that otherwise would never have had the opportunity of seeing the game at this level. However, 'professionalism' was to remain a denigration for several more years. Even in the late 1930s, when I was asked to escort across England a young Hungarian team that included their future international star Zuzy Körmöczy, I found the coach on the train, which had been reserved in my name, plastered with notices: 'Reserved for the Tilden Circus'! The slur was intentional and an old confusion between our names was still going on.

Within a short time all the major players in the world, excluding Borotra, but including Cochet, Fred Perry, and Donald Budge, became part of the Tilden 'Circus'.

After the war Tilden left the cold winters of Philadelphia for California where he could play tennis outdoors all the year. But for Big Bill the next eight years were a tragic slide to poverty and public degradation.

The one light of his life at that time was Gloria Butler, whose father had sponsored Bill's tour of the Riviera in 1930. 'Angel Child', as he had always called Gloria, suddenly reappeared in his life, with affection, sympathy, and financial support.

But he was already too far gone for more than temporary salvation. All but a few friends, such as Gloria and, generously, Vincent Richards, deserted him. 'Big Bill' died of a heart attack on 5 June 1953 while packing his tennis bags to set out on his eternal quest for yet one more tournament to win. True to form, even the USTA did not consider his death worthy of an acknowledgement, not to mention a tribute.

So ended sixty years of contradictions: inferiority, superiority, arrogance turned by fate to humility, victory, defeat, and victory again, insults to his national representatives but an immense pride of his nationality.

Big Bill Tilden remains one of the great immortals of American sport.

13 The Two Helens

Fate, coincidence, chance, call it what you will, the story of two young girls with the same first name, who were reared on the same street, were educated at the same school and college, were coached by the same man, who lived at different times in the same house, and were both to become American and Wimbledon champions, is one of the strangest of all tennis sagas. Outside their tennis, however, Helen Wills and Helen Jacobs, of Berkeley, California, had nothing in common. On or off the court they exchanged only a few dozen words in fifteen years of treading parallel paths on the international circuit.

The fact that Helen Wills ruled the circuit unchallenged was accepted by all the girls except Helen Jacobs and her refusal to pay homage to Queen Wills lent credibility to a picture of antagonism. There were also dark rumours of religious differences and differences in sexual preferences. In the 1920s such matters were not publicly referred to, so these aspects are best countered with Tristan's reply to his king about Isolde, 'What thou asks thou shalt ne'er discover.'

Helen Jacobs has said, 'There was no feud', but the lack of outward communication between the two Helens put an obvious question mark over their relationship. For those who wished to emphasize their differences some evidence of a deep rift was not difficult to discern. Helen Wills was extremely class-conscious and highly discriminating in everything from friends to fashions. She always aligned herself with all the 'right' people: royalty, famous politicians, the top names in the arts world. In hotels, only the London Dorchester and the George V in Paris were good enough. She was a talented painter and her works were exhibited in galleries from coast to coast. Beyond all this, Helen Wills's father was a doctor whereas Helen Jacobs's father was 'in trade'.

Helen Wills had a natural ability to excel and projected the impression that everyone should automatically recognize her superiority in whatever area of life she chose to favour.

With the exception of Garbo, I have seen all the best-looking women in the world face-to-face and in the beauty stakes, Helen Wills was very definitely in the top league. I sat opposite her one evening in the relaxed atmosphere of Noordwijk's Huis ter Duin

Hotel when we were both playing in the 1932 Dutch championships. She had a flawless complexion, while her facial bone structure and her finely chiselled features were reminiscent of a piece of serene classical sculpture. In dramatic contrast, she had the Marlene Dietrich technique of fixing her beautiful eyes with sudden intensity at the exact climax of a conversation, and I remember thinking how truly lovely she was.

Wills was certainly the Garbo of tennis, always wanting to be alone and away from her fellow competitors. This, coupled with her determinedly detached nature and unchanging countenance, both unfamiliar in tennis, gave the world's sportswriters a field day. Arthur Guiterman wrote in *Life* magazine in 1929:

> The Journalists, a Ribald Race,
> Have named her Little Poker Face.

As she grew up, the 'little' was dropped, but 'Miss Poker Face' stuck appropriately throughout her career.

In complete contrast, Helen Jacobs was one of the world's friendliest souls and I often thought that the more Helen Wills became distant and aloof, the more Helen Jacobs wanted to please.

Jacobs had a Grecian profile, which endeared her to the photographers, though she never aspired to Wills's grandeur. Wills had too much respect for tradition to innovate anything; Jacobs, on the other hand, was actually the innovator of the first tennis shorts for women.

Wills achieved an all-time record of Wimbledon singles titles. Her personality was often considered remote and unfriendly so there were inevitably those who envied or disliked her. And these same people, spearheaded by Bill Tilden and Molla Mallory, went to great lengths to show their admiration and affection for Jacobs.

Whatever may have been the true nature of their relationship, Wills certainly used her racquet as a knife against Jacobs. Helen Wills first beat her namesake, 6-0, 6-0, in an early practice encounter in Berkeley in 1923. In 1938 she capped her legendary career with an unequalled eight wins at Wimbledon. She also won seven US national singles titles, and throughout made sure Helen Jacobs was forever the unhappy second-best.

Jacobs won the American championships four times and one Wimbledon title when Wills did not play. She beat Wills only once in all fifteen years of their rivalry, in 1933, in the final of the US national championships at Forest Hills, and even then she was robbed of a clear-cut victory because Wills retired as defeat stared her in the face at 0-3 in the last set of their match. Described as 'grossly unsporting', Wills's default brought waves of criticism and indignation, equalled only by those levelled at Lenglen when Suzanne 'coughed and quit' against Molla Mallory in this same championship twelve years earlier.

In 1933 Wills had a back injury and at the time I defended her stoutly. But this incident never lost its questionable overtones because her default made it academically possible for her to say she never lost to Jacobs, just as Suzanne was able to believe she never actually lost to Mrs Mallory.

Helen Wills was born in Berkeley, California in 1905. She recalls in her memoirs that the fascination tennis held for her as a small child was just how high she could hit the ball into the sky. 'Up, up,' she said. 'Where would the ball go if it didn't come down?' This, to me, typifies Wills's mental process throughout her life. Just as her vivid childhood imagination knew no bounds, neither did her quest for unparalleled achievement nor her determination for unquestioned status.

Wills admits that at the University of California her ambition was above all to earn honours and recognition. 'I had a complete lack of interest in learning for the sake of knowing something,' she said. 'I was, in the truest sense of the word, a 'cup-hunter' in the field of scholarship.' This same obsession pushed her career 'up, up' to records never attained by anyone before or since. Twice she retired, and twice she came back to fulfil her ambition of being the greatest Wimbledon singles winner of all time.

In her junior days, Wills benefited from the inestimable advantage of having Hazel Wightman on her side at every opportunity. Throughout the decade that spanned World War I a deep-seated rivalry existed between Hazel Hotchkiss Wightman and the Norwegian immigrant, Molla Bjursted Mallory who, in 1915, thwarted Hazel's hope of a fourth American singles title.

Women's tennis in every country has always abounded with bitchy theories, and it was widely said that Hazel trained 'young hopefuls' with the specific purpose of revenging herself against Molla. She was certainly successful in the case of one protégée, Marion Zinderstein, who put Molla out of the 1919 American championships, and then Helen Wills, who beat Molla regularly from 1923 onwards.

Wills was a newcomer to Europe in 1924 and came as a surprise to the English. Accustomed to the glamour and panache of Lenglen, the sophisticated Wimbledon spectators were unimpressed by the expressionless, phlegmatic look of the new American champion in her school uniform of pleated skirt, middy blouse, black tie and stockings, with three large buns of hair and an eyeshade.

That year Lenglen withdrew from Wimbledon, pleading 'the

aftermath of jaundice', and although Wills marched to the final, conceding only eleven games in five matches, she was still not experienced enough to win Wimbledon at her first try, even in Lenglen's absence. In 1924 the leading English girl, Kitty McKane, was Wills's final opponent. Wills won the first set and had four points to lead 5-1 in the second set. This should have given her a certain hold on the title, but she faltered and the patriotic crowds, not having seen a British winner since Mrs Lambert Chambers before World War I, cheered Kitty to a memorable comeback victory.

It was symptomatic of Wills's mental detachment that after the most important match of her life at that time, she asked the umpire the score! Kitty McKane won the title because she never allowed herself to forget it.

Wills was bitterly disappointed at her loss and wept afterwards in the dressing room. She has said it was the last match she ever cried over. She certainly had no further reason to cry at Wimbledon for she never lost there again.

Throughout her career, Wills was described as being slow and flat-footed, even 'padding about the court'. She was a big girl, tall, and later, very statuesque. Her concept was to achieve the best results with the least possible expenditure of energy. 'Because I saved my energy conscientiously,' she once explained, 'I kept a reservoir of stored-up strength and was considerably slowed-up in doing so.'

Hazel Wightman and Helen Wills won the Wimbledon doubles together that same year, and Mrs Wightman's spurring cry of 'Run, Helen' was heard so often that it became the fashionable taunt to shout 'Run, Helen,' to any girl who had problems in reaching a short ball.

Like Chris Evert Lloyd today, Helen Wills handled side-to-side baseline movement with the greatest of ease. Her only vulnerability was with short shots that moved her forward and, as with Chris Evert Lloyd, revealed her difficulty in becoming an instinctive volleyer.

The essence of Wills's supremacy was the sheer power of her service and ground strokes. Elizabeth Ryan, who won many world titles with Helen as partner, always said that Helen could be counted on for two and a half points every time she served. If she did not serve actual aces, her service strength was sufficient to enable Elizabeth to 'poach' for outright winners.

Wills won the American championships for the third time in 1925, but did not go to Europe that year.

After the Cannes match with Suzanne in 1926, a new Wills blossomed on the Riviera and in Paris. She and Freddie Moody became inseparable, enjoying the golden life, the *the-dansants* and the gala dinners. Later she was swept up in the romance and sophistication of Paris, inspecting the couture collections and ordering her dresses from the top-name house of Patou. Her teenage buns of hair were soon lopped to confirm with the new chic of her image.

Shortly afterwards, when she was struck down with appendicitis, some people said her tennis days were finished, but they grossly underestimated Helen's determination and ambition. She had out-shone herself in her gallant defence against Lenglen. Before the appendix operation she was already the unquestioned No. 1 in the United States, and in 1927 she was ready to show Europe the full extent of her continuing improvement.

Wills's first round at Wimbledon that year was against Gwen Sterry and is memorable for unusual reasons. Gwen, one of the best English players of the day, was the daughter of Charlotte Cooper Sterry, who had won the Wimbledon singles five times at the turn of the century. I made a dress for this delightful lady when she was already in her late sixties, and I made the first wedding trousseau of my new career as a designer for her daughter, Gwen, in 1932.

In Helen's opening match at the 1927 Wimbledon, Gwen lost the first set but won the second, and for a brief moment thought she would win the match by default. It was a cold windy day, and after losing the second set, Helen, without a word or comment, walked to the umpire's chair and put on her cardigan. This is an unusual thing to do after two hard sets, particularly without any explanation. But Helen Wills never acknowledged the need to explain anything, least of all her own actions.

In retrospect, it seems that the moment of putting her cardigan back on in that match marked a major milestone in Wills's career. For six years she was never again to lose another set, anywhere in the whole world!

Meanwhile, 'Little Helen', as the press called Helen Jacobs, emerged as a potential challenger to 'Big Helen' in the late 1920s. She was a tireless retriever, a dour and gallant fighter with an ambition to succeed undaunted by repeated setbacks.

Her backhand was particularly accurate and her ability to serve aces when most needed made her a formidable opponent. She was three years younger than Helen Wills and for fifteen years played the part of an understudy waiting for any chance to play the leading role so determinedly held by Wills.

And, just as certain players are notoriously injury-prone, Jacobs seemed to attract rebuffs and snubs whenever any improved relationship with Wills was attempted. A typical incident occurred in the spring of 1929. Jacobs was then ranked No. 2 in the US, right behind Wills, and that year the authorities announced that they would send only a two-woman team to Europe. Breaking with all tradition, the establishment asked Wills to choose her own partner. Her course of action was predictable. She deliberately passed over Jacobs and nominated the No. 3 ranking player, Edith Cross, to go with her.

For once Jacobs spoke up, and a group of San Francisco businessmen, incensed on her behalf, personally financed 'Little Helen's' journey to Wimbledon.

But Fate decreed she would meet Wills in the final. It was the first of four Wimbledon finals between the two Helens and Wills won all four clashes.

I still think some of the most sensitive moments of my call-boy* job at Wimbledon derived from the four times that I escorted the two Helens to the Centre Court for these finals. Because of Wills's status as Wimbledon champion, she became one of the very select group of women who were given membership of the Wimbledon Club and therefore had use of the members' dressing room, which was upstairs. But, before winning her one Wimbledon title, Jacobs was relegated to the 'middle' dressing room, which was downstairs. So, when they met I had first to call Jacobs, leave her near the Centre Court entrance, and then dash upstairs to collect Wills.

At the top of the stairs there was a long passage and a door that also gave access to the royal box. For security reasons the police insisted on this door being locked and the one and only key was quietly given to me in order to avoid a long detour for the players coming from upstairs to the Centre Court. In my copy of Helen Wills's memoirs she has written a personal dedication, describing me as the 'key man' of Wimbledon.

The first three of the four Wills-Jacobs finals took place before Jacobs earned the privilege of using the members' dressing room. On these occasions, after I completed the routine of unlocking and relocking the pass door, Wills would sweep regally down the stairs towards 'Little Helen'. I would see her stiffen slightly as she became conscious of the presence of her victim, but she always made it seem as if there was nobody there at all. In turn, Jacobs made it appear

---

*At Wimbledon, before regular TV coverage (which is now seen in all the dressing rooms) the players had no means of knowing when they were required to go on court for their matches. In 1927 the attendances were increasing daily and the new Club secretary, Dudley Larcombe, decided it was the Club's duty to the spectators to ensure against any delays between matches. This responsibility was given to me and, over the twenty-three years in which I escorted every player on to Centre and No. 1 Courts, the world press gave me and my function the show-biz description of call-boy.

natural that she had not seen Wills by talking earnestly to anyone nearby.

In my job I always anticipated these particular days with some apprehension though the whole ritual of our going on court together probably took less than five minutes.

The 1932 final was the only time when the frigid atmosphere surrounding us was relieved by a brief moment of levity. Near the doors of the Centre Court we passed the current Wimbledon chairman, Sir Herbert Wilberforce. Sir Herbert was a delightful, typically Victorian English gentleman. He was a high court judge who came from a long line of famous British orators renowned for their wit. He had snow-white hair, and every day wore a rose, fresh from his garden, in the buttonhole of his lapel.

Sensing and knowing the feeling between the two Helens, he greeted them with his most gallant smile and I almost detected a wink at me as he said, 'Come, come. You ladies aren't going to *fight*, are you?'

He received no response whatever from either of the Helens who probably said to themselves, 'What a stupid old man.' Later Sir Herbert said to me, 'I thought I might break the ice, but I fear I failed miserably!'

'There was no feud,' said Helen Jacobs repeatedly, but a factual interpretation of the situation must surely depend on semantics. Perhaps it is difficult to feud if those concerned never address each other.

14 The Queen of Ice & Snow

Helen Wills was never one to talk about herself, but one day during the Dutch championships at the seaside resort Noordwijk she confided to Elizabeth Ryan and me that she had strained her back, 'fooling around with Freddie in the surf'. This injury was to plague her for almost two years and contributed to her controversial retirement when she was in a losing position in the 1933 Forest Hills final against Jacobs. Wills played Forest Hills against doctor's orders, partly to avoid disappointing her doubles partner, Elizabeth Ryan.

Wills's win over Betty Nuthall put her in the final. In the other half of the draw Jacobs was to meet Dorothy Round, but then the rains came. The rain cleared on Sunday, but because of her religious beliefs, Dorothy would never play tennis on the Sabbath. Ironically, the rain started again the next day, dragging out the tournament to twelve days. On the eleventh day Jacobs and Round eventually played their semi-final on soaking wet turf, and while their match was in progress, Helen Wills asked if I would give her a gentle practice.

This in itself was significant. For the past three days she had only occasionally been tapping volleys on the hard courts during short breaks in the clouds. In normal circumstances Helen would have wanted a testing workout in preparation for her final.

I knew Helen's game well from long years of observation and I had played a couple of sets against her a few weeks before at Easthampton.

As soon as we got on the wet practice court it was obvious to me that something was wrong. She was not bending properly and was nervous to move. Putting all the circumstances together, I realized she was still having trouble with her back and wondered how she would play the next day.

Jacobs and Round were playing their match on the Centre Court inside the stadium. We were knocking up on the court immediately outside and I noticed that Helen was playing particular attention to the Centre Court score. Jacobs won the first set and had a commanding lead in the second when Round fought back and eventually levelled at one set apiece. At this point I thought I detected some distinct displeasure in Helen Wills. Later, I concluded that Wills had not the slightest apprehension about meeting Jacobs in the final. However, because of the bad time Round had given her at Wimbledon a few weeks earlier there was no doubt about whom she would prefer to play in the US final. Jacobs came back to win the third set decisively, and at last I detected a sense of relief in Helen Wills.

All this is to emphasize that what happened the following day came as a great shock to Wills – and to everyone else. The two Helens had met seven times in the States and Europe, and until this eighth clash Wills had never lost even one set to her rival.

The next day Wills made history by retiring to Jacobs at 0-3 down in the third set. It is a controversial event when any player retires from a match in a losing position. Everyone present on this occasion was stunned into silence when it became clear that Wills was giving up.

My memory of the incident compares exactly with the description recorded by Helen Jacobs, so I quote these words from her book, *Gallery of Champions*.

> Leading 3-0 in the third set I had changed ends. I turned to the ball-boy for the balls, speaking to him once, and then again, before I realized his eyes were fixed on the opposite court. I repeated my request before I turned to see that Helen [Wills] had walked to the umpire's chair and was reaching for her sweater.
>
> It was a confusing moment. I hurried to the stand as Ben Dwight, the venerable umpire, announced that I had won by default. As Helen put on her sweater I went to her. 'My leg is bothering me, I can't go on,' she said. 'Would you like to rest for a while?' 'No, I can't go on', she answered.
>
> I went back to the dressing room where Molla Mallory was waiting for me. A radio commentator had immediately asked Molla to broadcast a statement on the default in view of her similar experience with Suzanne Lenglen. She did, in biting terms, and was still full of it when we met.

I also recall seeing from my court-side box seat that Jacobs, in trying to show sympathy with Wills's distress, put her arm on Wills's shoulder. This gesture, for all its kind intentions, seemed repugnant to Wills and, before replying to Jacobs, she pulled sharply away.

In Helen Wills's account of the incident several years later, she wrote: 'If I had fainted on the court, it would have been thought a more conclusive finish to the match in the eyes of many on-lookers, for they would have been convinced I could not continue. Had I been able to think clearly I might have chosen to remain. Animals and often humans, however, prefer to suffer in a quiet, dark place.'

No matter how one sees this odd occurrence, Wills's withdrawal when facing defeat brought eerie echoes of Lenglen's 'Cough and Quit' episode in 1921, and Molla Mallory seemed delighted to elaborate on these in her broadcast twelve years later.

It is a strange coincidence that Lenglen and Wills, probably the two greatest women players of tennis history, were to lose only one major match after reaching their peak of world supremacy, and both times – by retiring – they could claim they were never truly beaten. A further coincidence is that both supreme stars retired on the same court, at the same Forest Hills Club, and neither star ever played there again.

Helen Wills did not play at Wimbledon in 1934, but she reappeared in the following year. Wills's meeting with Jacobs in that final assumed even greater-than-ever dramatic proportions. Once again Wills was to lose a set, and this time unquestionably faced defeat, when, after a ninety-minute tug of war, Wills found herself at 3-5 and match-point down on her service.

At this point Wills put up a defensive half-lob. It is said that Jacobs missed an easy overhead, but in fact Wills's lob was never high enough for a classic smash. Jacobs let the ball bounce and then found it too low for the easy smash off the ground she had anticipated.

I was in my customary place on the court with Dan Maskell. Dan and I knew just how much was at stake for both girls. Jacobs was extremely popular with the Wimbledon crowds, and there was an audible groan as she misjudged the match-point and hit her shot well down into the net.

Fate was again kind to Wills in the next game, as Jacobs was 30-15 on her own service, but put a certain winner a fraction of an inch outside the line.

I see from the umpire's sheet, which I still have, that the match lasted one hundred and seven minutes. By coincidence, though the score was 6-3, 3-6, 7-5, to Wills, each girl won exactly one hundred and seven points. As usual, Papa Lenglen was right. He always said that traditional tennis-scoring could be unfair to the loser.

Escorting Helen Wills back upstairs to the members' dressing room, and still tense with excitement, I was fumbling for the key of the pass door when to my amazement Helen flung her arm round me and embraced me. 'Isn't it wonderful,' she said. This occasion and during the match with Suzanne in Cannes were the only times I ever saw Helen allow her 'poker face' any outward emotion.

Wills had already won the American championships seven times. With this latest victory over Jacobs she reached the same count at

Wimbledon and also equalled Mrs Lambert Chambers's record total of seven Wimbledon singles titles. Afterwards Wills disappeared from England, this time for two years. In her absence Jacobs finally achieved her lifelong ambition by becoming the 1936 Wimbledon winner.

To everyone's amazement Wills re-emerged in 1938. The natural assumption was that her boundless ambition would give her no rest until she became the unquestioned singles record-holder of all time at Wimbledon. In her quest it seemed unbelievable that Jacobs would again be her final opponent; and again their match would be highlighted with drama.

Big finals such as the Wills-Jacobs encounters always produced a flood of telegrams from fans. I remember on this occasion there were ninety-six addressed to one or other Helen – with one in particular addressed 'The Two Helens'. I took advice from Norah Cleather as to what we should do about this. Before deciding, Norah felt she should read the contents. It was just as well for the telegram read: 'Good luck. Wish you could both win.' I think Norah was right in decreeing this particular message should not be delivered to either girl.

In 1938 Wills spared me the ordeal of walking down the long passage and the stairs from the members' dressing room between the two antagonists. I have often wondered if Wills also wanted to spare herself this tense moment, because, an hour before the final, she told me that when the time came for the match she would be on an outside court practising with Dan Maskell. After the tensions I had experienced in my call-boy duties at their three previous Wimbledon meetings, I was truly relieved to hear this.

At the start of 1938 Wimbledon's second week, Jacobs injured the Achilles tendon in her right foot. All week she had been receiving treatment from the players' favourite osteopath, Hugh Dempster. As I took the girls on to court, I noticed her ankle seemed very tightly bandaged and a slight swelling was already showing above the elastoplast.

In the first set, Jacobs was within a point of leading 5-4, but in an attempt to reach a wide passing-shot she turned awkwardly and gave a cry of pain. Helen Wills, with her usual detached air, put her lace handkerchief to her nose and appeared not to notice.

As the match progressed, Jacobs became more and more lame till Hazel Wightman, intervening as always, surprisingly appeared at the umpire's chair and told her she should retire.

But Jacobs, obviously remembering the reverse situation of their 1933 Forest Hills meeting, was determined to finish the match and allow Wills a clean-cut record for the history books. This was an

107

unhappy finish to Helen Wills's illustrious record. Many spectators were shocked by her relentless detachment from Jacobs's injury.

Her incomparable feat of losing only one singles match at Wimbledon in a fifteen-year span would normally have received a tumultuous reception. But she climaxed her career before an apathetic crowd, hushed in sympathy for her victim. Helen Jacobs records that after shaking hands on that day, the two Helens never saw each other again.

My long-time friend Will Grimsley of Associated Press recently interviewed Helen Wills, and his impressions only served to confirm my earlier memories of her. Will Grimsley described her as 'an elegant and lovely woman who looks twenty years younger than her seventy-seven years'.

Helen Wills told Grimsley, 'I read about fierce feuds I am supposed to have had with Suzanne Lenglen and Helen Jacobs. It was never so. We were of different eras – Suzanne older than I, Helen younger. I never had an argument with either of them.'

Grimsley comments, 'Helen Wills is still an aloof and very private person.'

The last time I had any contact with Helen Jacobs was through my tennis-dress business. In World War II she had been a commander in the US Navy and had since been appointed sports-fashion adviser to the elegant Saks Fifth Avenue Store in New York. She was as delightful as ever and gave my partner, Henry Turner, every assistance in his negotiations with Saks. Today she lives quietly in Easthampton, a summer resort about a hundred miles from Manhattan.

More than half a century has elapsed since Helen Wills won her first American and Wimbledon titles and Helen Jacobs began her frustrating challenges to the 'Queen of Ice and Snow'. But the strange coincidences of their similarities, their differences, and the curiously parallel paths of their lives must rank among sport's most famous rivalries.

15 Thirties Diary

In this chapter I have to go back some years, because my twenty-first birthday coincided with the second day of 1931 Wimbledon. My father contributed a case of Dom Perignon and Daisy, his wife, arranged a vast white-iced birthday cake decorated with twenty rosebuds and one full-blown rose.

The implications of the full-blown rose depressed me beyond words. The golden span of my adolescence in France was over. The Riviera tennis jet-set had virtually vanished as a result of the Wall Street Crash and the subsequent European depression. I remember thinking, 'My God, today I am supposed to be a fully fledged adult and I haven't even made a start on a real-life career.' To me, coming of age was a traumatic experience. That day I felt that I shared in the growing pains of all the world's teenagers.

I had tried to prepare myself mentally for the bottom rung of the dress-designer ladder in London, but I was still in love with tennis and the glittering life of the grand hotels. While I was looking for any excuse to postpone the unavoidable ending of my Riviera boyhood, a last chance came when a friend unexpectedly offered me a ticket for the Wagner Festival at Bayreuth.

I had been a dedicated Wagner fan since my early teens. In Nice there was a music library where one could obtain the score of any opera for a minimal subscription. By the time I was sixteen I knew most of Wagner's operas line by line. In 1976, I was to make the thirty-hour journey from Australia just to catch some of the *Ring* at the Opera House, which conveniently adjoins my Philadelphia home. Only later, when storing away the programme, I realized this was my seventy-fifth *Valkyrie*.

Bayreuth was, of course, an unforgettable experience. I chose a particularly lucky year because Fürstwangler conducted the *Ring* and Toscanini followed with *Parsifal*. I had heard my first *Götterdämmerung* the previous year in Zurich, also with Toscanini in charge. I had visited the Wesendock Villa in Zurich and had also been dutifully to Triebschen, near Lucerne, where Wagner's son and the wonderful *Siegfried Idyll* came to life.

Although I have never enjoyed Salzburg as much as Covent

Garden, the Scala or the Metropolitan, opera everywhere has given me some of my happiest moments. In 1944, at the height of the Allied campaign in Italy, we were quartered in the Rococo palace of Caserta. The palace was devoid of plumbing as we understand the word, but there were silver crucifixes in each of the eighteenth-century panelled mahogany horse stalls, and a beautiful private theatre in which the kings of the Two Sicilies had entertained their guests. Our American commanding officer, General Mark Clark, was also an opera fan, so the neighbouring San Carlo Opera Company was summoned from Naples at weekends to perform for us.

It was during my pilgrimage to Bayreuth in 1931 that the first ever devaluation of sterling took place. The French, who had welcomed British visitors and workers for at least half a century, took the opportunity to close ranks by making work permits compulsory overnight for all foreigners.

So, inevitably, my fourth summer as George Simond's assistant in Le Touquet had to be my last. This time there could be no turning back. After a year of working from a South Kensington bed-sitter as London's youngest couturier, I had to take on additional space because I wanted to set up in Mayfair and I had enough work for a staff of five. In fact, I could only afford to take two weeks away from work that year to maintain my job as call-boy at Wimbledon, plus a few days to participate in the Dutch championships.

In spite of this, 1932 was a particularly happy Wimbledon for me, as Suzanne Lenglen came back for the first time to the scene of her former glories.

Since her exhibition tour of the United States in 1926, Suzanne had lived in great happiness with a charming young American millionaire, Baldwin M. Baldwin. Because of his dark good looks and his money, Baldwin was nicknamed 'The Sheik', and I remember that Suzanne always called him 'Sheiky'. Rumours of a serious romance between Suzanne and Sheiky became newspaper talk in 1927 but were at first confined to the gossip columns because Sheiky already had a wife and a son. Nevertheless, Suzanne brought Sheiky to Nice a couple of times and it was generally accepted in the French press that she was *maîtresse en titre* in this affair.

After the strains and privations of her earlier stardom, Suzanne revelled openly in Sheiky's luxury life style. However, the dark clouds of her life gathered again in 1929. The feared but beloved Papa Lenglen died. Suzanne and Mama Anaïs lost the use of the Villa Ariem, and by 1931 it became clear that Sheiky was no longer interested either in divorcing his wife or marrying Suzanne.

Suzanne's reappearance in London was sudden and dramatic. During her idyllic interlude with Baldwin she seemed to cut herself off deliberately from her previous friends. Only the night before her return to Wimbledon, after six years' absence, Sophie Wavertree received out of the blue a telegram which said simply, 'Arriving tomorrow, Suzanne.'

I happened to be standing by the entrance to the Centre Court when Suzanne arrived, and she gave me a very affectionate greeting. Suzanne's shock return caught Wimbledon completely by surprise: they had no seat for her. Moreover, like Mrs Lambert Chambers, she had become a professional. Both had openly made money from the game and were therefore pariahs, unfit to sit with the simon-pure 'amateurs'.

As outcasts, these two immortals of tennis were eventually found seats together in a back section of the stand. But everyone noticed. 'Look, Suzanne! There's Suzanne!' the whisper went right around the Centre Court. Ex-King Manoel of Portugal,* Suzanne's partner in so many past fun matches at the Beau Site in Cannes, was in the front row of the Royal Box. When he saw her, he blew her a kiss.

In business I was fortunate that the many socialites that I had met on the Riviera came to me with their orders. This was probably out of curiosity, but these women also brought their debutante daughters, and within a year I was able to arrange my first showing of a collection. At the time my biggest upwards step was to receive a mention of my designs in *Harper's Bazaar*.

Suzanne Lenglen stayed on in London and soon interested herself in my new life. Having recently terminated her five-year romance she was once again finding a new life for herself. We shared in this experience, and I found myself even more fascinated than before by her lively interest in everything. Since she was no longer constantly in the public eye, she had become a delightfully relaxed companion. Perhaps also, because I was no longer her 'stable-boy', I was able to have a more balanced conversation with an Empress.

When the time came for my second dress show, Suzanne said she would like to be there and would also like to wear one of the models from my collection. She chose a pale grey, wool-knit suit with a scarlet shirt, showing her dark hair and colouring to great advantage. Suzanne always preferred strong colours for her tennis accessories and only wore the pale shrimp-pink bandeau and cardigan on the big days because she believed they brought her luck.

Suzanne turned out to be the salvation of the show. It was one of those days when everything went wrong: there were interminable stage waits. During one of the nail-biting delays, Suzanne, sensing the situation, said, 'Leave this to me. On that note she left me and

---

*It was the last match he ever saw. That night he died of a heart attack.

walked conspicuously the full length of the catwalk to greet some imaginary friend.

There were some two hundred restless people assembled in the Garden Room of the Mayfair Hotel. Even after six years' absence, almost everyone recognized Suzanne. For the few who did not, her professionally poised walk made it clear she was a world-famous star. The delays were quickly forgotten as she put on this impromptu performance to help me out of my embarrassment.

On another occasion she came late one evening to my design studio. All the staff had gone home, so she sat on one of the workroom tables, dangling her wonderful legs. As twilight faded into darkness we reminisced, wistfully recalling the many happy moments we had shared. I asked her opinion of the current stars, Helen Wills, Helen Jacobs, and Dorothy Round. 'They don't use the court as I did,' she declared, the vanity of her tennis supremacy echoing clearly in the darkening room. 'For men the court is not that big,' she said, 'But for women it is enormous. I used every centimetre of the court. Today's girls do not seem to comprehend the geometry of tennis. I had no need to serve aces.' In 1983 I often wish more of the women's circuit players understood Lenglen's logic.

The next night we saw a movie together and were both fascinated by Adrian's fabulous Hollywood designs for Joan Crawford. In the story, as the hero died he sang, 'All Night Through I Dream of You'. I remember Suzanne saying how wonderful it would be to die dreaming of one's lover. All the sad longings of her earlier privations seemed reflected in those few words.

By the summer of 1933 my business was growing fast and I felt that if I did not soon make the 'Grand Tour' of our ancestors, I might never again have the opportunity. So, I made my first trip to the States, travelling with Elizabeth Ryan. After playing in half a dozen American cities and spending a few weeks in old-style Hollywood, I went on with the young 1933 Japanese Davis Cup team and spent some more unforgettable weeks in the Far East.

I have always been compulsively attracted by journeys to faraway places. In my teens I would make special visits to the Gare du Nord just for the fascination of watching the Trans-Siberian Express gliding off silently on its ten-thousand-mile trek to Vladivostok. From Japan I was sorely tempted to make the return journey to England via Siberia, but decided instead to make the five-week journey by boat.

In 1934 I was back at work and the following couple of years proved a boom time for those of us involved in fashion. For they were the years of the passionate royal romance between the Prince of Wales and Wallis Simpson. Every hostess, every guest at every party seemed

112

to want to outdo the other with new dresses and more sparkling jewels. Then, with the King's abdication in 1936, everything went into reverse. None of the socialites bought anything for months. The fledgling British fashion trade that Norman Hartnell, Hardy Amies, Digby Morton, and I had pioneered and which was just establishing its first identity, almost owed its survival to the big theatre productions of the day.

Happily, the coronation of George VI and Queen Elizabeth in 1937 put everything back in place. The same year also brought London's first sight of tennis on television. I have a clear memory of the baseline on the primitive screens being arched like a rainbow so it seemed impossible for anyone to hit over the lines.

The historic Don Budge versus Gottfried von Cramm Davis Cup match took place at Wimbledon that summer. By this time Fred Perry had turned pro', so that the whole outcome of the Cup rested on the match between America and Germany.

In Germany, Adolf Hitler had been building up a massive military force, backed by far-reaching propaganda for the Nazi cause. This propaganda was to reach even to the tennis courts of Wimbledon, for the Führer was determined to build an Aryan race of super athletes. Max Schmeling's stunning twelfth-round knock-out of Joe Louis in Madison Square Garden in 1936 had delighted Hitler. But Germany's humiliation at the Berlin Olympics of the same year – a humiliation led by America's black athlete, Jesse Owens, who won four gold medals – had mightily displeased him. Now the Germans had the chance to show the world again: for three single days in history, the swastika fluttered over the lawns of the All England Club.

With the teams locked at two matches apiece, the crowd of seventeen thousand waited anxiously for the world's two best players to appear for the decider. The drama began in the dressing room. I was anxious that there should not be a moment's delay and was hurrying Budge and von Cramm out of the dressing room when the telephone rang: Ellis, the attendant, picked up the phone and called to Jon Cramm, 'Long distance for you, sir.'

As the switchboard operator connected his call, von Cramm, with his inherent Germanic instinct, stiffened and stood to attention. For the next minute or more he listened intently. The only words he uttered were, '*Ja, mein Führer*', which he said about eleven times. When he finished he turned to Budge and me and said, 'Excuse me, gentlemen, it was Hitler. He wanted to wish me good luck.'

With that I swept them both on to the Centre Court for what has been described by many of the world's most experienced tennis critics as 'the greatest match ever played'. In the presence of Hitler's sports minister — a guest in the Royal Box — Budge won for the United States 6-8, 5-7, 6-4, 6-2, 8-6. Less than a year later, Gottfried von Cramm was imprisoned by the Nazis: a dark foreboding of what lay ahead.

The year 1938 was probably my best year as a society 'couturier'. That season I made no fewer than fourteen wedding dresses for some of the year's most elegant weddings at St Margaret's, Westminster.

On 2 July 1938, Helen Wills achieved her all-time record at Wimbledon. Two days later Suzanne Lenglen died in Paris of what is now called leukaemia. All the official tennis bodies in England, remembering my Paris contacts, asked me to help out with the wreaths and tributes. Jean Borotra's faithful Suzanne Duboy was our salvation, and I remember calling her at least half-a-dozen times on that sad Monday morning.

Suzanne's girlhood friend and partner, Pierre Albarran, who came closest of all to marrying her, records that on his last visit to her within weeks of her death, she confided in him, 'The happiest years of my life were 1919 and 1920, the years I spent mostly with you and Alain [Gerbault].' The period she referred to was, of course, at the beginning of her career, when her ultimate supremacy, and all it cost her, was still unrealized. So Suzanne died, dreaming nostalgically of her youthful companions rather than of the many famous men who would happily have married her.

On 23 August 1939, I left my precious Riviera knowing that war with Germany was inevitable. I was not on quite the last Blue Train from Cannes, but almost. How well I remember that sad journey along the coastline, once the Land of Lenglen. As the train passed the familiar succession of red rocks protruding from royal blue bays, every inch of the way seemed more beautiful than ever, and I purposely sat with my back to the engine so as to savour every last moment of its romance.

In London, I found countless busloads of children being evacuated to the country, away from the anticipated bombing. They blocked every road from the city, but the last of the summer tournaments were still being played. I remember thinking, 'I may never play tennis again, so I might as well enter this one last time.' My partner and I won the doubles. I went home and buried the cup in the garden. I was not about to have Hitler bomb my trophy after the toil and emotion we had experienced that week.

On Saturday, 2 September, I paid off my staff of one hundred girls and told them that if war was declared there was no point in coming back. The previous night all the lights of London had been blacked out and were not to be relit for six years. Neville Chamberlain announced the declaration of war at 11.00 a.m. the next morning.

114

The Four Musketeers with the French Davis Cup team, 1923. Left to right: Jean Borotra, René Lacoste, Captain Muhr (non-playing captain), Henri Cochet, Toto Brugnon and B. Shortt

The Four Musketeers in 1958, exactly forty-five years after their first appearance together

Jean Borotra with Henri Cochet before the controversial Wimbledon singles final of 1927 that Cochet may have won with an illegal double hit *(London News Agency)*

René Lacoste with the ball machine that was originally his invention

Toto Brugnon with me at the Gallia Club, Cannes, 1926

Wimbledon, 1935. Helen Jacobs (left) with
Helen Wills Moody (right) before the ladies'
singles final. Two years previously, Helen
Jacobs had been the first woman to wear
shorts at Wimbledon *(Planet Agency)*

Helen Wills Moody in play at Wimbledon,
1935 *(Fox Photos)*

Above left: Fred Perry winning Wimbledon, 1934 *(London News Agency)*

Above right: J. Donald Budge in play at Wimbledon, 1935 *(London News Agency)*

Left: Baron Gottfried von Cramm paying his respects to Adolf Hitler

Alice Marble winning Wimbledon,
1939 *(Fox Photos)*

Alice Marble and Bobby Riggs
dancing the 'lap of honour' at the 1939
Wimbledon Ball after both had won
all their events *(Sport & General)*

All smiles as Maureen Connolly and Teach Tennant arrive in London in 1952 to take Wimbledon by storm *(The Associated Press)*

Queen's Club, 1952. Maureen Connolly had injured her shoulder that morning, forty-eight hours before the start of her first Wimbledon. Teach escorts her off the court after her win in the doubles final, which she had played very much against her coach's wishes

Susan Partridge (left) with Little Mo (right) in the ladies' singles final at Wimbledon, 1952

Maureen Connolly winning the 1953 Wimbledon final. The tell-tale strip of satin shows where I tore the dress down the centre at midnight, the previous night

Discussing a creation for Billie Jean King with Margaret Goatson Kirgin, my assistant for twenty-one years

One of my evening gowns for a presentation at Buckingham Palace. Official regulations required a twelve-inch train from the shoulders, the 'Prince of Wales' headpiece with white tulle veil, and twenty-inch white kid gloves. This dress was chosen by five different debutantes for the presentation balls of 1938 (© *Ted Tinling*)

The air-raid sirens sounded immediately, but it was nearly a year before the bombing began in London.

When eventually my flat was bombed, the last of the Christmas puddings that I had prudently made as the war started remained intact, but its basin was shattered and the tiny fragments of broken china made a clean white halo on the shelf around it. I felt a sense of personal grievance against the entire Luftwaffe for bombing my plum pudding and immediately reboiled it in a new basin.

Wimbledon's Centre Court was also bombed when Norah Cleather was in charge and living on the premises. Some years later, on V. E. Day, Norah and I sat down to lunch together. As a token revenge for what we had endured, we solemnly ate the bombed pudding and saluted it for its private victory over Hitler.

In 1939 and 1940 auxiliary services of all kinds were organized while the enlistment processes for the three main forces were being arranged. Everyone had to sign dozens of forms and declarations of his ability. One that was sent to me asked whether my education had been 'primary', 'rudimentary', or 'elementary'. I settled for 'primary' and often wondered if this was why I was kept in the Army for seven years.

In May 1940, ironically one of the loveliest Mays in the long story of wet English weather, we lived the true-life version of that remarkable film, *Mrs Miniver*. In nine days 338,000 men of the Allied fighting forces were repatriated from Dunkirk in the historic armada of thousands of little boats. For a short time the London parties and celebrations were such that one could have thought the war had ended instead of just starting.

At the same time some 30,000 Frenchmen opted to join General de Gaulle in London rather than General Pétain in Vichy. On a glorious June day, when the flowering English gardens seemed to refute the very existence of war, Bertie Gillou, a close boyhood friend from my Riviera days, arrived on my doorstep, penniless and wearing only some tattered clothing given him by the Red Cross. His ship had been sunk in an estuary off Scotland; he had swum ashore and hitchhiked to London.

The Gillous were one of the first tennis families in France: Bertie's father, Pierre Gillou, was the captain of the 'French Musketeers' and the architect of their Philadelphia Davis Cup victory in 1927; Pierre's sister, Katie Fenwick, was four-times champion of France before Marguerite Broquedis; and Suzanne Lenglen's closest confidant, Coco Gentien, was Pierre's nephew. I had been part of their tennis milieu since the beginning of my own tennis days.

Meanwhile all the circuit tennis players, awaiting their call to duty, played exhibition matches to raise funds for the Red Cross. On

Sunday, 24 August 1940, we played at a club in Mill Hill just north of London. The sirens wailed all the afternoon, but we still believed in false alarms. As we left the club and looked down across London's twilight, most of the skyline was lost in a flaming blaze. It was our first sight of the Blitz and we learned the next day that the London docks had been almost totally destroyed. The American press described it as 'indiscriminate arson'.

In those last weeks of summer, Bertie and I laughed and swam and sunbathed each morning. We read Proust and Verlaine and explored Shostakovich together in the afternoons. After the ritual Ritz Bar cocktail session we became happily caught up in the extravagant night life of a London that survives now only in the nostalgic memories of old men.

After Dunkirk, anyone in an official capacity was required to carry a tin hat and a gas mask at all times. When we went swimming on those glorious autumn mornings, it was still odd to see sun-bathers with tin hats and gas masks constantly at the ready. On one occasion, when the sirens sounded, I remember a friend reaching dutifully for his tin hat only to place it carefully over his private parts before dozing off again. We laughed hilariously at the time. In a week he was dead, hit by a bomb. In the circumstances, even the tin hat in its correct place could not have saved him.

Eventually I received my own call to the Army and, having shared with Bertie in the final wake for the old world, I was never to see him again. All the life-styles we and our fathers had taken for granted died then, never to return, even as ghosts.

Memories
Light the corners of my mind
Misty waters cull a memory
Of the Way We Were.

Scattered pictures
Of the smiles we left behind
Smiles we gave to one another
For the Way We Were.

Can it be that it was all so simple then?
Or has time rewritten every line?
If we had the chance to do it all again
Tell me: Would we? *Could we?*

Memories
May be beautiful and yet
What's too painful to remember
We simply choose to forget

So it's the laughter
We will remember
Whenever we remember
The Way We Were.

'The Way We Were', by Marvin Hamlisch/Alan and Marilyn
Bergman.
Quoted by agreement with Screen Gems-EMI Music Inc.

PART TWO

16 Fancy Pants

On a scorching August day in 1951, I was sweltering in the primitive customs shed of an airstrip on the Canadian border, when the customs inspector pulled out of my luggage some rather transparent nylon tennis panties I had promised to take to a friend in Toronto. In those days one could have unforeseen entry-permit problems: there had already been some difficulty over mine, and for a time it seemed doubtful I would be allowed to continue my journey. I felt cut off and miles from a friendly face. To add considerably to my bad temper, the inspector waved the flimsy garments around for all his colleagues to inspect.

'What, Mr Tinling, no lace this year?' he asked suddenly with a grin. The tension was immediately relaxed, and I was surprised he recognized my name. Such was the power of Gussy's panties. After that I knew my entry permit was going to work out all right.

The story of Gussy Moran and the lace-edged panties that I made for her in 1949 still remains one of the most unlikely happenings in the many legends of tennis. Gussy's panties caused shock waves that reverberated from Alaska to Antarctica. On the way they even led the English vicar of St Andrew's Church, Buenos Aires, to preach a sermon, the theme of which was the sinful implications of wearing this unsuspecting garment.

Thirty-four years later it is still amost impossible to understand how a yard of lace, added to a player's normal undergarment and barely seen at five-minute intervals, could cause such a furore.

Yet the 'Gussy sensation' was tantamount to a stripper appearing suddenly on Wimbledon's Centre Court. Even this might not cause quite the same buzzing of intercontinental cables.

In 1977 the extraordinary Gussy story was still prominently quoted in almost every review of Wimbledon's one-hundred-year history. To understand it one must also understand the unique news exposure of the Wimbledon championships and the out-of-proportion importance that can be attached to quite small happenings there. Major Wimbledon controversies have been related many times to items of women's tennis wear. In the past, these have been brought on by the chauvinism of a tennis establishment that did

118

not appoint a woman to its committee until 1982. Whether the *cause célèbre* was showing one's wrists for the first time, as May Sutton did in 1905, or Suzanne's frocks 'indecently' revealing a woman's natural silhouette in 1919, the resulting indignation stemmed each time from Wimbledon's erstwhile all-male philosophy at its worst.

Besides, before TV coverage, tennis was reported to the world exclusively by men. Today there are more and more women reporting the game. Had this been the case in 1949 Gussy's panties could not have caused the same shock reaction. Women journalists would never have accentuated the panties' sexual implications to the same degree as the men writers.

But very few things in life derive from a single cause, and like the roots of some ageing tree, the Gussy episode had its origins in a complex tangle of happenings that had gone before.

The era of masculinity in both the style and dress of women's tennis was spearheaded by Alice Marble in the late 1930s. It was carried over to the post-war years when Louise Brough, Margaret Osborne, Pauline Betz and Pat Todd arrived in the first plane to touch down in 1946 at London's new Heathrow Airport. The masculine look of the women players who came to prominence during the war years related to the regimentations of war, when it was unavoidable that unisex duties should lead to unisex clothes. One of the major factors in the explosive reaction to Gussy's panties was the conscious, and subconscious, revulsion against this masculinity that was still obvious in tennis even four years after the war had ended.

Christian Dior's Paris 'New Look' in 1947 created an international hunger for a return to femininity and sexual attraction in clothing. This was just beginning to find expression in the designer collections, but not yet in the sportswear of the late 1940s. In fact, Pauline Betz recalls that in 1946 sportswear hardly existed, and it was actually impossible to buy a tennis dress.

As I had been a pre-war designer of evening clothes and wedding gowns, and as I was also preconditioned to femininity by the glamour cult of Lenglen, I was the first to rebel against the uniform appearance of the post-war tennis players. I felt that, by looking like modern-day Amazons, the sportsgirls were renouncing their birthright. There was no 'Peacock Age' at that time: all the men looked alike, and it scandalized me when women also looked identical to one another.

For this reason, in the beginning of 1947, I conducted a strong campaign for femininity in tennis, demanding, to begin with, that the girls wear dresses rather than the severe shorts and culottes they all wore at that time. Joan Curry, one of the few British internationals who could demonstrate on a centre court that tennis wear could be pretty as well as functional, came to me. When I was released from the Army after seven years in uniform and picking up the threads of my dress-designing career, one of my first thoughts was to make her an attractive tennis dress. Soon afterwards, Mrs Hilda Gannon also came to me with a welcome commission. 'I would like you to design something very special for my daughter's first appearance at Wimbledon. As you know, Joy can look very pretty.'

By tradition, Wimbledon dresses had always been white. Although there were then no written rules, I had no thought of offending anyone. But I did suggest that a diminutive sky-blue or rose-pink hem could be added to an otherwise conventional white dress.

Joy Gannon, who was later to become the mother of Buster Mottram, now Britain's top-ranking player, made her Wimbledon debut in my 'new look' in 1947. She looked adorable, and apart from one flattering paragraph in a London evening newspaper, nobody regarded the coloured hem as the least bit unusual. In the following year, Britain's No. 1 player, Betty Hilton, approached me before the Wightman Cup matches. She said she thought Joy Gannon's dresses were charming and asked me to design her a tennis dress that also featured a coloured hem. The dress I made for her had a coloured hemline, but the hemline was a half inch wider than Joy's and with a zig-zag top edge to the colour. Betty duly appeared in my design in the opening Cup match.

Hazel Wightman, who had donated the Cup, was still captain of the US team. She had a very dominating personality and considered herself the First Lady of women's tennis. She had decided some years before that she was the ultimate arbiter of tennis etiquette around the world, and it so happened that she took great exception to Betty's dress. Moreover Betty lost to Louise Brough 6-1, 6-1. At the time this was the quickest Cup defeat on record, but I was still amazed when Hazel announced that Betty lost because she was self-conscious about the colour on her dress! The next day I was shocked to hear that Mrs Wightman had asked the Wimbledon committee to ban both Betty Hilton and Joy Gannon from wearing the dresses I had designed for them.

When I arrived at Wimbledon to carry out my usual call-boy duties, Hazel embraced me superficially and kissed me on both cheeks with the smug smile that she used on people she had just beaten in a match. 'No hard feelings, of course,' she said. 'But we DO play tennis in white, DON'T we?'

My mind immediately went back to an incident in 1933 when Hazel Wightman saw Helen Jacobs, dressed in shorts, about to go on court for a similar Cup match at Forest Hills. At Wimbledon earlier that year Helen had actually launched what was then the novelty of tennis shorts for women and looked particularly good in them. 'Take them off and put on a dress,' Hazel ordered her at Forest Hills. Helen had to dig out a soiled dress from her luggage.

This renewed example in 1948 of Hazel's tennis power complex reminded me of King Canute, so I told her that henceforth I would call her 'Queen Canute'. World frontiers had changed, civilization had barely survived its greatest threat, but Hazel Wightman believed she could hold back the tide of change.

A short time afterwards the suntanned, shapely form of Gertrude Agusta Moran arrived in Europe from California. The press soon discovered the name 'Gussy' had been substituted as a more polite version of 'Goosy', the nickname one of her teenage boyfriends thought appropriate. 'Gorgeous' was added later.

Even at first sight, Gussy looked to me like a person who loved life, enjoyed being attractive, and enjoyed the excitement she gave to men. According to her mother, she always went barefoot at home, never wore make-up, and slept in a T-shirt. This was innovative, to say the least, in those days. The late 1940s were the 'Lana Turner era' when curvaceous figures were emphasized. Gussy epitomized this with her provocative, sexy bodyline and a walk that had so much bounce she appeared to be treading on a succession of rubber balls. The length of her stride seemed unreal, but it was instinctive and not at all artificial. She had a beautifully modulated, laughing voice, and her skin had a lustrous California gleam. I thought of her as a person who actually shimmered.

This was also a time when American women's tennis probably enjoyed its greatest depth. When Gussy came into my life, she was, in fact, ranked fourth among the top ten women and was the US covered-courts national champion, which proves beyond argument that she was a first-class player.

For two years I wrote the first post-war tennis fashion column in a magazine called *British Lawn Tennis*, while Gussy did the same job in the counterpart magazine, *American Lawn Tennis*, so our names were well known to each other. Until 1949 we had never met, but Gussy wrote to me in the spring of that year telling me she was about to make her first trip to Wimbledon. She said she had Red Indian blood in her, and therefore was extremely fond of colour, always wearing bright ribbons in her hair, even around her wrists, and wanting as much colour as she could have in the clothes she hoped that I would design for her.

The day Gussy arrived in England I was playing in the doubles final of the Kent championships at Beckenham. All my bio-rhythms must have been on a high that week because, in addition to my fateful meeting with Gussy, I remember the semi-final the previous day was the one match in thirty years of tennis in which I managed not to make a single error. In that sense this was the best performance of my tennis-playing life.

Gussy came straight from Heathrow to Beckenham to see the finals, and we were introduced by Mrs George Pierce Butler, the mother of Monte Carlo's tennis angel, Gloria Butler. Laurie Pignon, of London's *Daily Mail* was standing beside me. Gussy and Mrs Butler sat in the court-side seats, and I was delighted Gussy was able to see me at my best in tennis. But a lot of the time my concentration wandered from the game because of Gussy's sexy, suntanned legs that I could not help looking at each time I went back to serve.

'I hope you're going to take care of my tennis dresses?' she asked me later. Naturally, I agreed happily, but when I went to show her some sketches the next day I had to explain that though there was no reference to 'all-white' in the Wimbledon entry form, I was convinced from Hazel Wightman's actions the previous year, some stringent restrictions would be imposed. Gussy stared at me in disbelief, and I realized the full degree of her disappointment. Such a situation was unimaginable to her. As well it might be!

Designing for a player as stimulating as Gussy, I first had to find a fabric that suited her ultra-feminine image. But in 1949 Britain we still had what were called 'Utility' restrictions on all fabrics and clothing: the government would not allow us more than five buttons on any dress; we were restricted to a limited yardage around the hem; the seams of every dress could not exceed a certain number. All this naturally posed a lot of problems for designers.

Looking for an appropriate fabric, I approached a number of my influential textile friends until Nance Ellis, then head of public relations at the Celanese Corporation, produced out of a secret drawer a highly prized, experimental sample of soft knitted rayon. More than a quarter of a century later this probably sounds very prosaic, but at the time it was an absolute curiosity and a pioneering miracle.

I thought of Gussy as a shimmering personality and, to capture this image, I decided to trim her dress with white satin. She had never seen satin on a tennis dress and was startled but greatly intrigued at the first fitting.

Finally, I took the finished garment myself to the Dorchester Hotel. Adding a spray of orchids from the lobby flower shop, I waited impatiently for her verdict. Gussy eventually 'phoned me from her suite that she was absolutely delighted with the dress but, three hours later, back in my office, I received another call. Gussy was agitated, asking what she was going to wear underneath.

I had been completely unaware that Gussy had always worn shorts, that she truly had nothing to wear under a tennis dress because she had never owned one. 'What you wear underneath is up to you,' I told her with some scepticism. 'I do not think your underclothes are my responsibility.'

Gussy explained that she was playing Margaret duPont in the semis of the Queen's Club tournament the next day and would not have time to go shopping for anything at all. We both became rather irritable and finally she said, 'You'll have to make me something. You promised to take care of my tennis outfits.'

I had a French fitter at the time and told her, 'We have got to make Miss Moran some panties.' She frowned, but eventually produced some panties made from the left-overs of the dress fabric. 'They look heavy and dull,' I said, when she showed them to me. 'We cannot have any colour, so let's try some lace around on the legs!'

My fitter returned with some dainty 'handkerchief' lace, and again I thought we had missed out completely, remembering Gussy's startling mahogany-tanned limbs. Spectators never see championship tennis from close quarters, and I felt what we wanted was some lace with a bold design that would at least be visible from time to time in the stands when Gussy served. We finished up with coarse cotton lace my mother would have called 'kitchen' lace, because it was often used on household linen. So the notorious lace panties were born – not out of some erotic urge, but through niggling attention to detail and a special insight into the ingredients required to project the character of the players I dressed.

My philosophy is that the ideal designer makes frames for pictures, and when the frame is more eye-catching than the picture the designer has done a bad job. I certainly did not devise the 'picture' of Gussy, but history seems to think I created the perfect 'frame'.

One has to remember that tennis dresses of that era were close to 'kilt-length,' which is one inch from the floor when the wearer is kneeling down.

Gussy's dress was exactly that length, so the lace-trimmed panties would only be seen once or twice every five minutes. Even so, it was said the lace 'drew the eye to the sexual area' and this deeply shocked the Establishment. But it delighted ninety-nine per cent of the world, and Gussy gave press photographers their new position for 1949 – lying flat on the courts.

Wimbledon's 'Ladies' Day' duly arrived with my prediction coming true. Notices were put up in all the women's dressing rooms, which read, 'Competitors are required to wear *all-white* clothing.'

The fireworks really began the day before Wimbledon at the annual Hurlingham garden party, arranged to give the players some carefree practice on grass when all the other clubs were closed under the no-Sunday-play rule. Gussy appeared in her new outfit, and before I knew what was happening, a friend came to me saying, laughingly, 'I think you've cost me my husband.' I was taken aback. 'What do you mean?' I asked. 'All the men are lying on their stomachs watching Gussy,' was her reply.

I went to the court to find some twenty photographers in this position. Out of the blue the *Life* magazine photographer appeared and asked for a court where he could take some exclusive pictures of Gussy smashing, guaranteeing a tantalizing peep of the panties. At the time *Life* was the world's most influential magazine. Overnight, Gussy was shown to the world not just as a tennis player but as a sex symbol.

The press reports were also world-wide and incredible. The next day, Gussy, locked in her hotel suite, was besieged by reporters wanting to know whether she was really going to wear the panties at her Wimbledon debut.

'Will she?' 'Won't she?' was the press room question of every hour. All the phone lines and the Dorchester switchboard were jammed as frantic editors demanded an answer for their deadlines. At Wimbledon the press boys even organized a bulletin board that reported Gussy's latest available answer from her hotel room. Every fifteen minutes a different forecast was posted.

In 1949, the chairman of Wimbledon was Sir Louis Greig, and all this was to prove the climax of his antagonism. The focus of interest had been taken away from actual tennis to something he considered vulgar and out of place, particularly since the press deliberately represented the whole subject with sexual connotations.

Eventually Gussy felt, and I think quite rightly, that the publicity was too much for her. She had a singles to play against a competent competitor, Bea Seal, today a well-known referee. Gussy's first match at Wimbledon was going to be a difficult one, so she wore some old shorts and a shirt. As soon as she appeared the crowd started a questioning chorus right around the stands whispering, 'Where's the lace?' The 's' sound reverberated across the courts, and Gussy at first thought she was being hissed.

Then the world asked the same question, 'Where's the lace?' and Gussy's indecision was interpreted as a masterstroke of showmanship and public relations.

Her next match was scheduled for the No. 1 Court. By now even I was on tenterhooks wondering if, and when, Gussy would appear in the panties outfit. To this day I make a point of never asking a player what she is going to wear before a match. Her tennis must come first, and I purposely avoid embarrassing the players or myself by raising a question that could lead to a disagreement.

But I was still officially the call-boy for the two main courts, and my heart was in my mouth when I went to fetch Gussy. With the immense publicity surrounding her, I now had a vested interest in what she was going to wear. It was one of those moments in life when one feels one's whole future depends on the outcome. I had the same gut feeling as on the day Suzanne was asked if she minded a thirteen-year-old boy umpiring for her.

However, for her second match, Gussy glided out of the dressing room, giving me a conspiratorial wink and wearing my dress with the much-discussed panties underneath! The huge crowd, feeling its curiosity at last rewarded, approved loudly and welcomed Gussy with its fullest roar of applause.

At the time so much emphasis had been placed on the undergarment, everyone forgot to consider the dress itself. The dress has certainly been forgotten in the years since. I always thought it a very pretty dress on its own merits, so I was particularly pleased with the crowd's applause. In fact, walking behind the two girls, I felt rather sorry for Gussy's opponent, Betty Wilford.

Then we saw a rush of reporters scrambling to their telephones. The official count said there were nearly one hundred present. The match was unimportant. Gussy was wearing the lace panties! On court, the photographers machine-gunned Gussy merrily, led by Bob Ryder of Associated Press whose afternoon's work earned him the 'Photographer of the Year' award. The *Life* magazine picture was also the 'Picture of the Week' feature.

Then the situation began to snowball out of all proportion. Gussy was inundated with requests for personal appearances – everything from hospitals and garden fêtes to judging beauty contests. The Marx Brothers, in London at the time, invited her to join their act. A racehorse, an aircraft, and a restaurant's special sauce were named after her. The following week she was voted 'Best-Dressed Sports Woman' by the US Fashion Academy. The whole thing was staggering.

Meanwhile the Establishment resorted to the time-honoured tactic, 'If you don't like something, just disregard it.' Nothing was said to me at all. There was even a cold war from my colleagues in the inner sanctum of Wimbledon. Very determinedly they made no mention whatever of Gussy in my presence. I could only go about my job as if nothing unusual had occurred.

The tangled story of my break with Wimbledon after 'the Gussy affair' actually originated before the war. In 1937 I was offered what was really an apprenticeship as the future secretary of Wimbledon. Dudley Larcombe was due to retire in a few years, and the committee made the proposal that I have a trial period under his guidance, no longer as temporary call-boy but as his bona-fide successor.

I had been slowly but steadily climbing the ladder of dress-designer prestige in Mayfair. The Wimbledon call-boy job was only my summer holiday hobby. I loved every moment of it, but I also needed to be as successful as possible in the remaining fifty weeks of the year.

Considering the Wimbledon offer of permanent employment was a real dilemma. To accept would put me back again at the heart of my beloved tennis. The job also offered unlimited social advantages, including contact with the Palace as well as other privileges well beyond my normal horizons. But the money was negligible, and after a great deal of soul-searching, I decided to stay with my dress-designing. So I wrote a polite letter of refusal, formally and correctly addressed to the secretary. The correspondence is still in my files, and I am still surprised when I read it. Apparently its substance was never conveyed to Sir Louis Greig, because he stopped me in the men's dressing room one day soon after and said, 'My dear fellow, I am so glad you are going to join us. I'm sure you are going to do a good job.'

Although I realized he was caught unawares, I had to say, 'I'm sorry, Sir Louis, but I have declined.' From that moment on our previously cordial relationship began an irrevocable slide toward mutual antagonism. Evidently Louis Greig's change of attitude toward me began to crystallize ever more with various happenings that involved me in 1947 and 1948. One factor was that Jack Kramer, after winning Wimbledon in 1947, made me a gift of six very loud, contemporary American neckties. They were extra-wide in the latest American style, and I was very proud of Jack's present, particularly as there were no ties at all like them in England. The second factor was a stupid incident in 1947 involving the bouquets of flowers that have since become a traditional part of every Wimbledon women's singles final. For years these were always sent by the secretary and the referee as congratulatory gifts to the two women finalists in the dressing room. In 1946 Pauline Betz and Louise Brough had been so delighted when they received the flowers that they automatically took them on to the court with their racquets.

The next year, when Louise and Margaret Osborne were due to play the final, Louis Greig and the new secretary, Duncan Macaulay, took me aside and said the committee had decided they did not want the women to take their flowers on to court. It was Greig's way of attempting to stifle any semblance of colour or intrusion into what he considered the 'proper' way of playing tennis.

'I think it's a great pity,' I replied. 'Last year everyone loved the new picture.' Greig murmured that there had been complaints, but Macaulay suggested, 'Why not leave it to the players' discretion?'

Greig's eventual decision was a typical example of his ambiguity. Nodding to Macaulay he instructed me, 'Leave it to the players. Don't tell them to leave the flowers behind if they bring them, but if they don't, don't raise the matter.'

When I went to fetch the players, Margaret asked me the leading question, 'Shall we bring the flowers, Ted?' My inclination was to say, 'Of course.' But after more than thirty years I am still glad I was scrupulously loyal to my job and replied, 'It's entirely up to you.'

'Right,' said Margaret and Louise with one voice. 'We'll take them.'

We passed Greig and Macaulay on the way to the Centre Court and I knew from their sickly expressions they thought it was because of me that Louise and Margaret were carrying their flowers. As far as Greig was concerned, it was just another tick against my name in his black book.

A third factor was the 1948 episode when Hazel Wightman delighted the Establishment with her disgust over the colour-trimmed dresses that I made for Betty Hilton and Joy Gannon.

With all this happening, the 1948 Wimbledon was the first of my life that was not to be a total enchantment. With my clash with Hazel and the banning of my dresses in her Cup matches two weeks earlier came the first and unexpected clouds over the previously idyllic relationship that I had always enjoyed with Wimbledon. Conversely, there was a new note of anticipation because I had decided this would be the first time I would actually compete in the Wimbledon championships. I was good enough to have played there several times before the war, but because I was being paid for my call-boy job, the so-called 'amateur' rules precluded my doing both things at the same time.

After the war I was persuaded to resume the call-boy job on an honorary basis. I had played twenty-six tournaments on the 1947 circuit, I was also captain of the top division Sussex county team, but I had never played at Wimbledon. My friends rightly pointed out that if I did not enter soon, I could end my playing days without ever doing so.

Fate scheduled my Wimbledon debut for my thirty-eighth birthday (once again a Thursday!). I need hardly say I went to the Club, proud as Punch, wearing one of my Jack Kramer ties, and without the thought that it would strike horror in the chairman's soul.

After my match I was changing quickly to resume my job and was adjusting my tie when Louis Greig appeared in the dressing room. He made some caustic remark I have forgotten and looked in revulsion at the wide tie. It might have been something unclean.

'Your ties are your worst enemy,' he announced scathingly. Astounded, I realized he was not joking.

'I'm not really sure about that,' I countered, very tactlessly, because of the unexpectedness of his attack.

This sharp exchange was merely a storm warning. From then on I sensed that I was unwittingly caught up in a gathering squall. Gussy's panties were at the eye of the hurricane.

17 *Where Fashion Lags Behind*

In 1948 although I had not met Gussy Moran, we had written some mutually admiring comments in our respective fashion columns three thousand miles apart. In one of my columns I had said, 'Men go mad, we are told, when La Moran smiles at them and swoon when she takes off her sweater. The sooner all our lads are sun-tanned from the blaze of her tropic eyes the happier we shall be.' Later, I was told these obviously lighthearted remarks had been found particularly obnoxious by Sir Louis Greig.

Ever since 1928 I had received, around Christmas time, Dudley Larcombe's curt invitation, 'I hope you will join us again for the championships. They begin on June — Yours sincerely.' This was his usual peremptory style. In 1949 I thought the new secretary's letter had gone astray because by the end of March it had not arrived. In April I received a 'phone call from Louis Greig, and immediately sensed the tension and irritation in his voice, in spite of the ritual hypocritical English opening, 'My dear Fellow'.

Greig explained why the customary invitation had been delayed. 'My committee feel I should stress a few points. Some of us consider your ties are not quite ... er ... that you ... er ... if you could just ... er.'

I cut him short. 'Let's not worry, Sir Louis. The time has probably come when we should all have a change.'

Wimbledon had been my personal wonderland for twenty-three years, and I still marvel that I could even have suggested severing a bond that meant so much to me. But I was not about to burn all my bridges in one 'phone call, and the conversation ended with my saying I would think about his invitation, and his words.

In early June I was still uncertain about what to do. I had made no further comment about going to Wimbledon since Greig's call two months previously. Then I received a call from the secretary, Duncan Macaulay. Macaulay and I had known each other for more than twenty years and had built up some degree of mutual respect while we were both on the Wimbledon organizing team with Norah Cleather in the 1930s. Duncan told me he was leaving London the following morning for the Paris finals and thought it only fair to have a firm decision from me before he left. I had 'played a leading part in the organization of the championships for more than twenty years,' was the reason he gave.

That evening, at his flat, we had a dinner, which will always remain in my memory, discussing every aspect of Greig's and my own feelings until three o'clock in the morning. Trying to be tactful, Duncan opened the discussion by saying, 'I think the press are your worst enemies.' All my life the press has been extraordinarily generous to me throughout the world and I was certainly not having my 'problem', which appeared to be what we were discussing, blamed on my newspaper friends.

'Funny you should say that,' I countered with this in mind. 'Sir Louis thinks it's my ties.' Duncan then told me how the comments in my fashion column about Gussy had incensed Louis Greig with their 'vulgarity'.

After six hours of discussion I was close to deciding my long stint with Wimbledon should finish. Conversely, as a friend, I did not want to let Macaulay down only three weeks before the biggest job of his life was due to start. So I promised to 'sleep on it' and write to him the next day.

I have the copy of the correspondence in my hand as I recount this story, and see that I said, 'In light of our long association I shall not let you down at the last minute. However, I trust there will not be too many regrets, *either on my side or in the Committee Box.*'

The Hurlingham garden party had taken place on Sunday, and Gussy's panties made headlines the following day before Wimbledon even started. Gussy did not wear the panties at Wimbledon until Wednesday, but the London *Daily Express* in spite of carry-over war-time limitations to six pages, made Gussy a front-page leader story for five days in succession out of the first six days of Wimbledon.

On Thursday Gussy, still shocked by the enormous amount of press exposure she had experienced, was scheduled to make her first Centre Court appearance. This was a third-round singles against the diminutive Chinese prodigy, Gem Hoahing, whose total height was less than twice the circumference of Gussy's most expressive dimensions. The combined emotions of the whole situation proved far too much for Gussy, and she was beaten.

At Beckenham, when Gussy just arrived in England, I had had difficulty concentrating because she sat in the court-side seats. At Wimbledon I was again involved in a men's doubles, but this time in full sight of the electric scoreboard of the Centre Court during Gussy's defeat. It seemed that each time I went back to receive our opponents' serve, the board flashed the message that Gussy had lost another game. My poor partner, George Godsell, was distracted and we also lost. I think it was to the Irish Davis Cup team, Kemp and Jackson.

The day after her singles loss, Gussy was surprised to be summoned personally by Sir Louis Greig. She told me afterwards she expected to be reprimanded about her panties. But he only told her that her mixed-doubles partner, Bob Falkenburg, had pulled out of the event.

The imparting of this type of information is strictly the job of the tournament referee and in no way the normal function of the chairman of the world's most famous tennis club. I have often thought, and so has Gussy, that in sending for her Greig intended, in fact, to upbraid her about her panties, but confronted with her personal charm, and hearing her lilting voice in his office, he backed down.

The cold war against me went on until my birthday on 23 June. I had played and lost my first-round doubles match at Wimbledon, and with other members of the staff I was having our customary late dinner in the Royal Tea-Room after the rush and pressures of the day.

The caterers produced an imposing birthday cake for me when, because of a late mixed doubles, Jean Borotra appeared and asked if he might join us. Seeing the birthday cake on the table, he immediately ordered champagne for everyone. Then, with his usual infectious chuckle, he exploded the whole situation by saying, 'I don't know if we should drink to your birthday or your panties.'

There was deathly silence. Jean looked startled, and I felt I was being engulfed in a wave of open hostility. The romantic club room that held so many happy memories for me in those twenty-three years of Wimbledon suddenly became a court room. And I was clearly being declared guilty. But I kept all my thoughts on the matter to myself until an incident at Queen's Club. Notwithstanding the championships, Wimbledon always closes for the middle Sunday.

During Sunday lunch at Queen's Club, which does not close, a member of the Wimbledon committee attacked me bitterly before all the members. 'How could you do something so tasteless having been with us for so long?' he asked. 'What do you mean?' I inquired. His reply was quick and caustic. 'You have put sin and vulgarity into tennis.'

This accusation really released my bottled-up feelings. In the previous week I had been asked innumerable times for interviews about Gussy's panties. I still hoped the ridiculous storm would blow over and refused all comment, although I never denied having made the panties. One of my feature-writer friends had already called me that morning and was annoyed by my silence. Now I was ready.

So on Wimbledon's second Monday morning a column appeared in London's biggest circulation daily that quoted me as saying I did not understand the Establishment's attitude because I had added at least an extra thousand spectators each day to the Wimbledon attendance. This set the stage for the eventual jealous showdown with Greig.

Gussy had refrained from wearing her panties outfit after her second-round singles. But she and Pat Todd reached the doubles final against the title-holders, Margaret duPont and Louise Brough. In spite of all that had already been written, the question of whether or not Gussy would wear the panties in the presence of Queen Mary once again hit the headlines.

Throughout the history of Wimbledon controversies, pressure was frequently put on Centre Court players by telling them, 'Queen Mary might not approve'. In fact, she was a sporting old lady who smoked in public when this was still considered a questionable habit for ladies, and she always enjoyed a good joke.

On the final afternoon Gussy called every thirty minutes from her Dorchester suite to ask, in a frenzy of indecision, whether Queen Mary would be there to see her match.

Queen Mary was then eighty-four, and the intense heat of the day had already raised questions in the midday newspapers about her presence. Louise Brough was involved in all three finals, and her doubles match against Gussy and Pat Todd could only be a late starter. Queen Mary often arrived at Wimbledon about 3.00 p.m. but that day it was not until four o'clock that her equerry called to say she had decided not to venture out in the heat.

When Gussy was told Queen Mary was not coming she hurried straight to Wimbledon. Her emotional conflict was at least partly resolved, and if she could only pluck up the courage she was free to show off on the Centre Court her panties and the pretty dress that went over them. Nevertheless Norah Cleather, who was in the dressing room at the time, told me Gussy put on and took off the whole outfit at least three times before deciding.

With the enormous publicity, Gussy developed an oversensitive self-consciousness. She began holding her racquet in front of her face when going on to court until the press photographers protested she was preventing them from earning their living. Another time she protested that all the passers-by stared at her on the pavement. 'They looked at me and their faces fell,' she said. 'What did they expect. A goddess or something?'

In spite of a really sincere ovation from the huge crowd, Gussy, with her self-consciousness aroused to the full, hardly dared bend down during the preliminary knock-up. One ball-boy tossed her a low ball and she watched it, frozen, as it rolled by her feet. Other competitors in the stands roared with laughter, and Gussy signalled them to be quiet. It was only after she let two or three balls go by untouched that she plucked up enough courage to hit a few strokes.

Louise Brough and Margaret duPont, astonished, lost the first four games, but then asserted their superiority to win in straight sets. This was the end of two unbelievable, certainly unforgettable weeks for Gussy. She then left London, but for me the real drama was yet to come.

After the finals Greig held a private cocktail party in his committee room to which guests from the Royal Box were invited on their way home. Greig asked if I would recruit some of the stars for the party. Already among his guests was the current Prime Minister, Lord Attlee, who told me with a sly smile, 'You've done a great job for tennis this year.' Next, Macaulay stopped me on the stairs to say, 'Princess Marina [then president of the Wimbledon Club] thought the panties great fun.' During the party Louis Greig shook me (as I thought) spontaneously by the hand and said, 'My dear fellow, thank you so much for coming to Wimbledon this year. We could never do without you!'

This was reassuring. Stupidly I believed it and went to the Wimbledon Ball relieved.

But somewhere, deep down, I had an instinctive feeling I was again at a crossroads in my life. Something had happened in the previous three weeks that was too big for me to analyse. It was the hottest summer night in ten years and I walked back to my flat confused and alone.

Thirty-six hours later there was a ritual farewell cocktail party for the players, which I had attended for years past with Norah Cleather. Greig, as chairman of Wimbledon, was asked to say a few words. This time, the usual pleasantries completed, his whole appearance suddenly changed, even the muscles of his face seemed to go into spasm. 'Never,' he thundered, 'never shall we allow our Centre Court to become a stage for designers' stunts.'

You could have heard the traditional pin drop with ease. Norah was so shocked she dramatically dropped her champagne glass. A hundred heads swivelled to see my reaction. Even knowing Greig's uncertainties, I could not forget the unnecessary congratulations so recently offered. I felt betrayed and offended in a situation in which I had no means of defence.

This was the crossroads I had sensed. Now the direction was quite clear. I went back to my office, wrote to Macaulay, and reminded him of my warning, 'I trust there will not be too many regrets ...' Indeed, I told him, I now had a great many.

The following year, as Gussy began once more to think of

Wimbledon, she realized she would need some more tennis clothes, and I received a letter from her sent from India saying, 'Make me something even more feminine than last year. *Let's Dig Deep!*'

The British press anticipated yet another dress controversy: headlines appeared asking if Gussy would be banned from this Wimbledon; others asked pointedly what would happen if she were banned. Louis Greig, still peeved over the 1949 'indignities' announced, 'Wimbledon needs no panties for its popularity.' In another interview he said, 'Tinling's clothes are designed to keep everybody's eyes off the ball.'

I was approached by the whole British press asking if I was going to dress Gussy again, but I released only the letter she sent me. Then, following demands that I give a reply, I issued a statement through the Associated Press to the effect that if Gussy wanted 'practical and attractive garments' from me, I would be happy to take care of her.

This was my first experience of the new era of communications, the first time I was able to have a dialogue with a client right across the world through the news media. Our dialogue soon raised another question, 'Surely if you design another Gussy sensation, Wimbledon will throw *you* out?'

It suddenly hit me that I had made no public mention of my break with Wimbledon six months previously. Now I decided to speak out because my own friends needed to know that I would not be in my customary call-boy position at the 1950 Wimbledon and would be asking the reasons why.

John Olliff, who was the tennis writer for London's *Daily Telegraph*, asked me about this, and he reported my differences with Louis Greig for the first time. Unbelievably, they made the lead columns on the front page. As soon as the first editions hit the streets I was besieged by all the other London newspapers. The first call came from the *Daily Mail* just before midnight. The phone rang all night without stopping, and by dawn reporters from the next day's evening newspapers were already on my doorstep.

Features and readers' letters went on for weeks. Hundreds complained about the 'dictatorial' attitude of Wimbledon attempting to impose its wishes on the players. Photographers from all over the world lurked round my design studio hoping to catch me snipping a piece of fabric that would give them a clue to my plans for the next 'Gussy sensation'. And it was not long before other designers started to get in on the act: Emilio Schuberth, one of Italy's top names, made Gussy an outfit that she wore at Beckenham, on the same court where we had met less than a year before. The week before Wimbledon Pierre Balmain, of Paris, staged a press show in London at which Gussy modelled his creation. Fortunately for me this was composed of yard upon yard of flimsy silk chiffon and was totally unwearable for tennis.

Finally Wimbledon was three days away. After almost hour-by-hour contact with Gussy from India, I had not heard one word from her in four months, so I called the Dorchester and said, 'What in the hell goes on? Is Schuberth dressing you, is Balmain dressing you, or am I? What's the score?'

Gussy was distinctly embarrassed and said she would 'explain everything' if I would see her immediately. She received me in an apricot-coloured negligée, looking absolutely divine. She said she became 'caught up with those guys' and really did not know what she was doing. She excused herself, saying, 'I guess I just got carried away. You know how it goes.'

I went back to my workrooms and slaved until the early hours of the morning of 'Ladies' Day', finally coming up with a shirt-and-shorts outfit in white Swiss embroidery. At that time I had never made any shorts, but I decided this was my best insurance against Gussy's self-consciousness. Although I was assailed by doubts all through the night, my instinct kept me working. Around 5.00 a.m. I cursed myself for a fool, but I have never regretted the effort.

Later that day the outfit was delivered to Wimbledon with a note, 'I thought you might not feel like a dress today, so how about this?'

All I could do then was to sit back and wait. Once again she was scheduled on the No. 1 Court where the panties had made their first Wimbledon appearance. Once again the crowd was seething with anticipation. The United Press International wire service put out a story that read, 'The lips of every woman and the eyes of every man are asking the same question, "What will she wear this time?"'

The wait was agonizing. This was the first time in my life I was at Wimbledon without any duties, which also meant without any privileges, so I had difficulty in even making my way to the free standing room, the crowd was so dense. Suddenly Gussy appeared for my moment of truth. My knees went quite limp as I saw her looking dazzling and as sexy as ever. The tight-fitting embroidered shorts seemed to enhance her already provocative long stride. The press quickly dubbed it the 'Peek-a-Boo suit' because the embroidery had holes in it and the deep suntan of her shoulders was visible through the shirt. Her appearance was a smash hit. Phone calls came from thousands of miles away, from California, from Latin America and Australia. 'We must have it,' they said. 'Reproduce this outfit immediately and send it over.'

Within a few months of Gussy's first appearance, lace was to be seen on swimwear, ski wear, leisure wear, and every other conceivable type of garment. We had initiated a tide of fashion progress, the irresistible tide Hazel Wightman – like King Canute – was unable to comprehend.

Thirty-four years ago destiny linked me with Gussy through the common cause of believing the word 'feminine' could be a reality in women's sports. Our association had to survive many storms and stresses before we emerged, amazed by the whole thing, perhaps a little scarred in the process.

Today, after two wildly publicized broken engagements and two broken marriages, Gussy lives in quiet solitude near the Pacific Ocean in California. She spends most of her time teaching tennis to incurably deaf children at a nearby clinic.

But together, in less than three weeks in 1949, Gussy and I changed the entire concept of how sportsgirls could look. Her name has already become a part of the folklore of tennis and in years to come her story will still be told, as a legend, wherever the game is enjoyed or discussed.

18 Little Mo

Maureen Connolly, all tiny sixteen years of her, appeared suddenly from the dressing room and confronted me, 'Hi! I like your work and I'm going to wear your dresses!'

I had never before seen 'Little Mo', as she was called, and in that first meeting during the Longwood Wightman Cup matches in Boston in 1951, I got the impression I was being addressed by an animated toy in which a rapid-fire voice tape had somehow been implanted. The spring was overwound. Her eleven words took less than eleven seconds. Then she was gone.

Already in 1951 this child prodigy knew exactly where she was at, but even she could not have imagined what her meteoric rise to stardom would involve. Within weeks she was to become the youngest player ever to win the American championships; within nine months she had captured the first of her three successive Wimbledons, and in two years she achieved what no woman had ever done before, the Grand Slam of the Australian, French, Wimbledon and the United States titles. For good measure she added the Irish championships, which were particularly dear to her heart because of her shamrock ancestry.

Maureen followed Alice Marble as the second of Teach Tennant's amazing prodigies. But history was to repeat itself in the cruellest way. Just as Teach and Alice achieved fame and glory together only to be followed by a bitter and irreconcilable parting, so, too, did Teach and Maureen.

Maureen, whose parents had separated when she was four, originally took to tennis because her mother could not afford her first passion, horse-riding. Maureen's mother was a church organist. She had desperately wanted to become a concert pianist, but she found her tiny hands could not span an octave. Having suffered the frustration of her own hopes, she centred her ambitions on a musical career for Maureen. But this was not to be. Hours of practice on the tennis court were one thing, but never, at any age, did Maureen see herself tolerating hours at the piano.

When Maureen had become the world's best tennis player, she piloted me on a nostalgic visit to the cracked, concrete San Diego courts in California where she had played her first tennis games because there was no cost involved. As a promising twelve-year-old she had been noticed on these very courts by a veteran player, Daisy Tree.

Daisy knew Teach Tennant by reputation. Mrs Tree wanted lessons herself from Teach, but doubted Teach would accept her. It was a convenient passport for her to call Teach and draw her attention to this obviously talented child. As it turned out, Mrs Tree's inspiration was an act of destiny for Maureen and made her own hopes come true.

The passing years never softened Teach's idiom. When Daisy Tree first brought Teach and Maureen together, Teach's opening comments were as matter-of-fact as ever. 'Right. Now let's hit a few and see what you can do.' No how-do-you-dos. No pleased-to-meet-you. In Teach's opinion such refinements were a complete waste of time.

Teach was quietly impressed with Maureen, but not at all pleased with the fact that the child was left-handed. At that time there had never been a left-handed world beater among tennis women, and in Teach's logic Maureen would have to become right-handed if she were to interest herself in Daisy's 'discovery'. But meanwhile Teach's solar plexus sent her the same message as it had about Alice Marble. Maureen could be a world champion.

So Teach agreed on a deal with Daisy Tree and began Maureen's training by spending countless hours making the youngster catch, not balls but racquets, with her right hand. What first appeared a reckless decision was soon acknowledged as a stroke of genius. In less time than some athletes need to get their first mention in sports columns, Maureen was already champion of the world.

In the spring of 1951 I was invited to make a personal appearance with my tennis designs at the Robert Simpson store in Toronto. In August I was invited back. On the way from London it was easy to stop off in Boston for the Wightman Cup matches.

America's leading player, Margaret Osborne, had recently married Willie duPont and was out of the team, but there were still four high-ranking Americans available right behind her, including the current Wimbledon champion, Doris Hart. Hazel Wightman in person was captaining the American team. She always seemed to enjoy ruffling feathers, and on this occasion took the unprecedented step of selecting Maureen, ranked at the bottom of the American top ten, to play No. 3 spot in the Cup matches. Her gamble, in fact, paid off as Maureen scored a straightforward win over her British opponent, Kay Tuckey. This was the first explosion in her fireworks ascent to the top of the world.

I had not met Teach Tennant since Alice Marble's triumphant night at the 1939 Wimbledon Ball. At our Boston reunion Maureen rushed off to practise, and Teach was only too pleased to sit down with me and my business associate, Henry Turner, to fill us in on the details of her latest exciting find.

Teach was euphoric about the golden horizons she saw for Maureen. But she explained she also had problems. She was already thinking about Maureen's probable opponents in future years. She considered the world's leading players, Margaret duPont and Louise Brough, past their best and in Teach's mind, the ranking No. 3, Doris Hart, was already the one to beat for Little Mo.

At that time Little Mo was extremely cute, with irresistible urchin-like appeal: before she began beating the top players they all liked her. For her part, Maureen idolized Doris Hart, but Teach was convinced that as long as this state of affairs endured, Maureen would never beat Doris. Detailing her plans to make Maureen the world champion as quickly as possible, Teach startled Henry and me by telling us how she proposed to overcome Maureen's adulation for Doris. She was conceiving a number of cruel fabrications which she was about to represent to Maureen as Doris's opinion of her.

Teach's unique success as a coach made her many enemies, but whatever was said about her in later years, she had an extraordinary instinct for strategic, psychological training of future champions. At the time, her strategy for Maureen was successful, but in later years the latter was to say that one of the major factors in her break with Teach was that Teach taught her only how to 'win with hate', never for the love of the game.

Her forecast that Doris Hart was the one to beat for Maureen took only two weeks to come true. The Boston hate campaign against Doris began in August. In early September Maureen found herself confronting Doris herself in the Forest Hills semi-final.

Throughout her life Maureen was – as Chris Evert Lloyd is today – a fundamental baseliner. After five years' domination by the trio of Brough, duPont and Hart, the best serve-volleyers ever seen before Billie-Jean King, it seemed inconceivable that any non-volleyer let alone this tiny dynamo, could get her shots either past or over these Amazons.

But as Teach hoped, by the time Maureen took the court she had come to despise Doris because of the things Teach had told her. In a windswept Forest Hills stadium Maureen shocked Doris and the world with a 6-4, 6-4 win.

That evening I wrote to Jimmy Jones, editor of the magazine *British Lawn Tennis*, in whose columns I had so incensed Sir Louis Greig, 'I see no reason why Maureen should lose a singles match in the next five years.' A comparable forecast could be made today about Martina Navratilova.

After Maureen's shock victory, Teach had tears of delight in her eyes. She was also excited because, in the final, Maureen had only to play Shirley Fry of whom Teach had a very mediocre opinion. On this subject, Teach and I had a heated argument. Having served my tennis apprenticeship in an era of incomparable baseliners, I have always known that a really sound baseliner much prefers playing a volleyer than someone of her own type of game.

Shirley Fry was a tireless retriever, who ran and ran and rarely went for outright winners. It was this defensive concept that made Teach derisive about her chances. 'No one can win playing negative tennis,' was her doctrine. In fact, we were both right because Maureen, though she beat Shirley Fry in the final, had a marathon match and a very narrow escape. Marathons against Shirley Fry were to be repeated at intervals throughout Maureen's career.

On the surface Maureen's 1951 Forest Hills victory as a mere sixteen-year-old was the start of a glorious rise to world fame. But underneath, she was quickly caught up in the treacherous emotional cross-currents of stardom. Her propulsion to sudden fame gave her a crash course in the facts of life. Almost within minutes of becoming the new American champion, Maureen, in the excitement of signing autographs, was tricked into signing a concealed cheque that was later cashed by a con man. This caused a lot of cynicism in her and made her very guarded against signing autographs for the rest of her life.

The dust had not even settled on her first major victory when she was shocked for a second time. Her mother, Jessamine, who had become Mrs Bertse years before, reassumed overnight the name Connolly, obviously on the strength of her daughter's success.

Then came the third shock. As a result of Margaret Osborne's marriage to Willie duPont, Teach arranged for Maureen to team up with Louise Brough. At the beginning Louise and Maureen were very friendly. However, in the spring of 1952, the child prodigy, with one major title, had the temerity to beat Louise who had already won fourteen American and ten Wimbledon titles.

From then on jungle law took over. Louise convinced herself that Maureen was her deadly rival. Maureen recounts that in their first hit together at Wimbledon a few months later, Louise was out to kill her, even in practice. This sudden switch in Louise's attitude played right into Teach's hands and accentuated her own plan of tempering Maureen into the hard steel that she knew would be needed for the road ahead.

Then the antagonism, which had been developing for some time between Teach and Mrs Connolly over Maureen's future, began to assume problem proportions. The two women's philosophies were polarized in that Teach clearly saw in Maureen a repeat, if not an improvement, of her success with Alice Marble. Mrs Connolly, in absolute contradiction, saw her daughter as a child being dragged out of her natural age group and pushed relentlessly toward stardom.

The first major confrontation between Teach and Mrs Connolly arose over Maureen's initial trip to Europe in 1952. Because Maureen was only seventeen years of age, Mrs Connolly was still her legal guardian and was determined to use her right to travel with Maureen to Wimbledon. She told Teach that if she did not go along she would refuse permission for Maureen to go at all.

The familiar spectre of tennis politics then appeared. Teach was convinced that if Maureen was to follow the usual pattern of playing the French championships before Wimbledon, she would most likely lose both, so Teach ruled that Paris would be by-passed in Maureen's first year in Europe. As a result, both the USTA and the French Federation filed formal complaints that they were missing a valuable appearance of tennis' latest box-office star. Predictably, Teach held to her theory, but only after bitter recriminations from all concerned. Teach's determination to have the final say on Maureen's plans made her as many new enemies among the Establishment as it had in her past association with Alice Marble.

Throughout the spring of 1952 in London I received letters regularly from Teach explaining in great detail the schedule she was setting up for Maureen's forthcoming visit. The prime reason for these letters was that both Teach and Little Mo were determined I should design her tennis clothes.

Teach always made her plans months in advance on the lines of a military operation: so-and-so would happen on such-and-such a date; Maureen's measurements were this-and-that; and the parties would arrive at London Airport on 20 May at 5.33 p.m.

A smiling photograph of Teach and Maureen leaving the plane at London Airport shows only the superficial happiness of anticipation. Behind the smiles, many far-reaching problems were already fermenting. This photograph was, in fact, the last ever taken of Teach and Maureen in harmony. As Maureen came down the steps from the plane, a newsreel company asked me to pose with her. Remembering Teach's usual proprietary domination over her protégées, I said, 'I hope Teach won't mind our doing this.'

The effect was dramatic. From that moment on I was caught in the full force of the storm. Amazingly, the childish look left Maureen's face like a discarded mask, her eyes narrowed, and in a metallic voice I had not heard before but came to recognize later, she replied, 'What I

141

do is my own business.' She was then seventeen and eight months.

Teach ordained that as Maureen's dress designer I should have preference the next day over all other business, and I was told to be at their London hotel for a 7.00 a.m. breakfast. When I arrived, a group of pressmen were already waiting in the foyer for the new celebrity to appear. As they pumped me for information, Teach swept Maureen past them with all the elegant disdain of a movie queen from the old school.

At breakfast it was immediately obvious that Teach was inadequately briefed about British post-war conditions: she ordered bacon and eggs for both herself and Maureen. Helpfully, my assistant rushed off to her home to collect some of her own egg ration for Maureen. Within minutes of returning she was off again to collect some towels that Teach wanted for Maureen's practice-sessions. Again, with war-time restrictions still in force, no towels were available. These may seem trivial matters now, but Teach's unfamiliarity with the altered face of Britain was to have far deeper consequences before long.

Teach finally allowed the press boys their interviews with Maureen, and it was astonishing in those days to see so many well-known sportswriters focusing on an immature girl of seventeen. While everyone discussed and demanded every intimate detail of her past, her present, and her future intentions, Maureen would seem suspended in a cloud of oblivion. Her expression would denote meditation on faraway things, and one could have laid money on her not having kept abreast of the discussion. Then, suddenly, something would be said that directly affected her or conflicted with her unerring instinct for what was right for Maureen, and she would spark instantly to life. Again the expression would change, the eyes narrow, and out would come some devastatingly opposite appraisal in the metallic voice I first heard at the airport.

Maureen had a star's natural gift for dealing with the press. Her first practice hit at the Surbiton Club attracted sixteen press photographers, and at one point she called to them, 'Are you getting what you want, boys?' This instinct for what is now called Public Relations, disgusted the English purists, but her unexpected professionalism endeared her to the press.

During those early weeks in London I noticed signs of increasing unrest between Teach and Maureen. Naturally Little Mo was showered with all sorts of privileges and gifts. Teach obviously expected to share in these, but Maureen failed to see this, and friction quickly arose from these small details because of an already inflamed situation. The final, fateful blow, which would have submerged anyone with lesser spirit than Little Mo, came when she injured her shoulder in a practice hit with Louise Brough before the Queen's Club finals, only forty-eight hours before the opening of Wimbledon.

Teach called me at 11.00 a.m., completely distraught. 'Do something, honey,' she pleaded. 'Something terrible has happened to Maureen's shoulder. She's in agony.'

During Teach's London visits with Alice Marble in the late 1930s, she had placed unshakeable faith in a well-known osteopath, Hugh Dempster.

Thirteen years had elapsed, but she asked me to alert him that Maureen needed immediate treatment. It was Saturday, and Dempster had already left for his country home, so I contacted my own specialist, Hugh Burt, Director of Physical Medicine at University College Hospital. Maureen was rushed to Hugh Burt, and he diagnosed only a sharp attack of fibrositis. He said this could be allayed by some weekend heat treatment. But by a curious and fatalistic coincidence, he was going on leave that day and could not see Maureen again.

Meanwhile Hugh Dempster had been told on the golf course about my phone call and decided to sacrifice his Saturday so as not to miss the opportunity of including the new celebrity among his patients. Teach was happy to take Maureen to see Dempster, but his diagnosis was the complete opposite of Hugh Burt's: a badly torn shoulder ligament. 'The girl risks life injury if she plays again,' Dempster warned Teach.

Maureen, exasperated by Dempster's diagnosis, wanted desperately to believe Hugh Burt, but Dempster's pronouncement terrified Teach who still had great belief in him. The question was, which of the two Hughs was right?

Later, at Queen's Club, Teach was inundated with questions from an eager press. Louise Brough was not reticent. 'She's supposed to have hurt her shoulder,' Louise was telling everyone, 'but I can't help thinking she's got a great alibi there.'

Teach then made a serious tactical error. Instead of explaining the situation in detail and gaining press sympathy, Teach sat alone, on the Queen's Club terrace, a thunder-cloud expression on her face, muttering again and again, 'No comment, no comment'. With Teach saying nothing and Maureen shut away in the dressing room, reporters had little evidence to go on.

Maureen pulled out of the Queen's Club singles final, but then appeared in the doubles final, validating Louise's suggestion as far as the press was concerned.

But as Maureen was dressing, she overheard a reporter calling in his story that she was injured and would not play Wimbledon at all. Throwing a bath robe around her, Maureen rushed out of the dressing room and threatened the reporter with dire results if he did not cancel his story immediately. I doubt if he ever recovered from the shock of being confronted by a half-dressed teenager behaving like a bouncer ready to throw him out. Apart from illustrating the undercurrents of Maureen's character, this incident clearly demonstrated her determination to play Wimbledon, whatever Teach or any doctor might say.

The following day, Sunday, Maureen, Teach and Mrs Connolly locked themselves in their suite with the telephone ringing incessantly and half a dozen reporters camped outside their front door. Maureen, who felt instinctively she did not have a severe injury, kept saying she was determined to play at all costs. Teach, terrified that Dempster's diagnosis might truly jeopardise Maureen's whole future, was nearly hysterical. Mrs Connolly saw the whole situation as an opportunity to prove herself, repeating endlessly that their trip should never have taken place at all. Years later Maureen recalled that the events of this day brought her close to an emotional breakdown.

That Sunday night, on the very eve of Wimbledon, I had two phone calls within thirty minutes, the first from Teach, the second from Maureen.

'Against all advice,' Teach told me, 'this self-willed, headstrong, stupid girl will be playing Wimbledon. You must tell her what she's to wear. Her shoulder is badly damaged. This will be her only appearance and probably the last match of her career.'

Maureen was next. It was midnight. In a remarkably calm voice she said, 'When I play my Wimbledon match I shall need a warm jacket.'

I had to ask carefully, 'Will this be your only match?'

'Of course not,' she said with scorching scorn in her voice.

'But I thought you were badly injured?' I could picture the eyes narrowing.

'That's what Teach thinks.' The metallic tones were again unmistakeable.

As I left the underground going to Wimbledon on Monday, the newsboys were all shouting 'Little Mo doubtful!' I still believe that it was the newspapers, all declaring she was unlikely to play, that finally determined Maureen to compete.

Some time previously, Teach had already planned a few days' absence during the first days of Wimbledon to greet a close friend who was coming by ship from the United States, docking at Liverpool. In Teach's absence Maureen made her Wimbledon debut as planned. Against Mrs Moeller on the No. 1 Court she won her match fairly easily, and shortly afterwards decided on the action that was to change her whole life. She marched alone to the secretary's office and said she wished to call a press conference.

In those days, this was an unheard-of thing for any player to do, let alone a junior. Even the most hardened journalists were startled when they received her summons. They were startled even further when Maureen told them coldly that, henceforth, she would consider herself her own mistress and had no further intention of listening to Miss Tennant. 'She does not represent my views,' she added. 'Anything she says is without my authority and I intend to play on through Wimbledon.' All this was said in Teach's absence in Liverpool and without her prior knowledge. Mrs Connolly was conspicuously absent from the whole scene.

Teach never really recovered from the shocks of those few days. On Saturday she had been aghast that the perfectly-tuned machine she had built could break down. Now she realized that it could not only right itself but could go on without her. Little Mo, the 'Automaton of Tennis', also proved to be automatic.

'I shall never understand why she could sell me short in this way,' was Teach's heart cry. 'Obviously I don't count any more. I have lost all affinity with her mental attitude.'

Naturally I too was distressed by the course of events and embarrassed by not knowing the real depth of the chasm between them. Would I still consult Teach about Maureen's clothes, or had Maureen also assumed authority in that department? All I knew was that they still shared the same suite. I would have to wait and see how matters turned out before worrying about the following week's dresses.

Maureen's immediate future posed a more pressing problem for Wimbledon. The referee was besieged for answers by the press and the office staff were inquisitioned hourly by the ticket-holders.

Three of the top administrators of American tennis, Russell Kingman, Perry Jones and Bill Kellogg, were at Wimbledon but because of Teach's past belligerence toward all of them, they were too nervous to speak to her in the early stages of the conflict. However, immediately after Maureen disowned Teach, they approached Mrs Connolly.

Maureen had already consulted two specialists. Perry Jones' proposal was that he would arrange a consultation with a third specialist, but with one condition: Maureen must agree in advance to abide by the decision of the consultant of his choice. Little Mo's first reaction was predictable. She argued that she need not necessarily submit to anything or anybody. It took three hours of discussion to overcome Maureen's obstinacy, but her mother's pleadings and Perry Jones' reasoning finally won her over.

The third specialist was selected in conjunction with the Wimbledon committee. Maureen was taken 'incognito' – in absolute and totally unnecessary secrecy – to see Dr Knowland, the leading authority on physical medicine at Kings's College Hospital. The inevitable result of the secrecy was that, on her way to the hospital she was shadowed and embarrassed by reporters in a convoy of cars who chased her right across London.

Maureen said later she felt her very life in the balance as she waited for the third specialist to pronounce judgement. Finally, his verdict was identical to Hugh Burt's. With the application of some intensive heat therapy she could play on at Wimbledon. In her memoirs Maureen said she was already embracing Dr Knowland before he finished his diagnosis. But being cleared to play Wimbledon was only the first obstacle. Now she had to climb over a series of difficult hurdles to survive.

In her third-round match Maureen came close to seeing her Wimbledon dream evaporate against the English international, Susan Partridge. Although the match was not played on the Centre Court, Susan lost the first set easily from stage fright. But as soon as she recovered her composure she exploited Maureen's difficulties by slow-balling. This plan enabled Susan to win the second set and lead 5-4 in the third set.

Maureen recounts that, despite all the dramatics of her much-publicized split from Teach, from years of instinct she still looked for Teach's support and searched desperately for her in the stands. Instead, she saw only her mother.

It is widely accepted that minor injuries can be quite severely aggravated by nervous tension. At this point in the match Maureen seemed suddenly to become aware of her shoulder injury. In obvious pain she served double faults on both the first and third points of the tenth game. These brought her to within two points of defeat.

While all this was happening on court, there was a hilarious moment for me in the stands. After Maureen's second double fault a spectator directly behind me said, 'What a silly girl. She obviously can't serve from the right court. Why doesn't she just serve every time from the left?' In spite of this spectator's brilliant suggestion, at 15-30, Maureen served still another fault on her first serve. Somehow she managed to scramble the point for 30-all. A low moan rose from the gallery: the partisan crowd had eagerly anticipated the English girl reaching match-point.

What then ensued can never be better described than by Maureen in her own story, *Forehand Drive*.

For me, looking back on a brief span of star-rising, star-crossed tennis years, there is one dramatic moment when I knew this was my year, this was my hour, this was my time to become a champion. There could be no waiting. It was not the stuff of which headlines are made, but my heart knows a total stranger propelled me to the world championships at the age of seventeen.

At 30-all, suddenly piercing the tense silence, a young voice rang out clear and bold: 'Give 'em hell, Mo!' I stood stunned, paused, looked and saw a US Air Force boy. His face was a flash of youth, shining and glowing with friendliness. I did not know him. I had never met him. But truly, in that second, I was lifted to the heights by a stranger. I smiled and said: 'Thank you,' in a fervent whisper.

Truth can be stranger than fiction. If it seems incredible to believe one ringing cry of encouragement can turn the tide of a hopeless match, I say only: it happened!

Maureen's lifelong friend, newspaper columnist Nelson Fisher, originated the nickname 'Little Mo,' because he compared her 'firing power' to that of the battleship 'Big Mo', which frequently berthed at her hometown of San Diego.

In the Wimbledon semi-finals, Little Mo had once again to face Shirley Fry. She was naturally apprehensive and, to make matters worse, the whole day's programme was washed out by the rain. Nelson Fisher takes up the story of that day.

> The night before playing Shirley Fry, Maureen needed loosening-up after a long, rainy afternoon of tiresome stalling before a postponement was announced. Late in the evening Ted Tinling served as Little Mo's sparring-mate on the indoor wood courts of Queen's Club. Maureen vented a forty-five-minute stream of high-powered balls his way but the man pounded them back and provided the American champion with a very good workout.

The result against Fry was devastating. Maureen won in straight sets, more easily than in any of their other encounters.

In the final Maureen faced Louise Brough, still her doubles partner but no longer a friend. Louise was out to regain the title she had won three times in succession in earlier years.

Maureen had never possessed a ballgown. In 1952 it was inconceivable to attend the Wimbledon Ball in a short dress. Win or lose, Maureen intended to be there, so in the first week of Wimbledon she had asked me to create a special dress for her for the big night. To her delight, I suggested a mist-blue silk chiffon that was to have a horse-shoe spray of pink roses featured on a billowing skirt.

With the pressures of Wimbledon production in my workroom,

the dress was only completed late on the morning of her final. In consequence, I had to take it myself to her hotel, and I arrived at 11.30 a.m. less than three hours before the start of her match.

In spite of the late hour I found no one in her suite. Apparently Mrs Connolly had decided to take Maureen shopping with her. At noon Maureen and her mother returned together. Maureen snatched the dress from me, and in a matter of seconds both their characters were revealed to the utmost. Maureen held the dress in front of her, inspecting it in the full-length closet mirror. She suddenly looked twenty years older. The eyes narrowed to slits and the voice became even more metallic than I had previously heard. 'If I don't make the champion's speech in this dress tonight,' she said. 'I SHALL TEAR IT TO PIECES.'

I excused myself, saying, 'I must leave you now. The car is already downstairs waiting to take you to Wimbledon.'

There were less than two hours to go before Maureen's first Wimbledon final, the greatest opportunity of her life. I never believed Mrs Connolly had the slightest comprehension of the situation surrounding her daughter. Even so, I was flabbergasted to hear her say to Maureen, 'Honey, why don't we have a nice lunch here and go to Wimbledon later by cab?'

I did not wait for Maureen's reply.

Ninety minutes later she was on court against Louise, then playing her fifth singles final at Wimbledon. Louise served for the first set, but Maureen managed to break back, and from then on she always looked a certain winner. The voice of the unknown stranger had projected her to the world championship!

For Teach, a moment of personal tragedy came at the Wimbledon Ball that same night. A memory of the last Wimbledon Ball I had spent with Teach flooded into my mind. Alice, in her 1939 champion's speech, had made a gracious and generous tribute to Teach, the woman who made her everything she was. This time the knife was twice twisted in the wound. In her speech Maureen made no reference whatever to Teach, and the added callousness of the praise she accorded to everyone else, down to the ball-boys, was inescapable.

When the music started, Teach, sitting next to me, whispered, 'Dance with me, honey.' As I made lame attempts at lighthearted conversation, Maureen and Frank Sedgman, the men's champion of the previous day, completing their lap of honour together, moved toward us. I saw a chance of breaking the intolerable tension, some hope that I could win Teach a friendly glance. Deftly, I piloted her to within inches of her erstwhile protegee. For a second their eyes met. Then Maureen turned coldly away.

Teach's irreconcilable break with Alice Marble had been shattering. Now she had to face another future alone. Twice she had given her all. Each time destiny, and her protégées, flung it back in her face.

19 Maureen

The morning after the Wimbledon Ball, Maureen was due to fly to Dublin for the Irish championships. With her Catholic upbringing and her Irish ancestry she was very excited about this visit to her spiritual home. Within days in Dublin she became such a favourite that most of the Monsignor Bishops and the Cardinal himself were keen to attend her matches.

Nancy Chaffee, a very attractive and amusing American-ranked player, who often described herself as the 'poor-man's Gussy Moran', was at Wimbledon in 1952.

'Are you coming to Ireland?' Little Mo had asked her. 'Are you crazy?' Nancy replied. 'Do you think I'd play you where they'll put Holy Water on the balls?'

After Maureen's final snub to Teach at the Wimbledon Ball, Teach had deep soul searchings about whether to make a break there and then, but she decided that for her 'public face' she would go to Dublin with the Connollys. To avoid further publicity the two maintained what Maureen later described as a 'sham truce'. However, in Ireland it was obvious that the emotional scars had furrowed too deeply and the 'sham truce' was already terminated. Maureen and her mother returned home to California, but Teach returned alone to London.

Although Maureen kept on winning, I believe she lost a lot of her star quality after her parting from Teach. Though the supreme tennis skills were still there, the absolute confidence of stardom, which Teach infallibly imparted, seemed to have disappeared by the time she reached the American championships at Forest Hills in September.

Maureen's 'kid-wonder' days were so focused on tennis she had had no time or inclination to have playmates or to make friends of her own age. At Forest Hills, for the first time in her life, Maureen was playing the role of defending title-holder of a major championship. Yet instead of projecting the star status she had earned from years of preparation and at great emotional cost, she looked more like a little girl lost. Without Teach's hour-by-hour counsel, she seemed disorientated and disconsolate. I remember she was so much alone she even passed the time helping out in a local hairdressers.

Meanwhile Teach roamed around as aloof and alone as Maureen, avoiding conversations and greeting her few friends with only bluff, artificial joviality.

Nevertheless, in the second week of the championships and, in spite of all that happened at Wimbledon two months before, Teach and Maureen had a momentary reunion. For a few fleeting minutes, the flame of success that illuminated their alliance for four years flared brightly once more. Maureen suddenly found herself facing defeat against Shirley Fry in the semi-final and in desperation turned again to her former soulmate.

The Fry-Connolly match was originally scheduled for the centre court, but at the last minute was switched to an outside court. Shirley won the first set and was well on the way to winning the match when the tournament officials decided to move the girls onto the centre. They should have been there in the first place. It was one of those actions that tennis organizers decide upon without a moment's consideration for the players' feelings.

The switch unsettled Shirley's concentration. Once on the centre court the match changed to a desperate point-by-point struggle in which Maureen only just managed to save the second set and the match. Then, in the ten-minute interval that was allowed in those days in a women's three-set match, Maureen rushed straight to Teach's waiting arms in the dressing room. The ability to revitalize players and restore their confidence when in trouble, was always one of Teach's almost uncanny gifts. In this moment of self-doubt and danger for her supremacy, Maureen found herself in dire need of Teach's magnetic influence and reassurance.

As soon as I saw this astonishing back-track, I knew Maureen would make short work of Shirley Fry in the third set. In fact, she lost only one more game. To win the 1952 American championships and retain her title, Maureen still needed Teach's help. I have always wondered if, at the time, Teach could have suspected this was to be their final moment of harmony.

Three weeks later Maureen and Shirley met again at Perry Jones' Los Angeles tournament. There, Shirley came closer to winning than ever before, taking the first set and having three successive match-points at 8-7, 40-love, in the second. I watched the match from a court-side box with my lifelong friend Elizabeth Ryan, and I remember saying to her, 'The big season's over now, and if Maureen gets out of this match on her own, she will never need to go back to Teach.' Elizabeth readily agreed with me. We were not being cynical, just acutely alert to the tennis facts of life. We were both convinced the Forest Hills loving reunion was no more than a temporary expedient to overcome an unexpected emergency.

Maureen pulled the Los Angeles match out of the fire, beat Shirley Fry without Teach's help, and, unhappily, proved us correct.

It was impossible not to admire the defiant, dominating spirit of both women. However, whatever Maureen's mental process in her actions toward Teach, I believe she could have achieved the same purpose with less exposure of her inexorable self-will.

The split with Teach left a vacuum in Maureen's life and it was again Perry Jones who came up with a solution to her problem. Jones was the czar of the Californian Association that gave financial backing to Maureen's tennis. After Maureen finally beat Shirley Fry without Teach's help, Jones also realized that the hitherto implacable Connolly-Tennant association was finished once and for all.

But Maureen was still the top box-office attraction for Jones' Association and an important source of its revenue, so he needed a new coach and a new chaperone for her without a moment's delay. Harry Hopman, of Australian Davis Cup fame, had made repeated offers to help Maureen if she ever went to Australia. Then, like today, when there is a performer of world-wide importance, everybody wants to get in on the act. Jones had already planned a world tour for Maureen that would begin in Australia at the start of 1953. He therefore decided that Hopman's wife, Nell, herself an international player, would be an ideal companion for Maureen. She would also be Jones' reliable watchdog for the financial interests of the Californian Association, so he set up a deal there and then with Nell Hopman.

In outlook, Nell was a striking contrast to Teach. Above all, she had a much softer, more amateur approach to life. Two years later Maureen confirmed this dramatically when she said Nell taught her to 'win with love, not with hate'.

At the start of 1953 I received a cable from Maureen saying, '*En route* to Australia. Nothing to wear.' The coronation of Queen Elizabeth was approaching and I had already designed a Coronation Collection for New York Seventh Avenue reproduction. Inescapably this featured royal crowns, and when Maureen's summons came I still had crown trims on my mind. Almost automatically I put them on the dresses that were flown out to Maureen in Australia.

'Gee,' Maureen said delightedly when she received the shipment, 'Ted must think I'm a queen.' The idea was only slightly premature. It was 1953 when Maureen became Queen of Tennis by taking the Grand Slam of all the world's major titles. Seventeen years were to elapse before Margaret Court became the only other woman to achieve this same feat.

After touring the Southern Hemisphere, Maureen and Nell made the Italian championships in Rome their first European stop. Nell was a compulsive sightseer. Her journeys with Maureen took her to many famous places she had not previously visited, and in purposeful contrast to the manner in which Teach directed Little Mo's career, Nell arranged excursions, theatres, and a 'dolce vita' in miniature to replace Teach's stern disciplines. In Rome anyone could be excused for not concentrating on tennis.

The Italian championships were then played in the famous Foro Italico — Mussolini's attempt to outdo the Caesars. Fringed by cypresses, the dark terracotta of the arena contrasts magically with the royal blue of the sky. Marble terracing climbs towards almost constant sunshine, and the perimeter is watched over by twenty larger-than-life statues of civic dignitaries. Beyond the stadium the legendary hills of Rome zigzag in a blue haze, and the whole vista has a scented quality of romance only comparable with Provence.

The Foro Italico centre court is the largest in the world. It has also the slowest playing surface outside Paris. In setting up Maureen's 1952 schedule, Teach had shown her deep tennis insight by preventing Maureen from including Rome or Paris on her first trip. The contrast of unpredictable Wimbledon turf after hot sunshine and slow clay would be too great for any newcomer to absorb successfully at first try.

Whether because of the 'dolce vita' distractions with Nell, or because of the unfamiliar, slow Roman courts, Maureen proved Teach's theory correct by losing the Italian championship to Doris Hart.

In Rome, rumours were already buzzing that Maureen was in love. Later, in Paris, I certainly found her changed. Four international titles represented a tremendous fulfilment, and her previous brittle eagerness had blossomed into a glowing warmth. The transformation was accompanied by a mature and thoughtful interest in her clothes and new figure-consciousness. 'I'm giving up chocolates and pastries to stay under ten stone,' she told me.

Although she denied being engaged, Maureen was wearing a square-cut amethyst ring, the gift of Norman Brinker, the American Olympic equestrian whom she had met through her own passion for horses. In previous years Teach frequently complained that Maureen's habit of playing truant to go horse-riding was damaging her tennis, though such pessimism was scarcely justified by her results.

As a motherly companion, Nell Hopman had all the qualifications needed to help a flowering teenager in the throes of her first love affair. As Maureen's business manager, on behalf of Perry Jones, she also kept a tight rein on compulsive shopping. The missing element was Teach's uncanny ability as a tennis coach, a quality Nell was never able to replace.

After losing the Rome final to Doris Hart, Maureen was very disturbed about her form and her inability to get accustomed to the soft clay courts of Europe's mainland. In desperation she recruited Fred Perry to advise her, and after hours of evening practice with Fred she would also come to me for long consultations, asking how the meteoric Suzanne Lenglen remained so supreme in these slow-motion conditions.

Maureen had good reason to be apprehensive because Doris Hart loomed between her and her first French national title. To reach the final she also had to beat Susan Partridge, the English girl who brought her to within a hair's-breadth of defeat ten months earlier.

Meanwhile, on St Patrick's Day of that year, Susan had married the French charmer Philippe Chatrier, today President of the world-governing body of tennis. Susan had an outstandingly beautiful figure, and I made her a very striking bridal gown for the ceremony, at which nearly one thousand guests were present in Wolverhampton Cathedral.

When Maureen met Susan in the French championships both girls were on cloud nine for their own reasons; Susan just back from her honeymoon with Philippe Chatrier; Maureen at every mention of Norman Brinker.

Once again Maureen had a hard time, only beating Susan in a long three-set match. Nevertheless the high drama and tensions of the previous year were all gone. Maureen had already emerged from her youthful need for hate motivation. Little Mo was growing up fast and I doubt she would even have noticed if, this time, an unknown voice in the crowd had cheered her to victory.

The confidence Maureen gained from beating Susan a second time carried her to an easy revenge over Doris Hart in the final and to the second leg of her historic Grand Slam.

After Rome and Paris, the tennis scene moved to England.

Maureen's youthful victories and her public confrontation with Teach the previous year aroused enormous press interest in her return, and I found myself inundated in advance with questions: 'Have her subsequent successes changed her?' 'Has Maureen matured?' 'Is she really in love?' 'What will she wear?' So many journalists called me before her arrival, I decided on the then unprecedented step of inviting all London's women editors to a special reception to allow them to ask Maureen their questions in person.

More than a hundred writers, newsreel and television people accepted my invitation. Many post-war journalists had never previously met a tennis star in the flesh. This was the beginning of the public's involvement in the real personality and background of sports performers instead of hearing only of their sensational aspects. In retrospect, it was the forerunner of today's accepted media routine.

The following day, Maureen had warm and welcoming reports in the British press. I think all the journalists were relieved to find the metallic-voice tones and the unconcealed wilfulness of the previous year had worn off. We soon found ourselves caught up in the festive mood that pervaded England in that year of Queen Elizabeth's coronation. Nevertheless, we had one sad memory.

Maureen and I were playing our matches on adjoining courts at the pre-Wimbledon tournament in Manchester. Our matches happened to finish simultaneously, and we came off together laughing and happy, only to be greeted at the entrance by reporters who told us of Bill Tilden's death. Many of the young competitors in the tournament had never seen Tilden, but such was their respect for his fame that only a handful of players turned out for the parties that evening.

Beginning in Rome, we had all been on the road for six weeks, a long time in those days. After Manchester we converged as usual on London: in 1953 there was the added excitement of the Coronation to look forward to. Nell and Maureen were given front-line seats on the route from Buckingham Palace to Westminster Abbey, and remained starry-eyed from the spectacle all through Wimbledon.

Once back on the fast London grass courts, Maureen's tennis also seemed to fire, and in defending her Wimbledon title she lost only eight games to reach the final.

Looking back, however, I think the 1953 Wimbledon was probably one of the toughest I experienced. The pressures of my business were, fortunately, growing yearly. The aftermath of the press reception for Maureen also resulted in some new pressures.

With Perry Jones' financial backing, Nell was able to establish herself with Maureen in a luxurious suite in Grosvenor House. Jones was the first person since Helen Wills to declare that tennis stars deserved status. Life had never previously allowed Maureen a private sitting room in a hotel.

Unfortunately my devoting so much time to Maureen sparked some flickers of jealousy from Nell, and for a time I thought I was back in 1952 with Teach expecting to share equally in everything that was done for Maureen.

I calculated that Maureen needed nine or ten tennis outfits as she had nineteen possible matches at Wimbledon. Nell was unlikely to have more than six matches at most, yet she announced that she needed a different dress for each match. As the likely champion-to-be, Maureen was naturally concerned about having a particularly beautiful ballgown in readiness for the champion's acceptance

155

speech. As Maureen's official chaperone, Nell felt I should also provide her with an elaborate ballgown. Perhaps all chaperones are fundamentally alike, and my job again put me inescapably in the middle of an emotional tug of war.

For the third time in 1953 Maureen faced Doris Hart in the final. Having regained her form on the fast grass, she was no longer having sleepless nights about playing Doris. This time it was my turn.

I always encouraged Maureen to choose new styles for each Wimbledon, and, by the time she reached the final she had invariably discovered one feature from each dress she particularly fancied. For the last day I would try to embody all her fancies in a single new design, but we reckoned without the weather. After a late practice on the eve of the final, Maureen came off sopping wet. 'I just can't play in that high-neck dress tomorrow,' she panted. 'It's too hot, you've got to do something.'

I realized it would be useless to argue, although the dress was already awaiting delivery. It was a Friday evening, and my staff, of course, had already gone home. In a filthy temper I went back to my workrooms, hot and tired, and grabbed the dress. For speed, I ripped it right down the front. Only then did I realize there was not a scrap of the material left. By this time it was nearly midnight and I had nightmare visions of Maureen playing Doris in an old, soiled dress, and losing because of it.

Telling myself to keep calm, I tried to think. Eventually inspiration came. Finding an odd strip of white satin, I worked until dawn, stitching it to the torn edges and designing a low neckline.

That afternoon, when Maureen appeared for her final, a group of French journalist-friends who understood such things, rose to their feet and clapped. *'Bravo pour la robe!'* they chorused. It was very sweet music. Such near-disasters often made me wonder what the spectators would think if they knew all that goes on behind the outward façade.

Maureen beat Doris for the third leg of her Gland Slam in what many people still describe as one of the best-ever Wimbledon finals. Then the two girls met once again, in the Forest Hills final in September. This time Maureen was unplayable. Her drives on both wings had absolute firepower and seemed drawn, as if by a magnet, to the lines. I think this was the best match I ever saw Maureen play; so, recently I was amazed on finding a picture that revealed that there were less than three thousand spectators in the stands at the time. Even in the 1950s it was considered 'sissy' for men to watch women's tennis.

This was Maureen's third American championship. She had won Wimbledon twice, the French and Australian titles once, but at that time to be accorded the accolade of the Grand Slam, the news media required all these to be won in the same calendar year. Previously only Don Budge had achieved this. Now Maureen became the first woman to do so. Today the same situation would attract fifteen thousand enthusiasts, with sixty per cent of them men.

In the circumstances, I doubt if even the London press would have questioned the appropriateness of the crowns I had put on her dresses three months previously.

20 *An Empire for a Horse*

All her young life Maureen dreamed of owning a horse. She had started regular horseback-riding just as soon as her tennis brought in enough under-the-counter payments to pay for the expense. Teach, however, regarded all horses and riding as a dangerous risk for her star protégée, and they would argue repeatedly about the whole subject. In this respect Teach wasted her time. She could have realized, as she became familiar with Maureen's implacable obstinacy, that nothing she could do would keep Maureen away from horses. To Maureen, tennis was work. Riding was a relaxation that became a compulsive hobby. When I first came to know Maureen in 1952, her greatest desire in life was to possess her very own golden palomino.

Teach's attempts to discourage Maureen's obsession only resulted in Maureen playing truant from her tennis practices. The whole bitter argument would begin again when she returned, and Teach would get totally outraged.

But after Maureen won her first Wimbledon and retained her American title at the 1952 Forest Hills championships, Teach was no longer any part of Maureen's life, and her good friends, the Nelson Fishers, arranged a wonderful surprise award for her achievement. Upon her return to San Diego, they, in collaboration with the local Junior Chamber of Commerce and rich rider-breeder, Morley Golden, formally presented her with the thing she most wanted in life. Ironically, since it was this same horse that was eventually to terminate Maureen's career as supreme champion, the golden palomino was called Colonel Merryboy.

Throughout the spring of 1953, while Maureen was touring Europe with Nell Hopman and getting closer, title by title, to her eventual Grand Slam of that year, her mind was on other things: she was homesick for Colonel Merryboy and preoccupied almost daily about his welfare in her absence.

Neither Nell nor I had ever seen the horse, but Maureen chattered about it so incessantly we felt we knew every hair of its head. One day, at a dress fitting, even Nell was irritated into saying, 'Maureen, why don't you skip Wimbledon, go back and take care of the goddam horse.'

Nell's tart comment had the desired effect, and afterwards we were able to concentrate a bit more on the dress fittings.

Maureen's love affair with Norman Brinker was also blossoming at the same time, so it was remarkable, really that with two major distractions she was able to play the superlative tennis she did. However, once her Grand Slam was achieved, she had just one object in mind: to get back to Norman and Merryboy. Norman himself would probably be the first to agree that at that particular time no one was quite sure which of the two was uppermost in her mind.

I made the trip to California again that autumn, and almost within hours of my arrival, Maureen phoned me to say that I had to come out and meet with 'the Colonel'. We had lunch first at the Connolly home. I found Mrs Connolly just as contentious as I remembered her from the 1952 Wimbledon. There was even the usual embarrassing moment I had come to expect whenever Maureen and her mother were together. This time it was a Friday, and Mrs Connolly was scandalized when Maureen helped herself from a casserole of meat that she had prepared specially for me. Both Maureen and her mother were ardent Catholics, but Maureen had a special dispensation from the Pope to eat meat on Fridays before an important match.

Seeing Maureen help herself to the meat, Mrs Connolly could not contain her indignation. 'That's for Ted. You're not allowed to eat meat. You don't have a match today,' she remonstrated. Mother and daughter seemed just as polarized as ever, but Maureen just laughed. 'Ted is my big match today,' she said as she speared another sparerib.

After lunch Maureen drove me to Merryboy's stable. We did not even take the horse out, as she appeared overwhelmed with delight at just seeing her beloved pet. However, the horse showed no particular inclination to reciprocate, for as she went lovingly to feed Merryboy he tried to bite her. Again Maureen laughed off the incident saying, 'He's just in a bad mood today.'

In fact, nothing could really disturb her happiness at that time. She and Nell Hopman had just completed the first year of their association. Maureen had won every major title in the world except Rome, and Nell had been able to put in a very satisfying financial report to Perry Jones for his Californian Association. A few weeks later Maureen announced her engagement to Norman Brinker.

Everything seemed idyllic until, without warning, a stormy engagement period followed between Maureen and Norman. In that winter, Maureen's tennis enthusiasm suddenly lapsed alarmingly. Without Teach to insist on the daily practices, both Shirley Fry and Beverly Baker finally broke Maureen's long winning spell.

But these upsets all disappeared with the spring. Perry Jones reappointed Nell as chaperone for Maureen's 1954 tour. I was summoned to Paris as usual to discuss her new outfits, and in May the British journalists asked me to arrange a repeat of the previous year's press reception in London. There was only one problem. Harry Hopman had succeeded Fred Perry as Maureen's coach, so between them the two Hopmans now had complete control over Maureen's movements. When I met with them all in Paris, I became perturbed over Maureen's tennis attitude, and this led me to a head-on clash with Nell.

During the first four months of the year Maureen's tennis had been in the doldrums. She was bored, listless, and worried over her lovers' quarrels with Norman. She had spent a lot of her time just out riding or drooling over her horse. So I decided to speak up: about tennis, for a change, and not just about dresses.

Between Paris and Wimbledon there were competing tournaments in Berlin and Manchester. Nell wanted to see Berlin, where there was no suitable opposition for Maureen at all. All the top names were going to Manchester to familiarize themselves in good time with England's wet turf. I reminded Maureen of her lack of match practice. I told her that if she went to Berlin she could conceivably find herself playing Louise Brough or Doris Hart for the first time that year in an important Wimbledon match. Without any proper preparation she might have a bad time and no chance of recovery.

Maureen's reply was immediate and forceful. 'I'm playing Manchester.' Nell made no secret of her disgust at my intervention. What happened later completely vindicated my contention. In Manchester, Maureen met and beat both Louise and Doris on successive days. In the 1954 Wimbledon final, the exact situation that I had anticipated occurred. Suddenly Maureen found herself 2-5 down in the second set to Louise, but with the Manchester tests so successfully behind her, she was able to come back and win without the anxieties of a third set.

Within fifteen minutes, she came to tell me she felt she owed her victory to my advice. As this became the last championship match she was ever to play in her life. I was glad I had spoken up.

Maureen was still only nineteen. Yet within seventeen days of her third Wimbledon title, her whole tennis career would be terminated by an accident involving Merryboy. On 20 July, out riding with a party, Merryboy was frightened by a speeding lorry and threw her against it, breaking her right leg and severing all the muscles in her calf. Maureen was in the operating room for four hours and under heavy sedation for four days. Teach had been right about so many things, and so often Maureen had been unwilling to listen.

Maureen sued the trucking company for damages. Her comeback was long and painful, but, as always, Maureen refused to

160

acknowledge defeat. Her recovery began with such simple exercises as picking up marbles with her foot, then progressed to ballet class and eventually to some minor tennis hits. Her mind was always fixed on her future: she said she planned to defend all her titles in 1955 and, the following year would turn professional.

In January 1955 I heard from Nell that she was meeting Maureen as usual in April, and they expected me to meet them again in Rome or Paris to discuss Maureen's dresses. Later Nell recounted her full horror on receiving a late-night call in Australia from Perry Jones in Los Angeles, telling her that Maureen would never play tennis again. She had experienced a total setback in her recuperation.

In the subsequent court case it was said the accident prevented Maureen from earning substantial sums of money as a professional. Eventually, after years of legal argument, the trucking company was ordered to pay her a token sum of $100,000. By today's reckoning this 'token' would be more than a million dollars.

In March I received a letter from Maureen telling me she expected to marry Norman Brinker within three months and asking me to send some sketches for her wedding dress. She also told me of a strange incident that occurred while she was in hospital. A visitor was announced, and a few words revealed him as Martin Connolly, ex-US Navy boxer, her father. All her life she had been told he was dead.

Maureen's marriage was to take place on 11 June. Meanwhile in London I made her what I still think of as one of the most beautiful wedding dresses of my career. The fact that she invited me, from six thousand miles away, to make the dress for the biggest day of her life, aroused so much interest that Trans World Airlines offered to fly the finished product to California. The huge box, marked 'Precious Cargo', was even given a special seat.

After the stormy beginnings of Maureen's engagement to Norman, their marriage developed into a life of complete happiness. Their first home was in San Diego, later they moved to Arizona and eventually to Dallas. While Maureen was rearing two lovely daughters, Brenda and Cindy, Norman was establishing a nationwide restaurant chain. Today, his Willow Bend Polo stud, near Dallas, has taken him to riches and outstanding success.

The settlement awarded to Maureen in the court case brought the last contact between Maureen and Teach. Teach's summing up of the incident reflected the five years of pent-up bitterness she had experienced, 'A brief phone call, a brief, almost wordless visit, and a cheque for a very small sum left on my dining-room table.' To many of us this was a tragic final act in the interplay of two forceful characters. Both raised by each other to the highest peaks of success by their one-time mutual respect and affection.

In Dallas Maureen resumed short sessions of tennis and eventually became a much sought-after coach. Dallas also brought her a new partnership of lasting significance. There she met Nancy Jeffett, a former nationally ranked junior from St Louis. Together they organized clinics and exhibitions – anything that would help the development of junior tennis. Their aims became so closely identified they decided to work together, and as a result the Maureen Connolly Brinker Foundation was formed.

In the years between 1963 and 1971 the Wightman Cup matches alternated between Wimbledon and Cleveland, Ohio. When Britain's Ann Jones became captain of the British team, one of her first actions was to persuade Maureen to become the official coach to the British girls. In 1965 in Cleveland I was given the 'Marlboro' Award'. We discussed old times, of course, but without ever mentioning Teach. Maureen was as bubbling and effervescent as ever, and she was still wearing the square-cut amethyst ring which had told us so much about her first blossoming way back in 1953.

At my first meeting with 'Little Mo', when she gave the inescapable impression of being an automated toy, she was sixteen. How to explain that underneath the childish, giggling façade, there was a tough, iron-willed, and ruthless prodigy?

Designing her tennis wear, I decided to focus entirely on all the childish features that were appropriate to the lovable side of her. The inner ruthlessness and the iron will could best be illustrated, I thought, by the results on the scoreboard.

Alison Adburgham, one of London's best-known women editors at the time, perceived all this with great insight when writing about Little Mo's dresses. 'It is touching, reassuring, that this teenage girl, already at the pinnacle of world fame, should find delight in little things, in little cats with smiles, in furry poodles with sequin eyes, in dainty birds with fly-away wings which quiver as she runs.'

These were the trimmings I chose with deliberate care to show the world that Maureen was, at least in part, a lovable young person, regardless of her merciless dismissal of Teach and her inexorable determination to crush all opposition.

At the 1967 Wightman Cup matches, Ann Jones confided to us that Maureen already knew she had terminal cancer. She died, as she had lived, determined to defy Fate. In fact, on the day of her death in 1969, she had an assignment to cover Wimbledon for an American newspaper. But happily her name lives on, through the dedicated and continuing efforts of Dallas's Nancy Jeffett and England's Mary Hardwick Hare. In the past decade several millions of dollars have been raised in her name and devoted to the development of girls' tennis.

21 The Sunburned Country

My happy familiarity with Australian tennis now spans most of six decades. From Rodney Heath, Norman Brookes and Gerald Patterson to Peter McNamara and Paul McNamee; from Sylvia Harper and Mal Molesworth to Margaret Court and Evonne Goolagong. In the years between I have been privileged to enjoy the friendship of dozens of other Australian players, the girls and the fellas.

On my travels people ask me frequently, 'What makes the appeal of tennis so world-wide?' In essence I believe that spectators everywhere enjoy a one-to-one duel, but they like to see that duel conducted with chivalry. From its inception tennis elevated itself above some other sports by its inviolable code of gentlemanly conduct. The four French Musketeers proliferated these traditions through their innate gallantry. Successive generations of Australian men players have projected an admirable blend of sportsmanship and virility. The 'two Mcs', and before them, Ken Rosewall, Lew Hoad, Jack Crawford and other earlier players in the men's game; or Evonne, Wendy Turnbull, Mary Hawton and Nell Hopman and their predecessors, have invariably earned world-wide affection for their sporting personalities and often understated ability on the courts.

My first contact with Australian tennis was in the mid-1920s when Sylvia Harper, Esna Boyd, Daphne Akhurst and Floris Conway became the pioneer Australian women's team to tour Europe. I first met the top men players when the team of Norman Brookes, Gerald Patterson, Jack Hawkes, Jack Crawford and Harry Hopman came to the 1928 Monte Carlo Easter tournament to shed their sea legs before embarking on their Davis Cup crusade of that year.

That Easter week my boss, George Simond, was ill and I had to stand in as his understudy. It was a challenging week for me having to juggle with so many eminent names. The week went well, but I have often wondered what those tough Aussies really thought when confronted with a seventeen-year-old tournament referee.

Probably my longest continuing Australian association has been with the Brookes family. Norman and Mabel Brookes were very much part of the 'Upstairs' era of tennis. Their Domain Road home was one of Melbourne's most beautiful residences. Between the two wars they frequented all the stately homes and palace hotels of the Lenglen coterie. After World War I, when quite a few good players were emerging from 'Downstairs' backgrounds, Mabel continued to assume the role of tennis's Grande Dame, even among the cognoscenti of Wimbledon's Royal Box.

In the late 1920s the Brookes brought their three daughters, Cynthia, Hersey and Elaine, who were my contemporaries, for a summer holiday to Le Touquet. In that high-fashion setting I shared some fun games with Brookes (by then Sir Norman) and remember him as outwardly dour and serious but possessed of a sense of humour as sharp as his left-hand volleys. At times he would regale us with memories of his many long sea journeys from Australia when Mabel Brookes would pursue a relentless search for perfectly matching Pacific pearls. It seems that she never allowed the divers one breath of respite as she sat under a deck-awning; an imperious figure in all-white, tossing pearl after pearl back in the ocean because of some tiny flaw, imperceptible except to Mabel's demanding eye.

Lady Brookes's great-great-grandfather was the Governor of St Helena during Napoleon's exile and death there, so her five books of stories of St Helena and of her own pioneer childhood days in Australia make historic reading.

In the 1930s, Hersey and Elaine both married Englishmen, while Cynthia, by marrying the Lord Mayor of Melbourne, Sir Gengoult Smith, became that city's First Lady. So, for the 'big' days, when Cynthia's daughter had her débutante ball and later married in Melbourne Cathedral, and when Elaine was presented at Court in London, I was glad that Mabel chose me to design the appropriate dresses. In 1952, Hersey, after marrying golfer John Langley, induced the British Ladies' Golf Union to invite me to be the first couturier ever to design their Curtis Cup uniforms. And my association with the Brookes continued when Mabel (by then Dame Mabel) gave her all-important patronage to my first socialite dress shows in Australia. I soon learned that in Melbourne a Dame Mabel invitation had something in common with a command from Buckingham Palace.

In fact, the Brookes had long-standing links with the Palace. In 1907 Norman Brookes became the first overseas visitor ever to win the Wimbledon singles. By coincidence, the Prince and Princess of Wales, later King George V and Queen Mary, were in the committee box making the first visit of British royals to the Wimbledon championships. Naturally, the Brookes were summoned for congratulations and all four remained friends throughout their lives.

The ensuing years, from 1907 to 1914, were years of Wimbledon and Davis Cup domination by Brookes and his young partner from New Zealand, Tony Wilding. Between them they won a dozen Wimbledon singles and doubles titles and were primarily instrumental in winning the Davis Cup five times for Australasia in that short period.

Wilding had first competed at Wimbledon as a Cambridge undergraduate in 1904, and Brookes first competed a year later. Dame Mabel told me the two men developed an immediate affinity of minds. Probably the greatest regret of my tennis life is that I was too young to have seen Wilding play. Edwardian press reports all describe him as a wonderfully popular champion, probably the first international tennis star with charisma. In many ways a pioneer, he studied early automobile engineering. His personal quirk was to travel everywhere on his motorcycle, careering across Europe from château to schloss parties in the most remote areas, invariably winning the local invitation tournament and charming everyone with his good looks before speeding off to the next weekend gathering of Europe's aristocracy.

A 1910 Paris newspaper reports that Wilding 'stupefied' his many friends by announcing that he was shortly giving up tennis in order to buy and pilot his own aeroplane – certainly an astonishing statement from anyone at that time. But he evidently changed his mind, as in 1914 we find him still winning tournaments among the palm trees of the French Riviera. But by then he had become enchanted with the fourteen-year-old Suzanne Lenglen and partnered her in mixed doubles at the Cannes Carlton Club of later fame. That summer, with Marguerite Broquedis as partner, he reached the final of the Wimbledon mixed doubles. They undoubtedly impressed everyone as the 'beautiful people' of tennis, for the press had no inhibitions in describing him as an 'Adonis' while to this day Marguerite is still remembered by Jean Borotra as the 'Goddess'.

In the twilight of the *belle époque*, sports hero Tony Wilding was inevitably linked in Edwardian minds with his contemporary, hero-poet Rupert Brooke. Both represented an élite flowering of Cambridge sophistication, and both died as soldiers within fifteen days of each other. Wilding was killed in Flanders in 1915.

Together, Norman Brookes and Wilding brought the starry radiance of the Southern Cross to the tennis scene of their era. Dame Mabel has recorded a distressing account of these two men's final parting, on a grey, rainy morning in northern France, where the Brookes had gone to be with Wilding for what was to be the last weekend of his life. During World War I, while my eldest brother, Collingwood, was up at Jesus College Cambridge, my family rented a house in the city to be nearby at a time when the life expectancy of young men of military age averaged about four months. The house belonged to poetess, Frances Cornford, and her epitaph:

> *A young Apollo golden haired, stands on the brink of strife,*
> *Magnificently unprepared for the long littleness of life,*

though composed for Rupert Brooke still seems an apt eulogy for Tony Wildling too. By 1915 it represented a tragic glance at a society already obsolescent.

Although in 1919 Norman Brookes and his new Australian partner, Gerald Patterson, retained the Davis Cup, at Wimbledon's reopening that same year, Patterson took Brookes's title from him. To sufferers of tennis elbow, it may be some consolation to know that in talking to Patterson in Melbourne in 1953, he told me that even at the peak of his career he had never played a backhand shot without being in pain. As we talked we were watching the masterly ease of Ken Rosewall's backhand. No doubt Patterson was remembering the brute strength of his own ungainly action and the price paid in his era for lack of instruction and proven techniques to emulate.

Nevertheless, Patterson cannon-balled his way to a second Wimbledon singles title in 1922, and since Lenglen was then automatically winning all the women's events it was natural they should pair up to win the mixed doubles in 1920 and be frequently seen 'on the town' together.

When I first met the Australian men players, Harry Hopman was the rookie but Jack Crawford was the bambino of the team. If I recall correctly he celebrated his twentieth birthday during the Monte Carlo tournament where we met.

Hopman, one year older, was destined to become the captain, master-mind and dictator of Australian men's tennis from 1938 to 1967. But meanwhile he also distinguished himself as a player, particularly in doubles, winning the Australian championships twice with Crawford, and in mixed doubles when he was twice runner-up at Wimbledon. He also won the Australian mixed doubles four times and the US title in 1939 with Alice Marble.

But it was Jack Crawford who made the big headlines for Aussie tennis in the decade following our first meeting. In 1932 the tall American, Ellsworth Vines, beat Britain's Bunny Austin in one of the shortest and most decisive Wimbledon finals ever seen. At the time Vines looked totally invincible, – with the most awesome service ever seen before Ivan Lendl – yet the following year Crawford beat him to win Wimbledon, and with the Australian and French titles already in his pocket came to within a single set of winning Forest Hills. Had he done so he would have been the first Grand Slam winner, pre-empting by five years Don Budge's unprecedented 1938 achievement.

Jack Crawford remains in my memory the most modest and unassuming champion. Clearly, he had some very positive inner strength, but outwardly he gave the impression of being a rather anachronistic country squire, using an old-style square-topped racquet and always wearing flannel cricket shirts with long sleeves which he only rolled up to the elbow when the going got really tough. Crawford had asthmatic problems which made an immediate bond between us. In his day there was no question of sitting down or resting at end-changes, so he asked me always to be ready to take him a pot of tea if his match should go to five sets. I remember on several occasions going up the Centre Court gangway to leave a pot of tea – neatly set out with milk and sugar on a tray – on the umpire's chair. Today, when the players' unions have entangled themselves in a cat's cradle of pretentious codes and so-called guide-lines, the gentlemanly casualness of Crawford's matches seems, even to me, almost unimaginable.

In 1933 Australia sent us another rookie, young Vivian McGrath from Sydney, who really made Centre Court history by introducing to world-class tennis the two-handed backhand, since immortalized by Chris Evert, Borg and Connors. Then came young Adrian Quist (I say young because he is three years my junior). We first saw Quist in 1933, but in 1935 he began a golden fifteen-year match-winning spell. In those years Quist won the Australian national singles three times, the French and the US doubles once, and the Wimbledon doubles twice and, for good measure, a 'believe it or not' record of ten Australian doubles championships, plus forty-two out of fifty-five Davis Cup matches. Another Quist record I recall was in a Wimbledon Davis Cup match against Fred Perry. Then we experienced a real St Swithin's July day, when play was interrupted five times for rain. In all my twenty-three years as Wimbledon call-boy I was never required, on any other occasion, to get the players on court six times in one match. It must have been unbelievably trying for both Quist and Perry, yet remembering this incident in a conversation with Quist at Sydney's White City nearly fifty years later, we somehow managed to discuss it with almost affectionate nostalgia. Adrian also recalled that at 1950 Wimbledon he had partnered Gussy Moran, and was so distracted by the spectators' near hysteria over the outfit I had designed for her he was hardly able to get one ball over the net.

Until 1937, Norman Brookes remained the dominant force in Australian tennis, but Harry Hopman was appointed Davis Cup captain in 1938 and his team's 1939 win over the US successfully marked the transition from Brookes's to Hopman's reign.

In 1950 Harry brought his team to Wimbledon. Under the Brookes regime the team had resembled a gentlemanly cricket eleven on its way to a Saturday afternoon match in an English village. Harry's spartan approach went to the opposite extreme: he demanded long hours of training, rigid codes of behaviour and he instituted a system of fines for anyone breaking his rules. All journalists were refused direct access to any of Harry's players, who were instructed to say 'No comment. See Hop', to a degree where this became a joke answer throughout the tennis community. Harry was always concerned about the appearance of his players. It is said that in the days of steamship journeys, when evening dress was *de rigueur* in the dining saloon, Harry had one junior team member locked in his cabin for refusing to don his black tie and dinner jacket for the evening meal.

In 1951, Frank Sedgman won the American singles championship, the first Australian to do so in the seventy years of its history. Overnight Frank became another of Australia's sporting idols. In those early post-war days, most men could only obtain long, baggy, surplus navy issue shorts for tennis, so Harry asked me to make Frank some shorts that would fit him properly. In April 1952 I was playing on the next court to Frank in the Sutton tournament. Our matches finished simultaneously and I thought it could be an appropriate time to ask if he would like to have my shorts for the forthcoming Wimbledon. His reply was inevitable, 'No comment. See Hop.' The following week I was drawn in the mixed doubles at Bournemouth against Frank and his lovely wife, Jean, and I repeated the question. Frank disappeared into the shower, but on emerging, and without further preamble, signified his agreement with one single question, 'Gotta tape?' I have often thought that two naked men going through a measuring ritual in the dressing room of the very dignified West Hants Club would have made a world scoop for any photographer. This incident actually made history for me, because a few weeks later Frank won Wimbledon just twenty-four hours before Maureen Connolly, thus becoming the first of the twenty-two singles champions I have outfitted for their big day there. So, contrary to all possible expectations, my first Wimbledon singles champion was an Australian male!

In 1953 I made my first visit to Australia and was in Melbourne for the famous Davis Cup match when the eighteen-year-olds, Lew Hoad and Ken Rosewall were selected, the youngest team ever. I knew they would like some new shorts for their big moment so I cabled my London office and four pairs were specially flown out to Melbourne. I collected these myself from the customs at Essendon Airport and, after obtaining at least three permissions from Harry to visit the boys at the old Menzies Hotel, and three more before being allowed to speak to them, I delivered the shorts to Ken and Lew personally. They were delighted and danced round the room like kids with new toys. That year Tony Trabert captained the American team. His post-match speech was appropriate: 'We were beaten by two babes and a fox.' It was with this well-deserved reputation that Harry led his Australians to Davis Cup victory fifteen times in the next nineteen years.

Rosewall, Hoad and Maureen Connolly were all contemporaries. They initiated a new world of kids in international tennis. For two years the Hopmans reigned in supreme control as no one could approach either of the boys without Harry's agreement and neither could one speak to Maureen without Nell's permission. I remember wondering if this was a new style of tennis where no one over twenty would ever again win Wimbledon and the players themselves could never again be spoken to.

In 1926 I had played Toto Brugnon and Henri Cochet. In 1930 I played Bill Tilden. Between 1948 and 1952 I played John Bromwich, Frank Sedgman, Geoff Brown and Bill Sidwell, but I still hoped for the opportunity of playing the current Wimbledon champion, Lew Hoad. The chance came in 1957, in the second round of the Manchester tournament before Wimbledon. The men's singles had a 64 draw and Fate had given me the one and only unknown player, the one I was sure to beat in the first round. So much for over-confidence. My opponent turned out to be a dark horse and before long I found myself 3-6, 0-5, 15-40 down. But somehow a miracle happened and I scrambled home in the third set.

I was already forty-seven, and everybody laughed their heads off when the back seam of my Tinling-model shorts split just as I was about to go on for my centre court match against Lew. Even after emergency repairs the affair was still wild. Lew, of course, toyed with me at will, but at 1-1 in the second set I won Lew's serve on a net-cord. Thereupon, Tony Pickard, always one of Britain's brightest young squad members, leaped to his feet in the stand shouting, 'Come on fella. You've got the break. You've got him now.' There were 2000 spectators. Including mine, there were 2001 laughs.

Lew was always an easy-going tennis phenomenon and world-wide success did nothing to disturb his disarming simplicity. He won Wimbledon again in 1957, and late that night I left his celebration party only to return early next morning with the newspapers and the Wimbledon ballgown I had designed for his wife, Jenny. After a while Lew emerged from the bedroom wearing only a towel, a picture of idealized blond athleticism. 'You've had a wonderful press, Lew,' I said enthusiastically. 'The critics say you played the greatest....' He cut me short. 'What's Peanuts doing today?' he asked. Grabbing the papers he ignored all the rave reports of his final win over Ashley Cooper and settled down with his favourite comic strip.

By then, even Harry's flow of talent, drawn from an apparently inexhaustible well, was about to peak in the 1960s with the coming of Neale Fraser, Rod Laver, Fred Stolle, Roy Emerson and John Newcombe. Rod Laver, the little red-headed 'Rocket' from Queensland, possessed the most talent combined with ambition. He won Wimbledon four times, became the first tennis millionaire and the only player in history to win the Grand Slam twice. But as a pro' Laver was banned from Wimbledon from 1963 to 1967 and, had it not been for the International Tennis Federation's inexcusable delays in recognizing open tennis, his supreme talents could possibly have earned him ten Wimbledon singles crowns. As of today, the record books show Roy Emerson as having won the most international titles. Neale Fraser was my star client when he won the US title twice in 1958 and 1959 and Wimbledon in 1960. In contrast, Fred Stolle, while a fine doubles player, made history in a rather unhappy way by losing the Wimbledon singles final three years in succession. Tony Roche, partnered by John Newcombe, was certainly one of the great doubles players of our era. John Newcombe was the last of Hopman's great Australians and he, more than anyone, portrayed the essence of Aussie virility combined with outstandingly handsome looks. For Ken Rosewall their 1970 Wimbledon final together must have seemed like some drawn-out torture session as Newcombe's thundering aces kept coming and coming at him, particularly in the fifth set. Thirteen years later I was glad to read that Newcombe considers that set 'his greatest moment'. He recalls 'going into a zone'. 'Nothing else existed,' he says. 'The court, the ball and Rosewall were the centre of the universe.' With such high-powered concentration allied to ultimate technical skill, great champions win on the big days.

With some pleasant memories of John Bromwich, Ken Fletcher, Owen Davidson, Geoff Masters and Ross Case, we come now to the 'two Mcs'. With no wish to rob Peter to flatter Paul, I cannot recall many players more amiably sporting than Paul McNamee. When he beat John McEnroe in the 1980 French Open, Paul lost two vital set points on McEnroe winners, yet each time called 'good shot' with a smile. Unfortunately, this is mostly a forgotten courtesy nowadays. In fact, today's spectators are often so unaccustomed to the niceties of good sportsmanship, most of those present were mystified by what Paul had said. Together McNamara and McNamee have certainly revived world admiration for Australian men stars. One hopes the latest Australian whiz-kid, Patrick Cash, may perpetuate their example.

But apart from the world down-trend in court manners, what are the reasons for the decline in Australia's long-time near-invincibility in men's tennis? Why is the inexhaustible well of talent apparently drying up? In my view the answer is contained in four simple words: American dollars and American life-style. Until the 1950s there were only two classes of Australians, those who travelled and those who could not. It was as simple as that. The motivation to move into the group that was able to migrate annually to the Northern Hemisphere was enormous. But this was an extremely expensive luxury. Now the finance problem has been solved, first by 'shamateurism', later by the huge prizes that became available with pro' tennis. I remember players who gladly peeled potatoes in the galley below decks in order to make their way to the British circuit and Wimbledon. Today, any player who has participated in one Davis Cup tie or who has reached the semis of a circuit tournament, can look to a lucrative job and luxury living as king-of-the-castle coach in any one of a hundred American resort clubs. At first Australian sporting-goods manufacturers tried to sweeten the lives of their stars with undercover inducements to stay home. Jack Kramer initiated the Australian rot in the Sedgman, Hoad, Rosewall generation. Now the American dollar tide has become irresistible. Today, it is difficult to see how this trend could be reversed. There is no comparable situation among the women as the lack of visible international talent among young Australian women players is as inexplicably bleak and barren as it is at the present time in Britain.

From childhood, in the days of Australia's first world-famous 'Queen of Song', Dame Nellie Melba, I was brought up to have a tremendous admiration for Australian women. I still marvel at all they have achieved in sports, the arts, opera and ballet.

In the world of tennis Nell Hopman was no exception. I first met her when she came to Wimbledon on her honeymoon in 1934. With an immense dedication to the cause of Australian women's tennis 'rights', she was a forerunner of Billie Jean King, fighting an ongoing battle with intensely chauvinistic male administrators (at one time she was the only woman among seventy councillors on the Victorian State Association). I have often described her as the Emmeline Pankhurst of tennis.

A typical example of Aussie sportswomen's modesty is that after Sylvia Harper took Suzanne Lenglen to an unheard-of 7-5 set at Deauville in 1925, Sylvia never in later years mentioned this as an achievement. When I interviewed her on Australian national TV in 1979, she would only say, 'Yes, I played Suzanne. She was wonderful. It was a great privilege.' In the late 1930s two more charmingly modest Australian players came to Wimbledon, Joan Hartigan and Nancye Bolton. In 1956 Queensland's Fay Muller and Daphne Seeney were the doubles runners-up at Wimbledon. The following year Aussies Thelma Long and Mary Hawton were again the doubles runners-up and were later to play significant roles in the development of younger players, particularly Mary Hawton with Jan Lehane, Evonne Goolagong and Dianne Fromholtz.

But it was Nell Hopman who, after a two-year stint as chaperone to Maureen Connolly, obtained, single-handed, the Australian Wool Bureau's sponsorship, which in 1961 enabled the first post-war team of Margaret Smith (later Court), Lesley Turner, Jan Lehane, Mary Carter and Robin Ebbern to tour Europe and the United States. Again in 1965, and again almost single-handed, Nell raised the thirty thousand Australian dollars that enabled Federation Cup to be staged for the first time in Australia, and brought to the fore such eminent players as Judy Tegart and Kerry Melville.

Nell was an insatiable sightseer and always contrived to travel to Europe each year by a different route. In 1954 she decided to make her way to her Rome rendezvous with 'Little Mo' via South Africa and the Victoria Falls. The approach to the Falls threads through a narrow path bordered on both sides by six-foot-high tropical grass. Nell, walking alone, found her way barred by, as she said, 'a large baboon with menacing blood-red eyes'. Nell had piercing blue eyes and when the tennis community were told that a five-minute silent challenge had taken place between Nell and the baboon, none of us doubted which of them had worn the other down. In fact, the baboon did slink away, defeated, into the tall grass. Always ready to applaud winners in tennis, I thought it appropriate to embroider a red-eyed baboon on all Nell's tennis dresses of that year. Nell won the French doubles championship with Maureen. 'One look at that baboon across the net and our opponents had no chance,' quipped Maureen later.

But things did not always go so smoothly. Unfortunately, once Harry achieved success and fame in the men's game he firmly refused to take the slightest interest in Nell's achievements on the women's side. In fact it was only a half joke that when Nell wanted to discuss her hopes and plans or laugh with us, Harry would determinedly turn off his deaf aid. This was a great sadness to Nell and I think Harry missed a lot of fun. In addition, Margaret Court contrived a deep and bitter feud with Nell. From loyalty I was naturally on Nell's side in the quarrel, and for ten whole years Margaret and I never communicated on any subject. This made it difficult for me to dress her later, particularly as Margaret never missed an opportunity to make some sour crack about Billie Jean King, my most valued client at the time. However, in 1972, we eventually resolved our differences with the intervention of the Virginia Slims sponsors, who wanted me to dress all their stars.

In spite of this, from the dozens of Australians I have outfitted for the courts, I think I found Evonne Goolagong the most challenging. She always had a certain childish insouciance which must have infuriated her coach, Vic Edwards, as much as the other professionals who worked with her. At times, particularly when Mary Hawton first insisted that I dress Evonne, I felt I was grappling with a ghost, trying to grasp the essence of her elusive personality, so as to interpret this in her dresses. The real answer is that Evonne's beauty lies in the exquisite grace of her movements. When she is still, it seems impossible to capture her true identity. Yet this 'nature sprite' spontaneity is the heart and soul of Evonne's fascination.

In the Aboriginal language, Goolagong means 'tall trees near still water', and in 1971 I made her a dress on which we illustrated this scene with an embroidered landscape of gum trees beside a creek. 'A billabong for a Goolagong,' said the press. She wore it several times at Wimbledon and later, after Forest Hills, when Evonne was invited to appear on Hollywood's Dinah Shore Show, the whole studio was specially designed to match the sunburned colours of the Australian bushland. Evonne was momentarily embarrassed when Dinah asked her to play the didgeridoo, but fortunately there was another Australian on stand-by to demonstrate the art of playing this Aboriginal wood-wind instrument.

In 1972 I designed one particular dress for Evonne that I trimmed with lilac. Evonne liked the style so much that she asked me to make a duplicate, but this time trimmed with yellow. Evonne preferred the yellow-trimmed dress, but after two inexplicable losses wearing it I told her she would do best to burn it. She did not wear the dress again in England, but at Forest Hills I was returning from lunch with Gladys and Julius Heldman when I happened to catch sight of Evonne wearing the yellow-trimmed jinx dress. I couldn't believe she would resurrect this ill-fated garment for her American centre court début, but she was leading Pam Teeguarden 5-2 as we came in and Julius remarked, 'Well, at least she's not going to have trouble with that dress this time.' Following that comment, Evonne won exactly one more game in the match. Only last year in Sydney I asked Evonne if she had ever disposed of the dress.

'Oh yes,' she said. 'I gave it to my sister, Barbara.'

'What happened?' I asked.

'Oh she played one match in it which she lost and then gave up tennis for golf,' replied Evonne, casually. So much for superstition! Now, Evonne has found idyllic happiness with her husband, Roger

Cawley, and two lovely children. In 1982 it was a joy to see a renaissance of Evonne's unique grace and talent when she reappeared for a match at John Korff's Citizen Cup, which she lost to Chris Evert by only the barest of margins.

Working with Channel 7 TV-Sports', three young lions Garry Wilkinson, Peter Landy and Allan Stone, has been a constant source of stimulus and pleasure during my visits to Australia, not least because that ultra-modern medium has allowed me, on occasion, to throw the spotlight onto some of Australia's great champions of the past. These included Mal Molesworth – still sprightly when I interviewed her at the age of eighty – who was the first official Australian lady champion in 1922. I had met her counterpart, Rodney Heath, the first Australian men's champion (1905) when he had joined the inevitable social migration to Le Touquet in 1929 along with Randolph Lycett, probably one of the world's best doubles players. It was Lycett who dispatched me on my misguided mission to tell Suzanne Lenglen she was late for her mixed doubles against him.

Although it was Mabel Brookes's patronage which originally opened the doors to Australian society for me, it was Nell Hopman and Mary Hawton who in later years were always in there, lobbying for my cause in the belief that whatever I achieved, would ultimately add to the success of the Australian tennis scene. My admiration for both Nell and Mary was deeply sincere throughout our years of friendship and my comments here are intended as posthumous tributes to two ladies to whom not only Australians, but the whole world of women's tennis owe a significant debt of gratitude. More recently my much-valued relationship with Australia owes most to the current Executive President of Australian tennis, Brian Tobin and Colin Stubbs, his Director of Tournaments.

People who, like myself, delight in star-gazing, are often told that the skies of the Southern Hemisphere boast the brightest and the greatest proliferation of stars. In the past much the same could be said of Australian tennis, though today its stars shine, at least temporarily, less brightly. Nevertheless, there is still in Australia an 'old-fashioned' spirit of fun around. I remember being invited to visit a mid-week housewives' league at Illawarra, the home turf of Ken Rosewall, Ray Ruffels and the late Karen Krantzcke. On leaving I called to my hostesses, 'Mind you all win', and they chorused back, 'We don't play to win, we play for fun'. This was the most heartening statement I have heard in tennis for a long time and should be repeated daily at many other levels of the game.

It is now thirty years since I first came to Australia. This chapter was written during my eleventh visit and I confess to having an ongoing love affair with the country and its people since the first day. On every visit I have been fascinated with the straightforward niceness of Australians. Their kindness and neighbourliness are virtues which seem to be disappearing from the more sophisticated northern countries. When I saw 'A Town Called Alice' on American television, I was spellbound by the genuineness of Aussie sincerity, with its underlying yearning for things past and hopes not yet materialized. Songs like *Waltzing Matilda* and *Up There Cazaly* unlock what is to me the true feeling of the Sunburned Country. Each time I reread Thomas Wood's *Cobbers* I see the faded gum creeks again and the Southern Cross in its royal-blue midnight sky, and hope that Providence will allow me many more opportunities to return.

22 Madam Superstar

Wimbledon began in 1877 as a championship for men only. Even with Queen Victoria on the throne, it was a long way from being a woman's world. In 1879, however, one member of the All England Club did have the courage and foresight to propose a trophy for a ladies' championship event. The club committee rejected his proposal. Stunned by the rebuff, the member responded in his best Victorian English, 'I cannot but think the committee ungallant in passing by the ladies. They will, I think, come in time.'

To a limited degree, he was proved correct, as in 1884 Wimbledon capitulated to the extent of allowing the ladies their own event, although this was not permitted to begin until after the men's singles championship terminated.

I hope the spirit of that emancipated member was gazing down at a house situated in the exclusive residential area of Houston, Texas, on 23 September 1970, for there, at the home of Gladys Heldman, he would have witnessed a scene even his prophetic dreams could not have anticipated.

Finally exasperated by the chauvinism of the men who ran both amateur and pro' tennis, Mrs Heldman, the founder and, at the time, both editor and publisher of the magazine *World Tennis*, gathered together ten of the leading women players of the era and held a council of war.

The mood was such that on the very same afternoon at the local Racquet Club, having contracted to Gladys for the symbolic fee of one dollar, the rebels walked on court to begin the first-ever professional tournament organized for women and by women.

Inspired by Gladys Heldman, championed by Billie Jean King and financially supported by Joseph F. Cullman III, Chairman of the Board of Philip Morris, the world-wide conglomerate and also the parent company of Virginia Slims cigarettes, they initiated a crusade that was to change for ever the course of women's tennis. Marching behind the Virginia Slims banner, with its appropriate slogan, 'You've Come A Long Way, Baby,' the women moved rapidly up their very own stairway to the stars. As foreseen, ninety-one years before, the ladies had indeed 'come in time'.

176

For the record it should be said that the makers of this piece of history were the American players, 'Peaches' Bartkowicz, Rosie Casals, Billie Jean King, Nancy Richey, Val Ziegenfuss, Julie Heldman, and two Australians, Kerry Melville and Judy Dalton. Another American, Patti Hogan, joined originally, but was the one who withdrew when all ten were threatened with permanent disqualification by the US and international ruling bodies.

The part played by Gladys Heldman, one of the most remarkable and dynamic women I have ever met, provided the rock on which the whole rebellion stood. Without her extraordinary strength and powers of persuasion, nothing would have been accomplished. But, of course, from among those ten players, one name stands out like a beacon light. In the eyes of the public at large, it became Billie Jean King's revolution and, before long, it had spread far beyond the confines of a single sport. In a very real sense she has since eclipsed her great contemporaries in the feminist movement such as Gloria Steinem and Germaine Greer. She has, at various times in her life, become the most visible, the most controversial and the most admired woman of the moment. To millions of people round the world, she is instantly recognized as Billie Jean. Not always popular, not always right, she has, nonetheless, achieved as much, and in many ways considerably more for women's equality with men than anyone else in the past forty years. I personally nicknamed her 'Madam Superstar', and I cannot think of anyone more deserving of the title.

Though Billie Jean stood out from the crowd even then, I could not have predicted the extent of the fame that awaited her when I first set eyes on this little, bouncy tomboy of a girl with a loud mouth and a myopic gaze through owlish glasses at Wimbledon in 1961. As Billie Jean Moffitt she burst out of nowhere that year, an infectiously enthusiastic Californian chatterbox who was to delight the Centre Court spectators until they glimpsed the cold steel of ambition lurking beneath the happy exterior and, in true English fashion, turned away from someone exhibiting such a blatant and ruthless desire to win.

The origin of that desire can be traced back to the Los Angeles Tennis Club and the man who ruled the game in Southern California with a rod of iron, Perry Jones. It was Jones who unknowingly aroused Billie Jean's rebellious fervour during his 1955 junior championships. Billie Jean was only eleven years old at the time, but she was quite old enough to suffer the burning indignation of a kid from the wrong side of the tracks being made to feel out of place in a class-conscious environment. Her family was not poor but they felt socially inferior, and it was her father, a local fireman, who told her she must be more ladylike. He suggested she take up golf, swimming or tennis. Billie Jean chose tennis and spent the next few months working at odd jobs to buy her first racquet.

Less than a year after her first game, on the Long Beach public courts, she entered Perry Jones's junior championships. She was beaten in the second round but what embarrassed her more was the uneasiness she felt in the name-dropping atmosphere of the Los Angeles Tennis Club. She took her lunch in a brown bag while most of the other kids were able to order hamburgers in the coffee shop. Her parents were uncomfortable because they could not afford drinks at the bar upstairs with the other parents. All these little things lit a flame that was to billow into a fiery ambition.

The first flaring came when Perry Jones refused to include Billie Jean in a group photograph of the juniors because she was wearing shorts and not a dress. 'By that time I was really hooked on tennis. I loved tennis. I just dreamed about it, lived it. When I went to bed I took my racquet with me and looked at it. I saw myself playing at Wimbledon, the red carpet, the whole bit', she says now.

But instead of crying or imploring her parents to buy her a skirt, little Miss Moffitt thought, 'Who cares? It's small time. I'll show you anyway.' Far from forcing a kid into his line of thinking, Jones had sown the seeds of a revolution.

'I despised the whole system as a junior and although I wasn't sure how, I knew I was going to change it,' she recalled when we looked back on her childhood one day. 'The USTA and other governing bodies around the world made you feel obligated because *they* gave *you* the opportunity to play. They thought they owned you body and soul. Well, eventually I did play a part in changing the system and today it gives me total gratification to know this.'

Of course, before she could start changing the system she had to become a top performer on court and any doubts as to her abilities in this respect were removed when she beat the No.1 seed, Margaret Smith, at Wimbledon in 1962.

'That was the first time we had played but after that Margaret beat me fourteen straight times,' Billie Jean recalls. 'The fourteenth time was the final of Forest Hills in 1965. I led 5-3 in both sets but she won 8-6, 7-5. During the presentation ceremony, I realized I could beat her. I began to sense what it meant to have her killer instinct, what it meant to "go for the jugular". Suddenly I knew I would beat Margaret next time I played her.'

Billie Jean's instinct was unerring. She lost only eleven games in her next two meetings with Margaret and, with these victories, began her three successive years of Wimbledon domination. In the course of a decade, Wimbledon, the subject of her childhood dreams,

'The Way we Were' before Ted Tinling. Joy Gannon (now Mrs Tony Mottram, Buster's mother) with Mrs Betty Hilton (now Mrs Charles Harrison) in 1946

A mannequin models the dress worn by Britain's No. 1, Betty Hilton, with shoulder and hem trim in sky blue. Mrs Wightman successfully had the dress banned by the Wimbledon Committee after Mrs Hilton had lost to Louise Brough in it in the Wightman Cup, 1948

'Gorgeous Gussy' Moran, wearing the famous lace panties outfit in 1949. She added the coloured belt for the picture, as all colour was forbidden at Wimbledon that year

Beverly Baker of the United States being presented to the Queen by Lady Crosfield (centre). I am standing on the right, waiting to be presented *(The Associated Press)*

The Duke and Duchess of York, later King George VI and Queen Elizabeth, at Lady Crosfield's tennis garden party, 1924. The Duke was a keen tennis player and took part in the mens' doubles at Wimbledon

Vivian McGrath of Australia, 1933. He was the originator of the two-handed, sharp shooting shot from the left side

Australia's winning Davis Cup team, 1956. Left to right: Lew Hoad, Ken Rosewall, Harry Hopman (non-playing captain), Ashley Cooper and Neale Fraser

Above left: Probably one of the most graceful players of all time: Maria Bueno winning the Wimbledon final in 1960 *(Sunday Telegraph)*

Above right: Virginia Wade on her way to victory in the Wimbledon Centenary final of 1977

Left: Billie Jean King in action: winning the 1975 Wimbledon final. This was to be the last of six singles titles that she captured at Wimbledon

Wimbledon, 1972. The referee, Captain Michael Gibson, remonstrates with Rosie Casals over the design of her dress. She was sent off to change after the match had started, on the pretext that her dress 'advertised' Virginia Slims *(Syndication International)*

Joseph F. Cullman III, chairman of the Board of Philip Morris Inc.

Gladys Heldman, originator and organizer of women's independent tennis administration

The first mother to win a Wimbledon singles title since World War I, Evonne Goolagong Cawley. She is seen here with her husband Roger, daughter Kelly aged five, and sixteen-month-old Morgan *(Anne Rosengren)*

Martina Navratilova winning the tournament in Meadowlands, New Jersey, in 1982 *(Carol Newsom)*

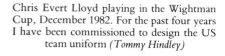

Chris Evert Lloyd playing in the Wightman Cup, December 1982. For the past four years I have been commissioned to design the US team uniform *(Tommy Hindley)*

Second to none: only H. L. Doherty (1902–6) equalled Björn Borg's record of five successive Wimbledon singles titles (1976–80)

Jimmy Connors to American columnist, Peter Bodo, 1983: 'My career has been a roller-coaster ride – great highs, and some tough lows' *(Paul Sutton/Duomo)*

Federation Cup, Tokyo, 1981. Her Imperial Highness, Princess Hitachi, welcomes the thirty-two participant nations. ITF President Philippe Chatrier (left) is about to respond, speaking also in Japanese. As ITF *Chef de Protocole,* this ceremony is my responsibility

Seven Wimbledon champions joined me to celebrate my fiftieth Wimbledon in 1982. Standing, left to right: Mrs Kathleen Godfree, Virginia Wade, Billie Jean King, Evonne Goolagong Cawley, Angela Mortimer Barrett. Sitting, left to right: Martina Navratilova, myself, and Chris Evert Lloyd *(Alan Davidson, Camera Press)*

became a stage for her greatest performances. She piled title upon title to equal the record of nineteen with Elizabeth Ryan. She became such a part of Wimbledon that her friend and one-time partner, Rosie Casals, who always calls her the 'Old Lady', describes Wimbledon's Centre Court as the 'Old Lady's House'.

By 1967, the little girl who had been left out of Perry Jones's photograph had grown into the best player in the world. If proof was needed, winning the elusive triple of all three events at both Wimbledon and Forest Hills is undeniable evidence. In terms of performance that year must surely stand as the crowning glory of her career. In long-term significance, winning the 'Battle of the Sexes' against Bobby Riggs in the Houston Astrodome in 1973, was probably the most important event in the history of women's tennis.

However, two years before that, when Billie Jean had married lawyer and promoter, Larry King, she had already started to make headlines in areas far removed from the green grass of Wimbledon's Centre Court. Along with fifty-three other signatures, her name appeared in the influential American women's magazine '*Ms*', under a bold headline that read 'We Have Had Abortions'.

Pioneers often shock, not least from a tennis court. Just as Suzanne Lenglen's little pleated frocks were said to be 'brazen' and 'indecent' in 1919, the idea of the world's top tennis star letting it be known she had had an abortion sent shock waves around the world in 1971. Billie Jean had to stand a torrent of criticism from all sides, including open attacks in the world's press and private letters of abuse.

Eventually her tennis started to suffer badly and she decided to take a break. It became her moment of truth. For the first time in her life, Billie Jean almost succumbed to the pressure. By March 1972 she was seriously considering permanent retirement. During one confused and confusing afternoon in Hawaii, while she and Larry were having a practice session, she seemed to change her mind every five minutes. By the time they had finished and were walking back to their apartment, Billie Jean had come to a decision. She was going to quit. That decision lasted just about long enough for Larry to start dialling the number of the Dallas organizers – their event was due to start the following day. But before he could complete the call, Billie Jean stopped him. 'No, I can't cop out,' she said. 'I don't care if I lose in the first round, I've got to turn myself around and Dallas is going to be the start.'

And it was. Many experts, including Nancy Jeffett, the queen of Dallas tennis, were predicting the first-ever meeting of the game's youngest and most popular stars, Chris Evert and Evonne Goolagong, in the semi-final. In anticipation of this unique occasion, Nancy had arranged a black-tie gala evening for the spectators in the court-side boxes, initiating in Dallas some of the elegance and glitter of the Royal Albert Hall. But, of course, Texans do these things in their own incomparable style and I rightly predicted that there would be millions of dollars' worth of jewels sparkling around the court.

With this in mind, for the first time I used rhinestones on a tennis dress, spreading them liberally on the special wardrobe I was preparing for Evonne for her American début. They certainly blended well with the glittering backdrop of Mrs Jeffett's guests. The only problem was that Evonne's eagerly anticipated first meeting with Chris never materialized that week. Billie Jean, 'turning herself around,' in no uncertain fashion, beat the young Chris Evert in the quarter-final, battling back in astounding, if typical, fashion from being one set and 1-4 down. On Nancy's semi-finals gala night 'the Old Lady' produced a repeat performance and beat Evonne. That was less than seven days after telling Larry she was going to retire for good.

Had she done so, the history of women's liberation, as well as the game of tennis, would have been entirely different, because, just eighteen months later, Billie Jean was to be drawn into another event. Again this took place in Texas, and so caught the imagination of the world that men and women from virtually every quarter of the globe were talking about a tennis match. For that one must not only thank Billie Jean's own audacity and unfailing sense of when to take up a challenge and blaze another trail, but also, of course, that irrepressible little hustler, Bobby Riggs. The first germ of this particular idea was planted by Riggs, himself the 1939 Wimbledon triple champion, at Forest Hills in 1970. During a practice session on a nearby court, Bobby suddenly jumped over the fence dividing Billie Jean's court from his and challenged her to a match. Riggs, forever looking for a new means of self-promotion, was sure he could beat Billie Jean despite being twenty-five years her senior. To do so would also inflict considerable damage on the new-found popularity and stature of the women's circuit – a fact that clearly did not escape the notice of Riggs and his male chauvinist associates.

Initially, Billie Jean ignored him. Then she said she didn't see what it would prove or how it could benefit the things in which she most believed. But Bobby had been taught obstinacy and persistence years before by 'Teach' Tennant.

In January 1973 we were all in Miami when Bobby renewed his attack. This time his target was Margaret Court. Margaret always found big-time exposure and money appealing. The combination of both proved irresistible. She soon told me she would be playing Riggs in a nationally televised challenge match in California in May, and asked me for a specially designed outfit for the occasion.

I think Margaret interpreted Riggs's challenge as something personal to her. She was a very self-centred person, and the responsibility she had to the whole cause of women's tennis may not even have occurred to her.

Billie Jean was furious when she heard Margaret had swallowed Riggs's bait. Her passion for defending causes close to her was instantly aroused. All her instincts warned of the risks to women's tennis if Riggs won. The relationship between Billie Jean and Margaret became even more tense than usual. Margaret's reaction was predictable. She interpreted as personal jealousy Billie Jean's opposition to her acceptance of Riggs's challenge. Meanwhile Billie Jean could do nothing but wait and pray that Margaret would win.

The Court-Riggs match held at Ramona, California on Mother's Day, proved a triumph for Riggs's hopes and ambitions. Margaret was a nervous wreck throughout the match and won only three games. The San Vincente Club is located at 1200 feet, hidden away among the Cuyamaca mountains behind San Diego. Margaret was quite unprepared for this altitude. She was also unprepared for Riggs's pre-match propaganda. All in all, she succumbed totally to Riggs's psychological warfare. For the final ironic twist, just before the match, her little boy, Danny, dropped her favourite tennis shoes in the toilet. The press described Margaret's performance as a 'Mother's Day Massacre'.

The preceding week, Billie Jean, Rosie Casals and I were in Tokyo. I was so determined to see Margaret's match, I left Japan before the end of the tournament. But Billie Jean and Rosie were in the finals and could not catch the same plane. Billie Jean had just reached Honolulu when she heard the end of the game on Rosie's radio. Billie Jean recalls her reaction, 'I went *bananas*. When I heard those scores, 6-2, 6-1, I knew I had to play Bobby Riggs.'

Billie Jean felt Margaret had betrayed the women's cause at a crucial moment in the development of the Virginia Slims tour. Her inner call obliged her to recoup the situation.

'Margaret had opened the door,' she said. 'Things had gotten out of control. I had to play Riggs. It was only a matter of time and place, and the money.'

I had the job of designing the all-important dress for the Great Challenge. I was particularly delighted because, that year, every major championship in the world had already been won by a player wearing a T.T. design. I thought Billie Jean would beat Riggs and this would be my Grand Slam.

The match was set for 20 September, only eleven days after the finals of the US Open at Forest Hills. August 28 was the day I was told. I realized I had no time at all and everything would have to be

181

decided, at latest, during the first week of Forest Hills. Even so, I would have to return to Europe to supervise the final touches of the dress in London and be back in Houston by 15 September. Understanding as always, Virginia Slims suggested my chief seamstress, Mrs Rose Stevens, come to New York to save time in this crisis. Billie Jean and her secretary, Marilyn Barnett, were staying at New York's La Guardia Sheraton.

When the date of the match was announced, Marilyn told me she had no fewer than 112 well-known sportswriters lined up for personal interviews with Billie Jean. I had to discuss fabric and designs with Billie Jean as a matter of urgency, so Marilyn put me at the top of the list. Mrs Stevens and I were allocated one hour at the Sheraton, at 9.00 p.m. on 2 September. I took Mrs Stevens in a cab from Manhattan. America was new to her, and she was dazzled all through the ride by the glittering Manhattan skyline. However, as we turned the last bend to the La Guardia Sheraton, the entire area blacked out and we just made it to the hotel entrance in total darkness. In the chaos of the hotel, we were lucky to be guided with one candle to Billie Jean's room by a mutual friend, Kris Kemmer. Even in the near-darkness I could see Billie Jean's room was a bower of red roses and other bouquets already sent by fans who expected her to win Forest Hills.

In Paris I had found a length of truly beautiful and unusual fabric, which was composed of opalescent cellophane stitched in wavy stripes onto thin nylon net. By candlelight all its rainbow shades shimmered like an oil slick in the sun. Billie Jean was ecstatic. 'I love it. I love it,' she cried. Then she retired to the bathroom with our one candle in a vain attempt to see how the fabric looked in the mirror.

Like the lights, the air-conditioning had failed. Marilyn had opened the windows, but the temperature outside was ninety plus. Awaiting Billie Jean's second verdict, Marilyn, Mrs Stevens, and I sat in total darkness, almost stifled by the scent of the massed roses. In such strange circumstances creations for big occasions can be conceived.

The following morning I dispatched Mrs Stevens back to London. She was caught up in Billie Jean's enthusiasm, but my long years had taught me to be ready for anything. 'We must have a standby dress "just in case",' I told her. On our way together in a cab to JFK Airport, with so little time to do anything, we decided on a remake of the dress that Billie Jean had worn winning Wimbledon. In retrospect, this was one of my luckiest decisions because it was the standby dress she eventually wore.

On 15 September I arrived in Houston with the two dresses. Mrs Stevens had done a good job, but Billie Jean, Larry and Marilyn

Barnett were hidden away so well that I could not find them. I was Gladys Heldman's house guest for the week. Eventually Larry called Gladys's home to say the *New York Times* wanted a picture of Billie Jean with me.

Billie Jean had not seen either dress. The big match was forty-eight hours away, yet nothing whatever had been said about the fit or the chance that the dresses could be wrong.

Larry met me and took me to Billie Jean's hideaway. After the photographer had left she at last said she wanted to try the two dresses. I had made her a simple button-down in the exotic Paris fabric. She looked great in it, and we were both delighted. Then her expression changed suddenly. 'I can't wear this dress,' she said. In less than a moment all the excitement was gone from her suite. By the looking glass she had done a routine of her usual tennis gestures, which included wiping the palm of her hand on her dress. 'I have never felt anything like this before,' she said. 'I could not risk upsetting my concentration with this strange sensation on my hand.'

We had silk-lined the inside of the dress throughout, but Billie Jean is extremely responsive to the feel of all fabrics, and I had failed to foresee that the outside surface of the cellophane might upset her, no matter how beautiful to the eye. I thanked all my lucky stars for the standby dress.

Nevertheless my face must have shown the disappointment I felt.

'I won Wimbledon in this style. It has "great vibes",' Billie Jean said. The Wimbledon dress had been white trimmed with lilac, while the standby replica was mint green with royal blue. I think Billie Jean was concerned to bring a smile back to my face because she quickly expressed enthusiasm for the soft colours. But I had one more problem. The previous night I had made a point of visiting the vast Astrodome for the first time, and realized that from many of the high balconies the performers would be almost indiscernible. The cellophane dress would have sparkled and shimmered; the detail of the standby dress could be appreciated from a distance of only a few yards.

On the day of the match, a friend, Ron Bookman, came to Gladys Heldman's house for lunch. We discussed my predicament and, with only six hours to go, Ron took me on a wild chase through Houston in search of some sequins and rhinestones. It took a while because nothing is near anything else in Houston, but eventually, in a rather unlikely looking shopping mall a dubious shop-assistant produced what I was looking for from the back of the store.

The motorcade of Gladys' house guests was leaving for the Astrodome at 4.00 p.m. At 3.55, perched on the edge of my bed, I finished sewing on about one hundred rhinestones and almost as many sequins. At last I felt Cinderella Standby could really go to the ball. It was not a wasted effort. Billie Jean's triumph over Bobby was bounced from the stratosphere to an estimated two hundred million colour television screens around the world. So, like tiny stars in the firmament, the dress glittered a great deal further than the uppermost balconies of the Astrodome.

In later months I received letters from four continents. Each one was as different as the indifferent colour reception being received by viewers in South America, Australia and Europe. 'How clever of you to put her in bright red,' said the first. 'I'm surprised you chose lilac,' said another. At least most of my friends in America, though television colour tones are not nearly as constant as in Britain, were able to detect the dress's true blue and green shades and seemed to agree with Billie Jean's appreciation of their subtlety.

At the Astrodome, Gladys Heldman gave her guests an entire row of gold-ticketed court-side seats. Chairmen of America's most powerful companies and conglomerates sat with us, including Lee Iacocca, then head of Ford Motors and, naturally, Joe Cullman of Philip Morris. Previously Joe had been a lone prophet of marrying business with women's tennis. Now Big Business was dotted all the way round the arena, sharing in a media happening of gargantuan proportions. The attendance total of thirty-five thousand was the largest – and still is the largest – ever to watch a single tennis match. The game, which had been feeling its way in the big professional world since emerging from the seclusion of its country club origins, had finally come of age.

Billie Jean King had made herself a bigger stage than even she had dreamed possible and, of course, she did not fail. Riggs tried everything he knew but Billie Jean kept control of her nerves and proved, with a 6-4, 6-3, 6-3, best of five victory, that she was not about to lose to a middle-aged man, however skilful, experienced, or cunning he might be.

I think the significance of the King-Riggs match will endure for at least fifty years. Small related events began the very next morning. At one bank where fifty women were employed, the entire female staff showed up for work on 21 September wearing tennis clothes. I'm not sure what they would have had to say about that at Lloyd's or Nat West, but in America the manager was also enthusiastic! The match was so widely discussed across the country that the head of one nation-wide sales group sent all his men to Houston so they would have an opening gambit for their sales pitch the following morning. The *Los Angeles Times*, which takes itself very seriously, led its front page with the story of the match and as the months went by, the tide of discussion swelled. People who had never previously given a thought to tennis were heatedly arguing the merits and demerits of a man losing to a woman, or a woman beating a man, according to their personal philosophies.

By playing, and beating, Riggs, Billie Jean made tennis an instrument of world communication as far reaching as the television image of her match. In her inimitable way, she had bounced tennis off the stratosphere.

Her victory at the Astrodome will certainly live longer in the memory than the sensational Palimony Case which surfaced in 1981 and arose from her relationship with Marilyn Barnett, even though it created almost as many headlines at the time.*

The whole thing erupted in April of that year when I was doing my usual job of introducing the players on court before their matches. We were at the Tournament of Champions in Grenelefe, Florida. Billie Jean, seeded third behind Martina Navratilova and Andrea Jaeger, was drawn in an evening match against the tiny 4ft 11in South African, Susan Lee Rollinson, who was ranked somewhere around eightieth in the world. Their match was the last of a long day's programme so, as was my custom, I went straight off to bed after completing the introduction.

However, the condominium allocated to me was well within earshot of the umpire's loudspeaker system and, as I tried to go to sleep, I became dreamily aware that Billie Jean seemed to be losing to this comparatively unknown player. Time after time I heard the umpire call 'game Rollinson', until I thought I really was dreaming and finally dropped off into an unbelieving sleep.

At 6.15 the following morning the phone rang. Rona Barrett, currently Hollywood's ace gossip columnist, had just announced on ABC's breakfast TV programme 'Good Morning America' that Billie Jean had admitted to a lesbian relationship with her former secretary. It seemed as if the whole world was looking for Billie Jean at Grenelefe but she had known, of course, what was to come and had already left the previous night so that she could be with her husband, Larry, in California.

Ana Leaird and I were the official press officers for the Women's Tennis Association and I sometimes wonder how we survived the day. Certainly neither of us want to experience another like it. Our phones were completely blocked with calls from dawn until dusk, by which time the place was alive with reporters. One national scandal sheet had a reporter there by 9.00 a.m. offering all and sundry

---

*Ironically, the Malibu beach house in which Marilyn had lived, and which became the focal point of the resulting lawsuit, was destroyed by the surf during the gale-force storms which hit the Californian coast in March 1983.

thousands of dollars in cash for 'personal revelations'. It seemed that every time Ana or I so much as spoke to a player there was someone eavesdropping behind a bush or a palm tree.

The whole thing came as much of a surprise to me as anyone. From my memories of that period, 1972 and 1973, Marilyn Barnett was a rather frail, erotic-looking blonde who had been – and, I believe, is again now – a Beverly Hills hairdresser. As Billie Jean's secretary throughout the frenetic weeks preceding the Riggs match, I found her extremely efficient as well as being bright and witty in a brittle sort of way. I could see that Marilyn could be an extremely entertaining companion, but I was never aware of the emotional bond between the two women that was subsequently revealed to the world at large.

Inevitably the splurge of publicity threw the spotlight on Billie Jean's relationship with Larry which, with her superstar status, was never exactly that of a traditional husband and wife. Larry is a charming, handsome, easy-going guy who has always tended to look younger than his age. He has obviously worshipped Billie Jean since his college days but neither seemed particularly distressed when they agreed to live separate lives quite early on in their marriage. Over the years it turned into a remarkable relationship because, on the numerous occasions that tennis or business brought them together, they always projected a mutual love of great depth and sincerity which, to me, far transcended the constantly recurring gossip about their individual romances with other people.

The day following Rona Barrett's bombshell revelation, Billie Jean decided on the extraordinarily courageous course of calling a press conference and 'admitting all' on nation-wide television. Her lawyers were desperately opposed to her doing this. She told me later that, in trying to weigh the legal advice against her instincts, she paced up and down in her hotel room for so long there was actually a threadbare trail on the carpet where she had walked by the time she had made up her mind.

At that initial press conference, with Larry at her side, she projected an image of great courage and sincerity admitting to the alleged association with Marilyn Barnett but adding that it had been over for some time. But that, of course, was not the end of it. Everyone wanted to interview her and, a few days later, she agreed to talk to Barbara Walters of ABC, probably television's most searching and abrasive interrogator. Yet, facing an audience of millions, I believe the frankness and braveness with which Billie Jean answered all Ms Walters's very intimate questions earned the admiration of huge numbers of the American public.

Billie Jean has always thought and acted at least a decade ahead of her so-called feminist contemporaries; hence the enormous amount of publicity she has received. But just as the abortion issue back in 1971 seems to have faded from the memory so, I feel sure, will the Barnett affair.

But if the details diminish in importance with the passing years, Billie Jean's place as one of the great women activists of her era is assured. So, of course, is her record in the game which offered the platform in the first place. She has broken factual as well as emotional barriers and it is these that will be remembered. Now she is, of course, the all-time record-holder of Wimbledon titles – a feat she achieved in somewhat bizarre circumstances in 1979 when the previous record-holder, Elizabeth Ryan, died at Wimbledon on the eve of her record of nineteen titles being broken.

Up to the 1978 Wimbledon the statistical comparisons between Elizabeth and Billie Jean were astonishing. At that time both had played in eighteen Wimbledon championships with Billie Jean having played 223 matches to Elizabeth's 221. By that year Billie Jean had suffered twenty-nine losses in all at Wimbledon – exactly the same number as Elizabeth. The major discrepancy, of course, was the fact that Billie Jean's championships included six singles titles while Miss Ryan's had all been in doubles. A final coincidence emerged when I discovered that both Billie Jean and Elizabeth had each benefited four times from opponent's defaults.

But statistics never tell the whole story. In my sixty years in tennis, I don't think I have ever come across two more indomitable and gutsier competitors than Elizabeth Ryan and Billie Jean King. Elizabeth recognized these qualities in the young woman whom, she felt sure, would one day surpass her record. 'Records are made to be broken,' Elizabeth always said, honouring her Edwardian code of ethics despite the immense pride she felt at her own achievements. 'If mine is to go, I would like Billie Jean to have it, because she has so much guts.'

That was indisputable. Few men or women would have persevered with an athletic career after suffering the kind of injuries endured by Billie Jean. Apart from playing against doctor's orders with heavy bronchitis at Wimbledon in 1974, she had knee operations in 1966, 1972 and 1976 and yet, in 1982, came within a set of beating Chris Evert Lloyd in the Wimbledon singles semi-final. For sheer persistence, she has no peer.

But then Elizabeth Ryan was also a remarkable woman who, for fifty-five years, was one of my closest friends. I first met Elizabeth, or 'Bunny' as many of her admirers called her, in my capacity as Suzanne's umpire in 1924. Suzanne and Elizabeth always played doubles together when they were in the same tournament and

Elizabeth also wanted me to umpire her matches. Our friendship eventually became very close, as is demonstrated by the collection of more than one hundred letters I have kept from her many journeyings.

Because of the current amateur rule, my paid umpiring job always precluded me from playing tournament tennis on the Riviera and this was my greatest frustration at the time. However, as Elizabeth frequently considered herself unfit and overweight she was always anxious for extra practice, even if this meant rising at some ungodly hour because all the courts were fully used for matches from 9.00 a.m. until dark. So practice-sessions had to finish by 8.30, a fact that in no way deterred me from travelling from my Nice home by train to Cannes, Monte Carlo, or Beaulieu, to play a couple of sets with Elizabeth before my day's work began. Even now I remember arriving breathless at the Beau Site to find her, racquet and balls at the ready, and grumbling because I was 'late' at 7.00 a.m.!

Before my later circuit-playing days I was already able to give Elizabeth a good work-out, though in over two hundred sets we eventually played I never managed to win even one until we practised in Zurich in 1930. Elizabeth was then so incensed with my 'breakthrough' that she actually accused me of cheating! But after that I improved enough to beat her regularly and, because I knew her game so well, was the one person who could help put her totally unique 'chop' stroke back on track when she struck a bad patch. For instance, in 1932 I made my first flight in a plane because I received a telegram from Elizabeth, who was playing the French championships, saying: 'Come at once. Can't hit a ball.'

During the last years of her life, when Elizabeth had reached the mid-eighties and was living near Sloane Square, I was again summoned, this time to answer a question that had become an obsession with her. She was obviously suffering from a sense of deep frustration and grievance that she had only beaten Suzanne in the first of their thirty-seven meetings and wanted to know the reason why. She said I was the only person in the world who could explain why she always lost to Suzanne. I tried to couch the obvious technical and physical reasons in the gentlest possible terms. In truth she had also been extremely unlucky that in the days before 'seeding' she had been drawn in an early round against Lenglen in five of the seven years of Suzanne's Wimbledon supremacy.

During that time, she was also brooding about losing her Wimbledon record. Despite her statement about records being made to be broken, she could not conceal her joy when in 1976 Chris Evert Lloyd and Martina Navratilova fought back against Billie Jean and Betty Stove in the doubles final after being 0-3 down in the third set.

A win for Billie Jean that day would have given her the record and, mid-way through that final set, Elizabeth insisted on being carried to the Centre Court doorway, determined to be the first person to congratulate Billie Jean on taking her own record.

Three years later in 1979, I dined alone with Elizabeth on the second Wednesday of Wimbledon and we discovered, after fifty-five years of friendship, that we both believed in reincarnation. She was full of good spirits that evening and we discussed a recognition signal should we meet again in some future place. In the meantime we set a more prosaic rendezvous for lunch in the members' enclosure on women's finals day. For the previous ten years, Elizabeth, with her two constant companions, Frances McKay and Muriel Thomas, had entertained me in this fashion and the lunch had become a happy ritual.

Unfortunately, however, I had to have minor surgery at Charing Cross Hospital on that Friday morning and, as a result of an infuriating delay, only arrived at Wimbledon five minutes before play was due to begin. I was ten seats away from Elizabeth and my last memory is of her and Muriel Thomas making questioning signs as to why I had not come to lunch. Muriel, who died herself very soon afterwards, told me that at the end of the women's singles final, Elizabeth said, 'And now for Billie Jean and my record.'

It was true that Billie Jean had reached the doubles final with Martina Navratilova, and was considered a certainty to win, thus finally gaining the record-breaking twentieth title. However, as everyone else knew, the women's doubles final was not scheduled until the following day, Saturday, so Muriel realized Elizabeth was confused and concluded that she was feeling unwell. Moments later Elizabeth said, 'I have terrible toothache. I must have eaten too many sweets.'

She was taken to the first-aid room where, after asking for some valium and a cup of tea, she collapsed. She was put, unconscious, into an ambulance and died on the way to hospital, aged eighty-seven. Twenty-four hours later Billie Jean duly won the doubles and broke Elizabeth's record. Destiny's timing for Elizabeth was unbelievable, and all her friends consider it marvellous that she was spared from seeing her beloved record actually surpassed.

I feel sure that the coincidence of Elizabeth's death will go down as one of the strangest fables in Wimbledon history, and it only remains now for Elizabeth and me to meet in one of our future reincarnations and reminisce about those extraordinary circumstances.

But if the life of Elizabeth Ryan came to a dramatic and timely end, the life of Billie Jean King goes on, searching for new frontiers to breach, for she is at all times a tomorrow's woman. I asked her once where she hoped to go beyond tennis. Her eyes lit up. 'Larry's always telling me: "Go ahead and see if you can become the first woman President of the United States." Can you imagine that?' Politics, television, something in public life are certainly amongst her options. 'Sometime, some place the answer will come,' she says, 'but you can bet I will do something more to change today's systems.'

I asked if she would confine her leadership to women's causes and that set off another torrent of rapid-fire thoughts. 'People put me in the women's slot because I happen to be a woman. But I feel that men as well as women are affected by what I have done. Men come up to me more often than women. Men have said to me, "You have made my life better by beating Riggs". Others have said, "You have made my life worse". Either way people are not indifferent. I hate people who are indifferent. The thing that makes me go is being a perfectionist.'

In the tennis community it is widely said that Billie Jean talks too much. Dressing-room gossip paints lonely pictures of her expounding passionately long after the last writer has left her press conferences. But creative thinking and the expression of her thoughts are the very essence of Billie Jean. And the essence is not sweet vanilla. Billie Jean is a star and in nicknaming her 'Madam Superstar' I did so because this implies the full gamut of her emotions from great loyalty, great professionalism and warm affection, all the way to deceit, bitchery and, at times, self-destructiveness.

The brightness of Billie Jean's stardom rubs off on her surroundings. When I have been with her I always come away thinking I must do better work. On most occasions she comes across as a warm human person. In 1973 my staff and I made our first dresses for her. She won Wimbledon that year and the following day arrived loaded with gifts of flowers and plants for my staff. This was a typical illustration of her thoughtfulness for those who collaborate with her. Yet in her bad moods Billie Jean can convey all the anger and turbulence of a demonstrator at the barricades.

In my lifetime two players, through the sheer force of their skill and pioneering personalities, have expanded the importance of tennis in everyday life to hitherto unconsidered proportions. By coincidence both have been women: Suzanne Lenglen and Billie Jean King. It is no coincidence, however, that both emerged as world trend-setters at the exact moment when women everywhere were themselves emerging from a chrysalis. Both women came unsuspectingly into a simple pastime. For both, tennis became a platform for their inspired leadership. Even the exposure of their human frailties on the centre courts of the world has served to forge essential bonds of communication with their followers.

Billie Jean, of course, is far from done. As we enter the age of the computer (Papa Lenglen would certainly have used computer techniques to plot and facilitate the course of Suzanne's matches), Billie Jean will be right there, matching the micro-chip word for word, thought for thought. She never gives up, not even when she goes to the movies. One might have guessed what her reaction would be when she went to see the film *E.T.*

'I loved it!' she told *Women's Sports* Magazine. Then she revealed what is really the heart and soul of her philosophy. 'But you know when those kids soar off into the sky on their bikes, I was sitting there in the theatre thinking, they are all boys — *not one is a little girl!*'

No, Billie Jean will never renege on her ideals.

23 Jubilation

Fred Perry and Virginia Wade, who have shared a common need to prove themselves despite totally differing backgrounds, will attend 1983 Wimbledon secure in the knowledge that their achievements have been recognized in unique and lasting fashion. The renowned sculptor, David Wynne, has been commissioned to make a statue of Perry which will stand proudly in the grounds of the All England Club, and in 1984, fifty years after he won the first of his three Wimbledon crowns, the gates at the South West Entrance will bear Fred's name. At Wimbledon, Virginia will not actually be cast in bronze, but as the result of her election to the Wimbledon Committee in December 1982, she has already been made an integral part of the All England Club's inner sanctum. If Fred is the first player to have Wimbledon gates named after him since the Doherty brothers, Virginia is the first woman ever elected to that exclusive group of men who are totally responsible for the running of the world's most famous championships. The honours accorded both are apt; Fred Perry is the last Englishman and Virginia Wade the last Englishwoman to win a Wimbledon singles title.

But, having noted that and noted, too, their somewhat un-English drive for recognition, I find it difficult to think of much else that Fred and Virginia have in common. Except, of course, that they both thought, behaved and reacted like the very real stars they were.

The pre-war male from suburban Ealing had to fight his way past solid barriers of social discrimination, while the post-war female grew up in South Africa, the land of ultimate discrimination, and then sailed through the tennis Establishment, enjoying instant acceptance as a young woman blessed with the correct manner, accent and pedigree. One the son of a Labour Member of Parliament; the other the daughter of a clergyman who rose to archdeacon. There was success in both their backgrounds, certainly, but, apart from choosing the game of tennis as a showcase for their hungry egos, the way they performed in that showcase differed in style, personality and speed of fulfilment.

Perry was born on 18 May 1909. By the age of twenty he had won the World Table Tennis Championships in Budapest. But in 1929 his tennis was only good enough to get him through the qualifying event for Wimbledon. Two years later, however, in 1931, he achieved the remarkable feat of reaching the semi-finals both at Wimbledon and Forest Hills; leading Britain through six rounds to reach the Davis Cup final; and proving his versatility by again winning an International Table Tennis title in Paris. Fred had a mercurial mind that was perfectly matched by his speed of foot. Whether it was factually true or not, he always seemed faster than his opponent and, after the change of ends, he was invariably ready to resume the battle before the other man. In all his matches pressure was the key. The dash and daring he brought to lawn tennis seemed an obvious carry-over from the rapid-fire sport played on the small surface of a table.

Perry's innate aggression was evident in both the physical and psychological tactics he employed. When psychology could help his cause, he never missed a trick. He was the master of one-upmanship. In the dressing rooms he had a sharp tongue and never missed an opportunity to make a penetrating comment, sometimes to the point of being extremely personal. On court, he was never averse to using a caustic one-liner to distract an opponent.

But neither his handsome hero's looks, enhanced so often by a flashing smile, nor his glib, wise-cracking tongue were enough to break down the barriers surrounding Britain's tennis Establishment at the start of his career. The fact that he finally succeeded in forcing people to accept him was due entirely to his belief in himself – a belief that eventually overcame the antagonism that was aroused by his way of speech, described as 'curious', in the strictly public school tennis world of those days.

It has to be realized that in tennis Perry was only the second Englishman after Pat Hughes to speak with a 'Non-U' accent. I often thought that Hughes, who went on to represent Britain many times in the Davis Cup and to win the Wimbledon doubles with Raymond Tuckey in 1936, also felt himself a marked man because of the way he spoke. In some ways his more conventional contemporaries treated him just as badly as a few whites treated Althea Gibson, the first black player ever to win Wimbledon, when she was struggling to break down barriers of a different kind in the 1950s.

Inevitably, in these situations, it needs someone from within the game with enough vision and pragmatism to come forward and take the black sheep into the fold. In Perry's case that man proved to be 'Pop' Summers, who quickly saw the benefits his company, Slazengers, would accrue should this abrasive and cocky youngster from the wrong side of the tracks realize his full potential. Summers knew enough about tennis to help Fred with his game as well as to tell him how to behave. And Fred was too basically practical not to listen.

As soon as Perry became Davis Cup material, Britain's famous captain, Roper Barrett, took over the role of mentor in much the same way as Herman David, Sir Brian Burnett's predecessor as Chairman of the All England Club, adopted a rebellious young Welshman called Michael Davies who was to become the British No. 1 in the late 1950s. In the pre-war days the attitude was very much one of 'as we've got to have the bloody upstart, we might as well knock him into shape and try and get the best out of him'.

For a while the best of Perry was more than many people were prepared to handle. It wasn't just his accent, but his consuming drive to win at all costs that ruffled the feathers of the more tradition-bound centres of the game. For several years I used to take teams up to Fenners to play against Cambridge University. The matches were played against the Light Blues over serene weekends where the noise level rarely rose above a ripple of polite applause, a muted call of 'Jolly good shot!' and, in the distance, the cry of a swan on the River Cam.

Perry's modern counterpart, Jimmy Connors – brash, arrogant and supremely confident – might just conceivably have been tolerated in such surroundings, on the basis of his being an American. But Perry was English, and after he went to Fenners with his Chiswick Park team a couple of times in the early 1930s, it was politely suggested that it might be best not to include him in future matches.

But Roper Barrett knew how to harness and mould Perry's burning ambition to the social demands of the times and, as the years passed, a strong personal affinity developed between them. Every time I took Perry and his opponent onto the Centre or No. 1 Court at Wimbledon, he always used to ask me where Roper was sitting. Then, rather in the manner of Ion Tiriac and Guillermo Vilas today, a strange series of signals would be enacted during the match.

Having already reached the semi-finals at Wimbledon and taken the French title at Stade Roland Garros the year before, Fred was to prove in 1934 that his great faith in himself was justified. That summer was unusually hot and dry, and the dust that hung in the hazy air was probably responsible for a strange epidemic that became known as 'Wimbledon Throat'. The infection was serious enough for sixty-three players to withdraw from the championships. Doctors likened it to a type of diphtheria. Perry and I were two of the lucky ones, but Dudley Larcombe and Norah Cleather suffered from the serious handicap of having to run the tournament virtually voiceless.

Amongst the top players, Gottfried von Cramm, the great German sportsman, suffered a severe attack but, typically, refused to scratch and lost badly to South Africa's Vernon Kirby. As the number of infected players grew and grew, only those with access to the privacy of the club offices knew how worried we really were. Eventually the drains were examined, the water tested and, late at night in the closest secrecy, sprays and syringes of potent disinfectant went into action against the insidious enemy.

The top throat specialists in London, Sir Milsom Rees and Ivor Griffith, were brought to Wimbledon every afternoon to examine and spray players' throats. When every possible precaution had been taken, it was finally decided to tell Buckingham Palace that it would now be safe for the Royal Family to come to Wimbledon.

Perry, of course, was fortunate to escape the epidemic but it was somehow fitting that so confident a performer should remain healthy and steadfast when so many around him were in disarray. Like the Grand Prix racing driver who reacts to a colleague's crash by putting his foot down even harder as he goes into the next bend, so Perry seized his opportunity and, after beating the reigning champion Jack Crawford 6-3, 6-0, 7-5 in the final, became the first Englishman to win Wimbledon since the Challenge Round was abolished in 1922, and the first player to put his name three successive times on the cup since the last of Tony Wilding's triumphs in 1913.

Fred knew he had been lucky, but luck is so often a companion of confidence. Writing about his victory some years later, Perry recognized that Fate had been on his side: 'Everything I did against Jack Crawford went right for me. And everything went wrong for him, including a foot-fault against him on match-point. Luck was on my side in the draw and in my matches, too. Luck, indeed, plays a very considerable part in any Wimbledon.'

But by the time Fred had beaten von Cramm in the finals of 1935 and 1936, any element of luck had become immaterial. The famous Centre Court had become his stage and Wimbledon a theatre for his matinée idol looks and aggressive skills. In three finals against worthy opponents Fred Perry dropped just twenty-two games in nine sets, only one of which he came remotely close to losing. Even with the rise of Don Budge – whom he beat in a monumental struggle at Forest Hills two months later in September 1936 to win his third US crown – Perry might have gone on to emulate Wilding's feat of four consecutive Wimbledon triumphs or, who knows, even the five straight victories achieved by H. L. Doherty thirty years before and Björn Borg forty years later. But, even in those days of pristine, pre-war sport, professional tennis was already becoming a reality and with it the prospect of legitimate money. All Fred's instincts turned him towards the rewards of a professional career but it would be wrong, I think, to imagine that the decision was an easy one for him.

Needless to say, the Establishment, having accepted him into their midst, were now loath to see him go. At the Wimbledon Ball in 1936, when his intentions of turning pro' at the end of the year were already known, various speeches from the top table pointedly 'regretted' his intention of deserting Britain's Davis Cup team. His speech in reply was typical. 'If anyone would like to make it worth my while to play another year,' said Fred, 'I would be glad to do so.'

That was Perry being his usual brash, cocky self but Norah Cleather and I, and certainly Fred's trainer and confidant, Dan Maskell who was then Davis Cup and All England Club coach, knew that this determination to establish himself as his own man in a newer world was causing him much inner sadness.

A month later, Perry led Britain to victory over Australia in the Davis Cup final at Wimbledon. It was the fourth time since he joined the team that Britain had won the Cup and, to this day, they have never done so again. Had we known the drought that was about to engulf the British game we might have drunk even more in the post-match celebrations. But before anyone got too tipsy, we decided to go back out onto the Centre Court to take a last look at the scene of triumph. The crowd had long gone and there were just a few groundsmen cleaning up amid the deserted stands. After a few minutes, Perry said, 'Let me stay here for a moment by myself.'

So we left him alone with his memories; standing proudly but sadly on the court that had seen him transformed into a world-famous figure, changing the course of British tennis history. He was twenty-seven and he knew, given the attitudes of the time towards professionalism, that he would never play at Wimbledon again.

But this was the private man that the public rarely, if ever, got to see. Considering the enormity of what he achieved for British tennis it was sad that he could not communicate better with the public of his era and so enjoy a greater degree of popularity.

Certainly his first Wimbledon victory in 1934 was overshadowed, as far as the spectators were concerned, by the triumph of Britain's girl prodigy, Dorothy Round, who won the women's title on the Saturday, twenty-four hours after Perry had beaten Crawford. That was the traditional sequence of play in those days.

Dorothy was a charming and modest champion. She had become a huge favourite even before succeeding Kitty Godfree as the first English girl to win at Wimbledon in eight years. And when she beat Helen Jacobs in a thrilling three-set final, the crowd were roused to a far greater pitch of excitement than that which had greeted Perry's victory.

Roper Barrett had volunteered to take a line during the women's final and he was just behind me as I escorted Dorothy Round back to the dressing room. Deafening cheers erupted all around us and even

King George V and Queen Mary, applauding from the Royal Box, seemed quite overwhelmed. Roper Barrett gazed wistfully at the frenetic scene and said to me, 'Fred could have had all this yesterday, if only he'd let them understand him.'

From a financial point of view Perry's decision to turn professional was fully justified. Even allowing for the disruption of the war years, it was estimated that he earned close to a million dollars between 1937 and the post-war decade – huge money for that era.

In my youth Fred was a warm and generous friend but after he launched himself into the manufacture of tennis clothing in the early 1950s, we found ourselves involved in a commercial duel over our relative dominance of tennis wear around the world. Today, with the smoke of battle behind us, we are able to reminisce happily about the countless dramatic encounters we fought and shared.

The more I think about Britain's last two Wimbledon champions, the less I feel they have in common. The inner compulsion to force themselves onto a stage and exhibit their talents; the iron-willed determination to be recognized; yes, these they shared. They both moved like panthers and both had the ability to produce winners at critical moments which, in itself, made them exceptional amongst British players. But, apart from their differing backgrounds, their respective talents, shaped inevitably by the eras in which they played, led them to the top by vastly disparate routes.

Perry was a spontaneous player who never changed to a lower gear once he had started his climb to the mountain top. He made a smooth, seemingly inevitable progression; advancing round by round with each year at Wimbledon and then winning both the US and French championships before reaching the ultimate goal.

Miss Wade, on the other hand, defeated Billie Jean King for a spectacular success in winning the first US Open in 1968, but then followed various fraught, meandering paths until she finally burst through the clouds nine years later to bask in the sunny glory of Centenary Wimbledon. Virginia's success that year naturally added a marvellous chauvinistic touch to the 1977 celebrations because, of course, it was Silver Jubilee Year for the Queen as well as being the Centenary of Wimbledon.

'As the Queen will be coming to present the Cup I think I had better win it,' Virginia joked during the press conference she gave after her first-round match. But then she became deadly serious. 'Actually, I feel very good about my chances. Despite all the disappointments of the past, I am absolutely confident in my ability to handle all the pressures and win.'

I know there were more than a few smirks amongst my tennis-writing friends when Virginia finished that little speech. One way or another Britain's best player had contrived to lose to all sorts of players who were not fit to tie the ribbon in her hair during a decade of Wimbledon disasters. So why, flying in the face of all logic, did she suddenly decide that this was to be her year?

A champion's arrogance has to provide part of the answer. Using the Jubilee and the Centenary as a spur to remotivate her pride, she based her argument on one simple and undeniable fact – that she was unquestionably the best player amongst her contemporaries never to have won Wimbledon. So therefore it must be her turn.

In the end the method by which she arrived at this conclusion did not matter. To Britain's great joy, she won. She played wonderfully well to beat Chris Evert in the semis, thus denying Chris a place in the final for only the second – and, to date, the last – time in ten years. Then, straining desperately to keep her nerves under control, Virginia overcame the pressure of being expected to beat a lesser opponent, finally defeating Holland's Betty Stove 4-6, 6-3, 6-1 to join Angela Mortimer Barrett and Ann Haydon Jones in a select trio of British post-war champions.

Miss Wade, of course, was a very different type of champion in both style and personality from her two predecessors. Angela and Ann were more conventional in their Britishness; quiet, determined girls who carefully analysed their talent and made it work for them through sheer force of will. Both offered remarkable illustrations of what dedicated hard work can achieve and their contribution to British tennis, by virtue of the example they set and their deep love of the game, was inestimable. Even though she was unlucky never to win Wimbledon, Christine Truman Janes was also an inspiration during that period and, because the British are so perverse about these things, probably attained a higher peak of popularity precisely because she always ended up the good loser.

Virginia, innately so much more of a star than Angela, Ann or Christine was also psychologically more fragile. However, that in no way undermined her commitment to a career that, in its longevity and achievement, is now quite remarkable. From her supporters' point of view it is only the failure to make the fullest use of two totally outstanding assets that adds a feeling of frustration for what might have been.

As her freedom from injury indicates, Miss Wade is an exceptional athlete. Her lithe and graceful movement on court has enabled her to avoid the kind of physical problems that have beset Billie Jean King and so many other leading players who, through the increasingly relentless round of competition, make unreasonable demands of their bodies. I cannot think of a British girl who was a better athlete than Virginia. Nor can I think of a British girl with a better serve. In fact I would go as far as to say that she has had the only really good serve we can record in 100 years of women's tennis in England. Despite having been given some wonderful examples of how to do it by American players – notably Helen Wills who, with Martina Navratilova, probably had the best women's serve of all time – there has never been an Englishwoman whose serve did anything more than 'pull the blind down' apart from Miss Wade.

I have my own theories about this. They may sound a little bizarre but the facts as I have witnessed them over the past sixty years seem to suggest I may be right. In my opinion, the ability to serve is inextricably linked to the environment of one's upbringing and is also related to the balance of male and female genes of which we all have differing proportions.

The fact that most British girls cannot throw a ball in the same way that American girls can, provides a lead into this argument. Until recently when several of the boys' public schools started admitting girls, the average English Miss who ended up playing a good standard of tennis, had been to a girls-only school where they played girls' games. In America, on the other hand, the Billie Jeans of this world were constantly competing with boys at boys' games like baseball. Faced with that co-ed challenge, a girl learned to throw a ball (thereby achieving the rudimentary basis of the service action) very fast indeed.

But one cannot ignore the more fundamental sexual aspects. Generally American women tend to be more masculine in their attitude, dress and behaviour than their British counterparts. In the States there is a strong desire on the part of many young women to adopt the aggression of the male, to wear men's clothes and to do men's jobs. Sometimes the situation is forced on them. Nancy Richey, a very pretty, feminine girl, told me that she began wearing men's shorts and a visor when she started playing tennis back home in Texas because none of the boys would take her seriously enough to play with her unless she dressed and behaved as they did.

In Britain, women have always tended to be less aggressive. One, possibly insignificant, result of this is a total inability to produce a dominating serve when they walk onto a tennis court. It may be difficult to prove but I am convinced the ability or inability to reproduce that service action (which is breathtakingly simple when demonstrated by macho men like Pancho Gonzales, the former British Davis Cup star Mike Sangster or today's Ivan Lendl) lies in the balance of one's sexual genes. I myself have never been able to serve fast, or throw a ball, so all this is very close to me.

People have tried to break down this argument by trying to equate the serve with the smash. But the two stokes really have little in common. Think of the great Ken Rosewall. By comparison with his peers, had a very poor serve, but could smash with the best of them. Virginia Wade has a tremendous serve and often can't smash to save her life. The difference lies not so much in the technical reproduction of the strokes but in the psychological equipment required to play them. When you go for an overhead you are already in the game. The serve, however, is the first thrust; the act of penetration, if you like, which initiates the whole performance, and that is something totally masculine.

Despite her feline grace and personal beauty, Virginia has always projected a strong streak of masculinity in her make-up which reveals itself in her dominating personality, her wide-shouldered, slim-hipped body and, yes, her ability to serve. It has also, of course, created problems in trying to find a man to share her life. Not because she is unappealing to the opposite sex, on the contrary, when she left to live in New York, eligible young men from all over Britain were lining up to catch the eye of this strikingly attractive girl. Several caught Virginia's eye but none could hold it for long. The result was that she never found the cultural kind of escort that her mind needed, combined with the physical kind of appeal she appears to want. In other words she never found a man 'whose plumage blended with his language', which was the essence of André Malraux's delightful reply when the last great love of his life, Louise de Vilmoir, asked him why he was so fascinated by her. For Virginia, plumage and language are as important in a male as, for the author of *La Condition Humaine*, they were in a woman.

There is no doubt, of course, that many possible suitors were frightened off by the haughty airs Miss Wade can adopt when she is less than pleased. This is true both on and off court. To say that she bristles when annoyed gives only a pale indication of what she is like. Mere hedgehogs bristle. An aroused Virginia is far more leonine than that. Her whole stance gives off an aura of high-level indignation emanating from every pore.

David Gray, during his days as tennis correspondent of the *Guardian*, once wrote that Virginia reminded him of Maria Callas playing Medea, and the comparison is wonderfully apt. Stimulated by that image, I was reminded while watching Virginia play Martina Navratilova of the great line from Puccini's *Tosca*, after Tosca has just murdered Scarpia, 'We shall meet before God!' Twice in the closing games, the umpire, Lee Jackson, chose to over-rule line-calls in favour of Martina and, at the end, when Miss Wade had lost, she marched up to Lee Jackson and said with a look that would have slayed them at La Scala, 'You've just cost me one hundred thousand dollars!' Her whole tone and manner at that moment was like Callas proclaiming 'We shall meet before God!', and the actual line would have been even more appropriate.

It had been a typical Wade reaction, exhibiting her capacity to make someone feel two feet tall despite the fact that Lee's feet were perched way above her in a chair that is supposed to offer a position of authority. That, when you think about it, is no mean achievement. But it stems, in part, from a personality that was always bursting with the need to project. It is not an uncommon affliction but it is very much a two-edged sword with the accent often on the negative. Of today's stars, Pam Shriver suffers a hundred per cent from it. In an earlier era, the former Wimbledon champion, Karen Susman, offered a prime example.

Rather than overcoming the problem, Virginia eventually lived through it and, once she started to get sufficient recognition and acclaim off the court, it became less of a problem. But of course with Miss Wade there was always that frozen lid of upbringing which prevented her from ever doing anything outrageous. In contrast, Miss Shriver has no inhibitions and no one to tell her it might be a good thing if she had.

In fact Virginia and Pam play similar games: suspect forehands; big serves (although Virginia's was more effective); and forceful, attacking backhands. Like the tall American girl, Virginia's backhand was her banker and it is a very difficult banker to have; not in any sense a gold chip investment. I would think that any girl with a one-handed backhand as their best shot in today's game must be considered vulnerable.

But apart from Virginia's athletic prowess, her greatest strength always lay, not simply in her powerful serve but in being able to summon that power when she needed it most. In that respect she did share something with Fred Perry — a very un-British, in-built confidence that enabled her to serve an ace against Americans when her back was to the wall. Perry wasn't a massive server by today's standards and aces were not his stock in trade but he did have that ability to pull out really big shots on the big points.

From a personal point of view, Virginia was a technical joy to make dresses for because she has always commanded public appeal, and her sensuous figure never changed an inch. In the sixteen years I dressed her, her measurements remained absolutely constant. Dear Christine Truman was quite the opposite, of course. In fifteen years I think she managed to be twenty-one different shapes. She used to make jokes about it when she came for a fitting. 'Oh, I think I'm back to my 1960 figure today,' or 'Why don't we try my 1962 pattern?'

Christine's size went up and down like a balloon depending on how happy she was or how well her forehand was working. But Virginia never changed and now, in her late thirties, I think she looks more beautiful than ever. If anything, her figure has improved and whenever I introduce one of her matches I make a point of saying, 'Miss Wade has confided in me that she is now thirty-seven but, as I think you will agree, she remains one of the most beautiful women ever to play tennis.' And they do agree. In fact when I made that introduction in Florida last year, I was interrupted by a loud and spontaneous burst of applause. There is no doubt that Virginia has created a wonderful public image for herself on both sides of the Atlantic.

Dealing with her on a personal level, however, is slightly different. Looking back, I found that I never felt really at ease with Virginia. I think it is a facet of her personality that she finds it difficult to be spontaneously gracious. And that is so important for me. I flower if people are gracious to me and I suppose I have been spoilt by the charm and gratitude of some of my other, equally celebrated, clients.

Although I am sure that Virginia was genuinely pleased with many of the dresses I created for her, she somehow found it very difficult to articulate that pleasure. I can remember one particular occasion when I was seeing her to the lift after a fitting at the Avon Estate in Kensington, where I had my design studio. She said, 'Thank you. I am very satisfied.' It struck me as the most extraordinarily stilted expression considering the relationship we had. It sounded like something one would say to the carpenter or the plumber!

Apart from dressing Virginia, I also acted as her agent for a few years. At the time I think I understood her mental state well enough to give her some sound advice, especially regarding World Team Tennis which suddenly sprang into being in 1974.

Virginia didn't like the idea of team tennis at all and, after a long talk at Queen's, she readily accepted my suggestion of setting a sum below which she would not participate. We very deliberately set her price at an exorbitant level. 'At least it will put your mind at rest,' I told her. 'There is nothing more to worry about. If they want you that badly they will know now that they are going to have to really tempt you.'

In fact, it was less than a year later that the New York Apples team came up with an offer that went quite substantially above the figure we had set and, of course, I told her that not only should she sign but should also leave me and join Mark McCormack's stable, which was then just beginning to cast its eyes on international tennis fame. 'You'll be in a world I can no longer handle,' I said, 'so you will need accountants and tax lawyers and all those extras that IMG will be equipped to provide.'

Then our partnership was severed completely a couple of years later when I moved to Philadelphia. I was having serious financial problems setting up my business in America, and felt that my superstar clients, who by then were making large sums of money, should start paying for the dresses I made them. When I explained this, Billie Jean, in her typically generous way, asked 'How many dresses did I have last season, Ted?' When I said 'Six', she immediately replied, 'OK, make me twelve.' In stark contrast, Virginia felt it would be more fitting for her status to be paid for wearing a bulk manufacturer's designs.

The tennis world had become a multi-million dollar marketplace and the pressures, which Fred Perry was probably better suited to handle temperamentally than Virginia Wade, were building all the time. To answer the question in the song, yes, it really was 'so much simpler then'. The choices were less complicated; the goals more obvious; the rules governing the way we behaved, socially, commercially and competitively, were more clearly defined.

I think Virginia often found it difficult to blend the lessons of her upbringing with the demands placed on an independent, international star. But she always carried herself with defiant dignity and ended up making the right choices for herself. There is no doubt at all that by virtue of achievement and qualification she is the best possible choice as Wimbledon's first-ever female committee member. It may be deemed difficult to add stature to such an august body as the All England Club, but Virginia Wade will consciously do that the moment she walks through the soon-to-be-named Fred Perry Gates.

24 Man of Destiny

It is not really surprising that I believe in reincarnation. In some ways I feel I have already been reincarnated once without having died. By any standards it must be the ultimate in *déja-vu* for someone to fill two separate but identical jobs some fifty years apart and to be selected both times in such amazingly similar circumstances.

I say this because it was while umpiring at the French championships in 1927 that All England Club officials came to know me, with the result that I was invited to join the Wimbledon championship staff that year. In 1982, having been reinstalled in Paris by French and International Tennis Federation president, Philippe Chatrier, this time as one of his personal assistants, Wimbledon Committee men again noticed me and evidently thought 'Why don't we have him back?'

On both occasions it was a major crisis over player relations that precipitated Wimbledon's action. In 1926 they were caught in a tragic misunderstanding with Suzanne Lenglen. In 1981 there had been a problem with John McEnroe. It has been said that one of my better virtues is mediation between warring factions, so it seems that in some cases the wheel of Fate really does turn full circle.

From a broader viewpoint, however, the game was naturally very different in 1982 from 1927. Tennis was originally introduced to France by the English, in winter time on the Riviera and at summer resorts, from Dinard around the Channel coast to Houlgate, Deauville, Le Touquet and several other long-forgotten rendezvous of the rich. That the seafront boulevard in Nice still bears the name 'Promenade des Anglais' and for sixty years was imperiously overlooked by a huge statue of Queen Victoria until the Germans threw it in the sea in 1943, gives only a small indication of the extent to which this whole glorious southern coast was once virtually an English colony. At the time ninety per cent of the participants in the north-coast events were also invariably English.

In French tennis only Paris, therefore, was a late-starter. The sophisticated and well-to-do Parisians at first disdained the new game as simply another English excuse for unnecessary outdoor exercise to be indulged in by foreigners at holiday resorts. In fact, as late as 1927, before the Musketeers first won the Davis Cup for France, the Paris Government was prosecuting its own tennis Establishment for non-payment of entertainment tax. The Government alleged that while 'true' sports such as rugby, football, athletics, even swimming, 'properly prepared young men for appropriate military service and were accordingly "worthily" tax-exempt,' tennis clearly fell into the frivolous and taxable category of leisure and entertainment.

Nevertheless, in 1882, five years behind Wimbledon, Paris did follow the English line by adding two grass courts to the Racing Club and, the following year, offering tennis for the first time at the Stade Français in the forest of St Cloud. In 1885 a more social-than-tennis club was laid out at Puteaux, a wooded island site in the Seine near Paris, though by initially naming this 'Le Club des Anglais', and excluding the word 'tennis' from the titles of the two other clubs, it seems that some guilt feelings as well as tax problems surrounded the whole enterprise.

Later, in 1891, the first French national championship was won by an English member of Puteaux, J. Briggs Esq. At the time nearly every tennis event in France was being administered and won by the English but after ten years, Paris suddenly recognized the game's potential and set out determinedly to gain control of the English-dominated resort clubs around the coast. In turn, this policy gave rise to newspaper editorials which fiercely advocated that all future French national championships be confined at least to permanent residents of France. Ultimately this was the rule until 1925.

Meanwhile, Parisian acceptance of tennis was also fortified by the emergence of France's first players of international ability, André Gobert, Max Decugis and Maurice Germot. At least Gobert and Decugis were Paris born and bred. Gobert became the first Frenchman to compete at Wimbledon and, with Decugis, was the first to win a Wimbledon championship. Having won the French national singles at St Cloud six times, the doubles an incredible total of fourteen times, and eventually amassed thirty-four national titles in France alone, Decugis firmly entrenched himself as the legendary father of French tennis, and certainly the pivotal influence in finally making Paris the titular headquarters of the game in France.

In retirement, Decugis lived on the Riviera. He died there only a few years ago, aged ninety-seven, so we had many opportunities of listening to his inexhaustible fund of historic anecdotes. One of his favourites was that while serving at Puteaux at the start of this century, he looked up not only to see Santos Dumont, the pioneer Brazilian aviator, becoming the first man to fly over the Eiffel Tower, but also to see Dumont frantically swatting, with his straw boater, flames that were coming from his primitive one-prop engine. Puteaux must have been, beyond doubt, the most romantic setting with its socialite ladies in their frills and furbelows, stepping daintily from their carriages to be ferried out to the island. Decugis vividly remembered one early national ladies' doubles championship final when, after an interminable match of high lobbing, the score reached five-all in the third set. Whereupon, one of the ladies made the dramatic announcement that she must leave at once. 'My carriage is here. My new consort awaits me at Maxims. In the name of Love I renounce my claim to the title,' she said, leaving her astonished partners with only the splash of the ferryman's oars echoing their surprise. Ironically, the names of the team that won by virtue of this passionate default are immortalized in gold leaf on today's French honour-roll, with prestige identical to such household names as Lenglen, Wills, Navratilova and Evert!

During these years one personality from the English camp was outstanding in defence of tennis's cross-Channel conduct and origins. This was my first boss, George Simond. Simond was a small, kindly man who even on the hottest days wore thick tweeds with a waistcoat. He was a shrewd mathematician and handicapper whose compulsive hobby was to devise 'fail-safe' systems for winning at roulette in Monte Carlo. In Edwardian days he had been four times a doubles semi-finalist at Wimbledon and once reached the final. In Europe he won the national titles of five different countries when even the French newspapers described him as *'l'agréable champion anglais'*. In middle age he became Europe's premier tournament referee and taught me as his assistant, almost everything I know about the problems of handling temperamental tennis stars.

But with Simond persistently exercising his deep-rooted English influence in tennis, an eventual confrontation with the autocratic and ambitious Paris administrator, Pierre Gillou, was as inevitable as the dawn. Gillou had risen to almost national-hero status as captain of the Musketeers when they won the Davis Cup for France. His chance to assume total authority in the last English stronghold, Monte Carlo, came in 1928 when the new Country Club was sited on French territory, a few hundred yards beyond the frontier of the independent Monaco principality. How well I remember Gillou storming into the new club to demand a complete re-draw of Simond's seeding so that the Parisian champion, Simonne Mathieu, would be in first place ahead of the English, German and Italian women George had selected on local merit!

In the 1930s and again from 1953 to 1963, Pierre Gillou served two ten-year terms as president of the French Tennis Federation, a forerunner to Philippe Chatrier who, this year, completes his own first decade in the same appointment. Looking back, I suppose it was because I had been so closely identified with French tennis in my teens that I was spared from banishment, for soon afterwards nearly every British worker was thrown out of French tennis, effectively ending what had been, in many cases, lifelong affiliations. I had been an umpire at St Cloud in 1927, and then I was lucky to escape the guillotine by Gillou inviting me to the new Roland Garros stadium in 1928, 1929 and 1930. Possibly my very close youthful association with his son, Bertie, or Bertie himself, may have influenced his decision.

Either way I was there and ready to umpire on the opening day of Roland Garros when the British and French women's teams staged their annual encounter which preceded the main championships. Just as Lenglen and Tilden outdated the old Wimbledon in 1921, the Musketeers' victory immediately outdated St Cloud. The new stadium was conceived to accommodate the eight thousand spectators expected to attend the first challenge round in France in July 1928. However, in spite of extraordinary wrangles with the landowners, the City of Paris, the new court was ceremonially declared open when Helen Wills played an exhibition set against her compatriot, Frank Hunter, on 18 May.

Play began officially the next day. I remember the installation of the first-ever electric score-boards, and also I recall being instructed on how to operate the dials on the umpire's chair so that the heavy steel frames, perched high above the original wooden stands, turned, like the pages of a huge book, to show the score point by point. Dudley Larcombe came for the finals. He quickly spotted this innovation and in 1929 Wimbledon had the improved electric-bulb version which remained unchanged there for the next fifty years.

But for more than half a century I have believed that I umpired the second match on that 19 May opening day. My records clearly say that in my match England's Betty Nuthall beat France's Mme Vaussard, 6-3, 6-2. Quite recently, France's leading sports newspaper, *L'Equipe*, wrote a feature on the beginnings of Roland Garros and authoritatively recorded the Nuthall-Vaussard match as the curtain-up on the new era. Of course I am now delighted to have authentication of the small part I played in this milestone moment in French tennis.

1931 was the year when I decided to leave the glamour summers of Le Touquet to become an aspiring one-room designer in London. So my French connection came to an end for twenty years until Fate, Chance, as you will, handed me the threads again, neither in Nice nor Paris, but at Le Touquet, exactly where I had supposed they had been permanently broken. Certainly, I would never have had the opportunity of returning to the French championships in an official capacity had it not been for Philippe Chatrier, the man I first met at Le Touquet that year.

In 1951 I had gone back for a nostalgic fun-week to play doubles with a friend. I found the famous casino a ghost of its former glories when, in the late 1920s, it boasted the presence of the Prince of Wales plus no fewer than forty British lords at a weekend gala dinner. However, I was interested to see what kind of players France was producing from the war-time generation. Chatrier stood out by miles as the juvenile lead, the dashing dark and handsome charmer who had been junior champion of France and who was fast heading for the fringes of Davis Cup level with a sports journalist's career in mind.

My first close association with Philippe came shortly after when the French decided to send an official team to the British hard courts championships in Bournemouth. At the time, through the chaotic misadministration of post-war Britain, we still had bread rationing. If one wanted bread at a restaurant or hotel, the three-course meal limit was reduced to two courses. Having been raised in France, the idea of Frenchmen eating a meal without bread was inconceivable, so I arranged a 'collection' among some of the other competitors. Most of us gladly surrendered our bread coupons to celebrate the return of our Gallic, and gallant, friends who were understandably shocked but also very gratified.

In 1952, Philippe became engaged to Britain's No. 1 player, Susan Partridge, who that year came within points of stopping Maureen Connolly's career before it began, and was also the current French indoor champion. Being present at the inevitable young lovers' quarrels between these two gave me an early insight into Chatrier's complex and intense personality. We had some comic moments when the three of us dined together. On some days they decided not to be on speaking terms with each other and while Philippe would ask me: 'Would you please explain to the English lady ...' Susan would say: 'Will you kindly tell your French friend ...' Then, in the spring of 1953, they had their fairy-tale wedding in Wolverhampton.

Philippe and I met, of course, many times in the next twenty years. Then in 1975, in addition to retaining the French Federation presidency he was elected President of the 110-member International Tennis Federation, the world-governing body. With this global responsibility Philippe has shown himself to be a man of many parts, a dreamer who makes his dreams come true, an activist and a poet much as his compatriot, André Malraux, de Gaulle's famous Culture Minister, was a man of extreme erudition who also formed his own fighting squadron in the Spanish Civil War. Both men, while jealously guarding their aesthetic and romantic principles, launched themselves vigorously into competitive politics. Malraux won some protracted struggles in the Chamber of Deputies. In his own country, Philippe has achieved to an unprecedented degree personal popularity and commercial success for tennis. As one example, when his presidency of France's Tennis Federation began in 1973 the total of individually affiliated players was close to two hundred thousand, using about seven thousand officially designated courts. In 1983, over fifteen thousand courts will be in use and the number of affiliated players will pass the million mark. This same electrifying success can be seen during the French Open, where the world's most famous status-symbol trade-names – Hermés, de Beers, *Vogue* magazine, Maxims, Lanvin – all clamour for on-site recognition at Roland Garros. Beyond this Philippe is engaged almost daily in fighting some bitter and tough opposition in the increasingly difficult world of international pro' tennis.

But in spite of my decades of friendship with Philippe, my return to officialdom at the French Open came about in a curious way. In 1978, under Philippe's direction, Roland Garros celebrated fifty years of its spectacular evolution. Past champions and tennis personalities from all over the world were invited, but I was not on the list. In all fairness, Philippe was very embarrassed when he discovered, but since he was not born until well after 1928 I gladly accepted that he genuinely did not know I had officiated there on the opening day. In 1979 he made immediate amends by inviting me to join his personal staff, a privilege I have enjoyed ever since.

Working for Philippe, I find him always an inspiring leader, but also an unabashed romantic. At its best tennis can evoke the traditions of Camelot. Philippe easily assumes the Arthurian chivalries of the game. Fortunately for me we had the same, if not concurrent, schooling in French upper-middle-class manners – manners based on respect: respect for one's self, respect for one's peers and for life's beneficial traditions. It was from respect that Philippe had the main gates of Roland Garros renamed 'The Gates of the Musketeers', and from respect that by personal treaty with Jacques Chirac, the Mayor of Paris, he had the street bordering the stadium renamed 'Rue Suzanne Lenglen', the first in Paris ever to be named after a sports personality. At Federation Cup, over which Philippe presides each year, he appoints me his *Chef de Protocol*, so again his respect for flawless etiquette ensures that we have no problems dealing with the royals and the heads of state in the various countries we visit.

As a personality, Roland Garros himself is not widely known. A popular member of the Stade Français, he was a man of vision, a young French aviator who saw faraway horizons and was determined to reach them. In 1913 he was the first man to fly the Mediterranean, from St Raphael to Bizerta, an intrepid adventure at that time. Then like Tony Wilding, he was killed in action in World War I. Philippe perpetuates Garros's vision with the improvements in his organization he extracts each year from his closest hench-men, Christian Duxin and Régine Tourres. Leading other members of his ever-faithful team, he has made the French Open, with Wimbledon, the most admired championships in the world.

The hundred-year road from Puteaux's Club des Anglais to Chatrier's quintessentially Parisian Roland Garros, was often a bumpy ride. After the initial antagonisms all was sweetness and light when Edward VII, with his enormous popularity in France as the amorous Prince of Wales, negotiated l'Entente Cordiale. We had sunshine and blue skies again when Lenglen and the Musketeers were enchanting Wimbledon, but distinctly frosty weather when English tennis officials were made *persona non grata* in France in 1932.

Now Philippe has paved the long road with sincere friendship and warm hospitality. The current Wimbledon chairman, Sir Brian Burnett and his wife, Val, are always among Philippe's most honoured guests. To French tennis, and to the hundred-plus nations who elect Philippe every two years as their leader, he has become their Man of Destiny.

He has been a Man of Destiny to me, too.

25 'Mr Communicator'

As I write this final chapter, there are two supreme players in the increasingly competitive world of women's tennis – Chris Evert Lloyd and Martina Navratilova.

In the closing months of 1982, every final of importance – the Daihatsu Challenge at Brighton, the Australian Open and the Toyota – were contested between these two great champions, and, of course, back in the summer, they had met in the Wimbledon final for the third time in five years. By the end of the year, Martina, with the French Open and Wimbledon titles heading her list of triumphs, had compiled the extraordinary record of ninety wins and just three losses while Chris, as holder of the US and Australian Opens, had enjoyed a year that was only marginally less spectacular, with seventy-six matches won and six lost.

Naturally I have followed the careers of both girls from their beginnings, and have grown to know and admire them as two of the greatest champions the game has seen. It would be unthinkable to end this life-long account of the game as I have known it without recounting at least a few of the experiences I have shared with them over the years. So, with the indulgence of my delightful editor, Margaret Willes, over matters of space and time, I must ask the reader to journey back with me for a moment to the early years of pro' tennis, more than ten years ago.

In the summer of 1970, Margaret Court was heading for her fourth US singles triumph as Forest Hills. Already the great Australian champion had won Wimbledon three times, the French four and her own Australian title on no fewer than nine occasions. Having duly won at Forest Hills, she seemed unstoppable until, just two weeks later, she suddenly lost a match to an unheard-of fifteen-year-old called Christine Evert. Had we foreseen then the golden tennis future that awaited the little teenager from Fort Lauderdale, we would not have been so surprised.

My own first sight of Chris was in August 1971. That year was probably the most hectic of my life. In March I had bought back from Tootals the ownership of my design business that I sold them six years before. My business partner, Henry Turner, decided to stay with

Tootals so for the first time in twenty years I was running a three-continent operation alone. During Wimbledon I was told that Gladys Heldman had arranged for July an extremely valuable personal appearance stint for me at America's most famous store, Neiman Marcus. In August the Wightman Cup matches were in Cleveland, Ohio. Virginia Wade, Joyce Williams, Christine and Nell Truman from the British team, as well as the US captain, Carole Graebner, and her players Val Ziegenfuss and Julie Heldman, all required dresses from me. Then, from Cleveland I had to make a forty-eight-hour dash to Milwaukee.

In my last years in England I was Chairman of the British Association for Tenpin Bowling (my second sports love). Our lads had won the previous world championships four years earlier, and our women bowlers had since become champions of Europe, so I really wanted to be in Milwaukee, where our teams were trying desperately to uphold their prestige against twenty-two other nations. To cap all this, Joe Cullman and his Virginia Slims people called me to Houston to appoint me official designer to the Slims circuit, giving me exactly nine days back in London to prepare my ideas and sketches.

In the decade from 1965 to 1975, before I left England to live in America, I made twenty-eight trips to the United States. During most of these I contrived a stop-over with my very close Philadelphia friends the Fernbergers who, by organizing the world's most important men's indoor event, have become a mainstay in the fabric of global pro' tennis. Philadelphia also stages another important event, the eighteen-and-under girls' international championship on grass, and it was during my 1971 rush visit, when the Fernbergers took me to this, that I first saw Chris Evert. I need hardly add that she was winning and already so adaptable that she made a rotten grass court look quite good. Only days later, in Cleveland, Chris put the entire female tennis community in shock by beating Virginia Wade and Winnie Shaw, Britain's Nos 1 and 2 players, with a total loss of six games. In September she played her first national championship at Forest Hills. There she fought off six match-points against Mary Ann Eisel, dismissed the experienced Frankie Durr and Lesley Hunt, and went on to an amazingly self-composed semi-final against the eventual title-winner, Billie Jean King, before fourteen thousand spectators.

During Forest Hills, America's *Ladies' Home Journal* decided to give tennis awards to Hazel Wightman, Gladys Heldman, Chris Evert and me. Hazel was then eighty-four, Gladys unchanging and ageless, Chris was not yet seventeen, and I was in my sixty-second year. We could hardly refuse, though it was a strange mix of ages that lined up in the stadium for this event. But the luck of the draw put me next to Chris Evert and I admit that after nearly fifty years of observing champions in bud, in flower and in fading glory, I looked forward to this chance of meeting our tennis world's latest budding prodigy.

I think the quality of self composure most stands out in my memory of this initial close-up of Chris, though I also recall, as we met, a sharp flash of Bette-Davis-like appraisal, and an instant 'Are you dangerous? If not, what can you do for me?' scrutiny. This mannerism was, of course, quickly camouflaged by success, and today Chris is all glamour and charm, communicating pleasure to every spectator. But in the ten years of her evolution to world stardom, she has treated us to several layered phases. In 1974, American columnist Jim Murray wrote, I thought appropriately at the time, 'Chris plays like some bored guy giving lessons to creaky old ladies', and then, 'Chris is so shining white you should wear sun-glasses to look at her.' My particular response at one stage was to compare watching her play to being in a launderette where one's interest is only aroused by some bright handkerchief or one's most intimate garments revolving mechanically past the glass window. Over the years, however, media descriptions of her warmed noticeably, from 'Ice Maiden' through 'Miss Cherry Pie' and 'Unsuspected Romantic' to 'Most Gracious Lady'. Certainly we have in turn been awed by her Everest remoteness, dazed by the accuracy of her pistol-shot strokes, and perplexed and enchanted by her 'love doubles'. In addition, Chris has already earned a whole chapter of technical tennis history for the universal appeal of her two-handed backhand, which has revolutionized women's tennis. Lastly, for me personally, designing her wedding dress remains an unforgettable pleasure.

For contractual reasons I never made dresses for Chris until she asked me to undertake her American team outfits for the 1978 Federation Cup in Australia. The next week she asked, 'How much notice do you need for a wedding dress?' At the cup champions' dinner, a gracious thank-you note was delicately pencilled on a Christian Dior handkerchief, but added below came the message, 'Don't forget you still owe me the most important dress of all.' Of course, I was delighted, though, apart from the dozens of socialites in my couturier days, Chris's wedding dress was the fourteenth I designed for a tennis star. (No. 13 was Christine Truman's, but at the time I never dared tell her.)

Chris chose white satin and Chantilly lace, which we re-embroidered with two thousand seed pearls. Reporting the wedding, New York's unique profile columnist, Dave Anderson, wrote, 'On or off court, Chris is as smooth as satin, as traditional as lace and as durable as those pearls.' Jean Rook, the 'Empress of Fleet Street', headlined in England: 'Chris is a Pearl of a Bride', so our choice of design was internationally validated.

I have often told Chris that with her flawless baseline technique, and by not being a compulsive net-rusher, she could play on for ever. I feel sure her myriad fans hope she will.

I first saw Martina playing in the French championships some ten years ago. She was then an anonymous, rather over-weight teenager, but already providing one of the recurring shocks she gives regularly to the tennis community. On that day she was demolishing Nancy Richey, the top-ranking American in the tournament.

In those years, players from the Communist Bloc were still confined to drab shorts and shirts; I remember one girl telling me they had no option but to obey their sports ministries and take whatever was issued to them by their state. Martina's shorts were colourful and different from everyone else's, with one front-patch-pocket in bright red and its opposite number in blue. To the perceptive eye she was already signalling her determined individuality as well as her wonderful natural ability.

A few months later, in Washington, she beat Chris for the first time. Only recently she told me she will never forget the sleepless night that followed that dramatic 7-5 third-set tie-breaker.

In 1975, Martina left her home and country for America. I had done so just one month previously, so I sometimes think we shared a few moments of soul-searching. Soon after Martina's arrival in the US, partly in celebration and partly to counteract any momentary self-questioning, I made her two really startling tennis dresses – both white, but with trails of bright flowers climbing from the hem-line. These elicited from Marilyn Fernberger the comment, 'So we're into shower curtains now.' The *New York Times*'s Neil Amdur quoted Martina, 'Ted understands me perfectly,' she told him. 'Those dresses are wild, just like me.'

In 1978, Martina's first Wimbledon singles win confirmed the superstitions every star holds, one way or another. Six months earlier I had made her an all-white dress with a fine gold pin-stripe. It was elegant, but I thought it looked very dull indoors under bright lights. Yet, surprisingly, this became Martina's 'lucky' dress for that season. After she won five Virginia Slims circuit tournaments wearing it, plus for the first time the ultimate Slims championship, her current coach, Sandra Haynie, said to me, 'That goddam dress has stains and holes all over. Can't you make her a duplicate?' Eventually, after searching half the American continent for the same fabric, my persistence paid off from the back shelf in a small store in Dallas. We re-made the identical dress, but my staff inadvertently used slightly different buttons.

During Wimbledon I noticed that Martina was wearing the duplicate for most of her matches, but I recognized from the buttons that she had gone back to the original – holes and all – for the final. When I congratulated her later on her win she looked surprised. 'Thank you. I have never yet lost a match in that dress,' she said, as if just wearing it made the result a foregone conclusion.

I had designed Martina's dresses since 1974, but her first Wimbledon singles title put her advertising value to aspiring bulk manufacturers far beyond any considerations of mine. However, in June 1979, when she was already leaving me for a large contract, she asked me at the very last moment for some Wimbledon dresses. I used white, of course, but in desperation through lack of time I thought we could trim one dress with some pre-embroidered peacock motifs that we already had in the studio. 'Peacock feathers are considered universally unlucky,' my long-time manageress, Margaret Kirgin, insisted. 'Well, Martina is different,' I remember saying. 'Hopefully, she will think exactly the opposite.' And so it turned out. The peacocks became Martina's good luck symbol of that Wimbledon. In fact she was so confident in them that she answered one surprised reporter's question forty-eight hours before the final, saying: 'Of course I shall be wearing my peacock dress.'

Personally, I have no doubt that Martina has now the finest serve-volley game of any woman ever seen. She has perfected a concept first shown us by Elizabeth Ryan before World War I, improved by Alice Marble and the great Brough-duPont-Hart trio, and taken to its previous peak of effectiveness by Madam Superstar, Billie Jean King. On her serve, Martina takes maximum advantage of today's relatively permissive foot-fault rules that restricted her serve-volleying predecessors. In addition, she has a fascinatingly imaginative concept of actual strokes, with all the daring and risks this implies.

Martina is twenty-six months younger than Chris and could dominate the game for the next decade, or at least for as long as her inner fires provide the incentive. She has lately transformed her former 'Gucci-speak', bejewelled, jet-set image into that of a serious and highly-tuned athlete. She gives great credit for this to her coach, Renée Richards, and to her trainer friend, Nancy Lieberman, herself America's top female basket ball player.

But who's counting? Though all the great stars have needed deep emotional bonds with someone in the stands to reassure their innate doubt and fears, when the chips are down, out there alone on those huge centre courts, winning big finals is very much a do-it-yourself process. And among women, as this goes to print, it seems impossible that anyone could be better equipped for winning than Martina.

So from Chris and Martina, back to my surprising, but happy return to the world shrine of tennis.

I first went to work on what was then called the 'Wimbledon Championship Temporary Staff' the day before my seventeenth birthday in 1927. In 1982 I re-joined that select group. Naturally, a great many things happened to me in the years between. I have already described some of the highlights, but on the day before my seventy-second birthday, Tony Samstag wrote in the London *Times* a sensitive view of this intervening period:

> The beautiful people of tennis gathered yesterday on the eve of the 105th Wimbledon tennis championships, to welcome one of their own back to the fold after thirty-three years in the wilderness. This is how the object of their affections, Mr Ted Tinling, the former dress-designer and all-round outrageous personality, describes his years of disgrace since he shocked the pants off a rather more impressionable public with the little lace confection he whipped up for 'Gorgeous Gussy' Moran [in 1949]. He is to take his place at Wimbledon today as official trouble-shooter, heading a Liaison Committee that will attempt to mediate in any conflicts arising between the players and the All England Club during the tournament. Unofficially, of course, he has never been away, and yesterday's brunch party, at the Royal Garden Hotel in Kensington, was his thank-you to about 200 friends and associates on the eve of his 50th Wimbledon.

My guest-book tells me that twenty-five Grand Slam title holders came to support me, including Kitty Godfree who won in 1926 and was therefore the current champion in my first year at Wimbledon. Six other lady champions, together with Rosie Casals and Tracy Austin, came too. From the men champions, Fred Perry, Neale Fraser and Arthur Ashe came, while Jimmy Connors was represented by his lovely wife, Patti. Other guests included Wimbledon Chairman, Sir Brian Burnett, and the Lawn Tennis Association Chairman, Jim Cochrane, and Philippe Chatrier paid me the additional compliment of flying specially from Paris. It was a very emotional occasion – and an unforgettable one for a less pleasant reason. Only nine days before I had to have a knee cartilage removed and left hospital too soon for comfort for my celebration and for my nostalgic return to Wimbledon.

After the thirty-three years 'in the wilderness' it was certainly great to be back, particularly to celebrate my Golden Jubilee in the very same All England Club offices where some of my happiest moments were spent – long ago. There was also a strange feeling of paradox in reviving old relationships with old friends and forming new relationships with new friends. By 'old' friends, I mean players like Jimmy Connors, Chris Evert, Tracy Austin and Rosie Casals and a host of others who have known me nearly all of their tennis-playing lives, but have never considered me in the context of being an official at Wimbledon.

I soon got used to people saying, 'Oh yes, I remember my Mother telling me about you.' Indeed, Mother could have given them a very accurate description of my duties, as I was invited back for precisely the same job as the first time around.

Astrologers always tell us that anyone involved in communications has an influence from the planet Mercury strongly visible in their charts. Mercury symbolizes, of course, the 'wing-footed messenger'. Whether or not one believes in horoscopes, destiny certainly threw me in the deep end of communications right from that day, back in 1924, when I first umpired for Suzanne. And probably by sheer coincidence, I do have a very dominant Mercury in my stars.

Looking back, I see now how often it has fallen to me to communicate and to interpret people and things to other people. Umpiring already comes into this category, as an umpire is communicating the score and the state of the game to the spectators. Certainly designing so many wedding dresses, I had to be very sure not to convey the wrong message. 'How dare SHE be married in a white dress' is a comment I heard more than once from a bridesmaid's bitchy mother. Even in the Army, where one's job was essentially decreed by someone else, I was the guy who drew the short straw and was kept in khaki for two extra years in order to organize the unprecedented pool of interpreters for the Allied Control Commission. This was well and truly unprecedented as, in spite of the many wars won by England since 1066, no one, until 1945, had found it necessary to talk to the losers in the losers' own language.

Tennis is an unending story of winners and losers, so perhaps this experience is one reason why I seem able to communicate with both categories. In my eight years as designer to the Virginia Slims circuit, I contrived over one thousand different dresses for the players and in each the main intention was to communicate the wearer's particular qualities and personality to the spectators. There were winners' and losers' dresses there too. I always made winners' dresses for Virginia Wade and Martina because they so often won. (Virginia always looked as if she was winning even when she was losing.) Conversely, some girls always seemed likely to lose, and I tried to ensure they did not over-communicate their misfortune by wearing some violently visible creation.

Destiny never let up in chaining me to this role, sometimes as an unwilling go-between. In 1970, when the International Federation and Lamar Hunt's WCT group went to war with each other for the first time, through my long friendship with Michael Davies and Derek Hardwick, the major opponents, I was inextricably caught in their complex antagonisms. Sports writer J. L. Manning even wrote, 'How sick can a sport be when it needs a dressmaker to solve its problems?' Suffice to say that we did eventually all sit down together; Hunt's thirty-two players, who were determined to boycott 1971 Wimbledon, all turned up in good order and I shall always be proud of this memory.

Billie Jean King and Rosie Casals have proved wonderfully loyal clients of mine for the past ten years. At 1982 Wimbledon, Billie Jean King wore her blue-flower-trimmed dress when the chairman made her a presentation on winning her hundredth match. She wore the same dress so often in reaching the singles semi-final that Chris Evert said she really hoped she would not see it across the net when they eventually met. For as long as Billie Jean and Rosie want my dresses, I could never let them down.

But when I was seventy, three years ago now, I found that my enthusiasm for reaching my workrooms at 8.15 every morning was no longer as it had been. Moreover, there were currently no new frontiers to cross in tennis design, so once again communications took over my life.

In 1982 I spent more than thirty weeks in my role as Mr Communicator, I was *Chef de Protocole* for World President Philippe Chatrier and his ITF team – David Gray, Paolo Angeli and Ann Haydon Jones; I returned to the revived Virginia Slims circuit; I helped to publicise the younger members of the Women's Tennis Association with television interviews and such-like; and, above all, I was invited to work at Wimbledon again. I find the life that I have always loved very stimulating – even more so now that it is updated by the sunrise of the computer age where, at the touch of a few keys, I can obtain and communicate instant important information about the world of tennis.

Since returning to Wimbledon, I suppose it was inevitable that I be asked many times how I was received by my young bosses who form the Championships' Committee of Management. One answer is that my age is actually an asset because everyone realizes that I have seen nearly all of it before in my previous 'incarnation' there. Naturally, many of the personalities are new and dozens of improvements have been made, but whenever I was in doubt, I turned to Chief Executive, Chris Gorringe. I told him several times that I felt like a rookie signal-man on Clapham Junction, but Chris unfailingly told me when to pull the correct lever.

Some people – particularly overseas journalists – told me I might find Chairman Brian Burnett 'difficult'. Before retiring from the Air Force, Sir Brian was an outstanding Commander-in-Chief, and I believe there are times when a Commander-in-Chief is justifiably 'difficult'. In fact, he was charming to me throughout and was always receptive to sensible suggestions – as were the young heads of his committees. Admittedly, during the war I had worked in the close entourages of Bernard Paget, Maitland Wilson, Montgomery and Eisenhower, all field marshals or five-star generals and all commanders-in-chief. At each GHQ the senior aides had a 'club' where in terms of grapevine communications we owed nothing to MI5, so I returned to Wimbledon knowing that at least I was reasonably 'house-trained', and knew the language expected of me.

There again, communication was the name of the game. This was particularly obvious when the Chairman gave me the opportunity of introducing players to him personally, and they were all delighted. It was on one such occasion that a player dubbed me 'Mr Communicator'.

As to our beloved game, no matter what emerges to startle or change the way it is played, managed, viewed or reported, the developing omnipotence of the computer will play an ever-increasing role. I feel this strongly because I believe it is now a mistake to be over 'national' in tennis. Philippe Chatrier's world-governing body has already 111 members, and the dialogue that will be necessary amongst all these when tennis returns to full status in the 1988 Olympics will give the game even wider horizons.

For my part, I just hope to see more great players, whatever their race, creed or colour. For, whatever their background, they are a joy to behold for their strength, their skill, their personality, and, hopefully, for their chivalry.

How understanding it was of Fate to allow Elizabeth Ryan the final hours of an illustrious life watching a game of tennis! For my part, I find that I am as easily enraptured and as fascinated by the spectacle and drama of it as I was all those years ago, when tennis was part of a different world. So much has changed, yet the essence of the sport is still intact and my love of it remains undiminished – yes, even after sixty years.

Appendix

A Brief Biography of Suzanne Lenglen
Written by Charles (Papa) Lenglen in 1926

In June 1910, Suzanne Lenglen, who then was eleven years old, received as a present her first tennis racquet, if that dubious instrument could properly have been called a racquet. It was one of these toy affairs that can be found in any toy shop, and at the time I did not think that she would make better use of it than other children of her age.

At first I paid little attention to her, allowing her to play with her little friends on the tennis court which I had constructed in my garden. At the end of about a month, however, I was so pleased by the dexterity which she showed with her toy racquet that I ordered from one of the Paris manufacturers a racquet which was both light and well balanced, made especially to suit a girl of her age.

Then, in order that I might get a more definite idea of what she was capable of, I often played with her. The progress she made was as rapid as it was surprising. Even at that youthful age she showed signs of her developing genius for tactical execution.

In the month of September, that is to say only three months after she started, we visited a friend of mine, Dr Cizelly, who lived at Coize, near Chantilly. The doctor was a great tennis enthusiast and owned a court – a rare thing those days in France. It was there that Suzanne played her first game before a gallery.

The annual Chantilly tournament was about to commence when I decided to enter my daughter, then aged eleven. Suzanne was entered in the handicap ladies' singles, with a handicap of plus 15, 3-6 (i.e., she received one point every game and two points every other game). She came through four rounds and took second prize.

A few months later, when I returned to Nice, I applied for her admission to the Nice Lawn Tennis Club, of which I was a member, and by special dispensation, as children were not allowed at the club, I obtained permission for her to play on Thursdays and Sundays, the days when she had no school. The Nice Club and the other Riviera clubs were frequented by some of the best racquets of the world, including the American champion, J. B. Alexander.

I used to go to the club every day in order to study the strokes and the manner of play of these great masters of the sport, with the ultimate purpose of teaching my little Suzanne the best points of each player.

The play of the English women consisted mostly of long, rapid drives placed accurately along the lines, and impressed me by its great regularity and calm, reasoned placing. But I must admit I had eyes only for the play of the men, who astounded me by the remarkable superiority of their methods.

Why then, I asked myself, should not women adopt the masculine method? It seemed to me that with a well directed course of training any woman could be taught the game as it was played by the men, although naturally she would be unable to play it with the same degree of force.

With this idea in mind, I waited expectantly for my daughter to gain a little more experience, in order to start her training in masculine methods.

It was necessary for my daughter to do an enormous amount of work before she could show any appreciable results in this direction. She had need of all her tenacity of purpose and all the help given her by her comrades at the Nice Club.

I was well seconded in my endeavours by Alvardo Rice, Secretary of the Nice Club, who took a great interest in Suzanne and to whom I would here like to pay a tribute, for he was one of the finest men the sport has ever known.

At thirteen, Suzanne was chosen by the Nice Club to represent it in an inter-club match played against the club of Bordighera, Italy, for a Challenge Shield offered by Mr Rice. The Bordighera Club was composed largely of English players who wintered on the Riviera.

When the day of the match arrived, Suzanne, accompanied by her mother, went to Bordighera. They were warmly welcomed by the women of the club, who, thinking my wife was the opponent sent by the Nice Club, directed her to the dressing room to change into her tennis costume. Their surprise was great when my wife, pointing to the diminutive Suzanne, informed them that there stood the representative of the Nice Club.

Surprise and curiosity gave way to amusement, which soon changed to chagrin as my little daughter carried off the victory in the two matches in which she played.

The next year, in January 1914, G. M. Simond, the well-known English tournament player and referee, entered Suzanne in the Carlton Club of Cannes tournament, with the hope of seeing her meet

Mrs Winch, at that time one of the best English players. She also was entered in the mixed doubles, in which she won the first prize with the great Anthony Wilding, who had expressed a desire to have her as a partner.

She encountered Mrs Winch in the finals, which lasted three long and gruelling sets. The victory fell to Suzanne, then fifteen, and she was warmly congratulated by her English opponent.

At the beginning of the third set, Suzanne was so fatigued that she wanted to default. I pointed out to her that her opponent was equally tired.

'It is not good tennis, then,' she replied, 'it is courage that will win this match' – that was how she won.

From that day to this, all opinions to the contrary notwithstanding, I maintain that my daughter has proved to all unbiased spectators, that she is as courageous a player as any who ever stepped on a tennis court.

This victory, which no one would have dared to forecast, caused quite a flurry in tennis circles on the Riviera and in England, where the high standing of Mrs Winch was well known.

The directors of the Nice Club frankly admitted they had thought the victory an impossible one for Suzanne and began to interest themselves greatly in my young prodigy. For me it was the direct factor that decided me to devote myself entirely to her training.

Since the career of Suzanne is somewhat wonderful throughout, I would like to tell of the following incident, which took place during a vaudeville performance given in the Casino Municipal de Nice in 1912. Among other vaudeville turns there was a hypnotist, accompanied by a medium who served as his subject.

They performed experiments in mental telepathy, thought reading and fortune telling. The woman, her eyes blindfolded, said she would try to answer any question in the mind of any person in the audience.

I concentrated on the following question:

'Will my daughter one day become champion of France?'

In a few seconds the medium answered – 'Better than that – Better than that.'

Suzanne is today champion of the world.

Index